DESIGNING
LEARNING PROGRAMS
AND
ENVIRONMENTS
FOR STUDENTS WITH
SPECIAL LEARNING NEEDS

DESIGNING
LEARNING PROGRAMS
AND
ENVIRONMENTS
FOR STUDENTS WITH
SPECIAL LEARNING NEEDS

Edited by

PHILLIP J. SLEEMAN

Director
University Center for Instructional
Media & Technology
Professor
University of Connecticut
Storrs, Connecticut

LOUIS V. MESSINEO

Superintendent of Schools
Director of Instruction and
Pupil Personnel Services
Tolland Public Schools
Tolland, Connecticut

D. M. ROCKWELL

Security Training Associates
Memphis, Tennessee

CHARLES C THOMAS • PUBLISHER
Springfield • Illinois • U.S.A.

Published and Distributed Throughout the World by
CHARLES C THOMAS • PUBLISHER
2600 South First Street
Springfield, Illinois, 62717, U.S.A.

With THOMAS BOOKS *careful attention is given to all details of manufacturing and
design. It is the Publisher's desire to present books that are satisfactory as to their physical
qualities and artistic possibilities and appropriate for their particular use.* THOMAS
BOOKS *will be true to those laws of quality that assure a good name and good will.*

Printed in the United States of America
CU-R-1

Library of Congress Cataloging in Publication Data
Main entry under title:

Designing learning programs and environments for
    students with special learning needs.

    Bibliography: p.
    Includes index.
        1. Exceptional children--Education--United States--
Addresses, essays, lectures. I. Sleeman, Phillip J.
II. Messineo, Louis V. III. Rockwell, D.M.
LC3981.D47   1983   371.9′0973   82-16796
ISBN 0-398-04770-7

CONTRIBUTORS

RANDY ELLIOT BENNETT
Director, Special Education
Educational Testing Service
Princeton, New Jersey

ETTA M. BISHOP
Assistant to the Director, UCIMT
University of Connecticut
Storrs, Connecticut

RICHARD H. BLOOMER
Professor & Director of School Psychology
University of Connecticut
Storrs, Connecticut

JAMES G. BUTERBAUGH
Salt Lake City, Utah

CHARLES C. D'AREZZO
Director, Learning Resources Center
Community College of Rhode Island
Cranston, Rhode Island

RUTH WORDEN FRANK
Reading Consultant
Rochester, New York

RICHARD L. GORHAM
Director, UCIMT Product &
Instructional Development Division
University of Connecticut
Storrs, Connecticut

KATHLEEN L. HAMMOND
Ph.D. Candidate — Psychology
University of Pittsburgh
Pittsburgh, Pennsylvania

v

ALMA JEAN HARRINGTON
Assistant Professor
Middle Tennessee State University
Murfeesboro, Tennessee

MARY KATHERINE HAWRYLUK
School Psychologist
S. Brunswick Public Schools
S. Brunswick, New Jersey

JO MARY HENDRICKSON
Vice President
Continental Learning Systems, Incorporated
Nashville, Tennessee

ROBERT J. ILLBACK
Director, Student Services
Fort Knox Dependents School
Fort Knox, Kentucky

STEPHEN LAWRENCE
Psychologist
Enfield, Connecticut

JOHN LEACH
Associate Professor of Education
University of Connecticut
Storrs, Connecticut

RONALD LOIACONO
Director of Research & Evaluation
Cooperative Educational Services
Norwalk, Connecticut

CHARLES A. MAHER
Co-Director
School Planning and Evaluation Center
Rutgers University
Piscataway, New Jersey

ALFRED J. MANNEBACH
Professor
University of Connecticut
Storrs, Connecticut

LOUIS V. MESSINEO
Superintendent of Schools
Tolland Public Schools
Tolland, Connecticut

PATRICK R. PENLAND
Education and Library Science
University of Pittsburgh
Pittsburgh, Pennsylvania

JEFFREY C. PINGPANK
Attorney
Avon, Connecticut

D.M. ROCKWELL
Security Training Associates
Memphis, Tennessee

GERARD ROWE-MINAYA
Associate Professor of Educational Administration
University of Connecticut
Storrs, Connecticut

ROBB RUSSON
Instructional Designer
Utah State University
Providence, Utah

FARHAD SABA
Director, Telecommunications Division
University of Connecticut
Storrs, Connecticut

ROBERT A. SHAW
Professor of Mathematics Education
University of Connecticut
Storrs, Connecticut

PHILLIP J. SLEEMAN
Director University Center for Instructional
Media & Technology and Professor
University of Connecticut
Storrs, Connecticut

VYKUNTAPATHI THOTA
Professor of Instructional Media & Technology
Virginia State University
Petersburg, Virginia

RICHARD W. WHINFIELD
Professor, Vocational Education
University of Connecticut
Storrs, Connecticut

DAVID L. WILSON
Director of Corporate Communication
and Training
Hartford, Connecticut

DAVID W. WINIKUR
Director, Bureau of Pupil Personnel Services
New Jersey State Dept. of Education
Trenton, New Jersey

PREFACE

THE decade of the eighties will continue to witness significant modification in the design and delivery of instruction to students unable to progress academically as well as their peer group, and to students who are *not* given appropriate opportunities to develop their special abilities or talents. Conservative estimates of students who need *special instruction* represent approximately half of the school population. Federal Public Law 94-142 allocates funds up to 12 percent of the population who have been identified as handicapped. The majority of the fifty states estimated that approximately 5 percent of the school population are gifted and an additional 5 percent are talented in specific areas. Federal and state legislation for remediation and additional instructional services for educationally disadvantaged is generally estimated to be about 20 percent of the total school population. Regardless of the validity of these estimates, they cannot be ignored as they reflect federal and state statutes, community mandates, and most importantly, the learning needs of the students.

With the increased demand to justify and validate programs to the federal and state courts, state departments of education, and the local school community, it has become essential that learning programs and environments become clearly articulated and designed. To coincide with the laws and current educational thinking, it is essential that programs follow the normalization principle (mainstreaming) whenever possible, i.e. students should be educated with their peer group. The integration and design of programs and learning environments for students with special needs is a new challenge for educators, as it involves new and expanded roles for all members in the educational and social agencies.

A positive response to this challenge will lead to a new level of educational excellence for *all* students. On the other hand, if done poorly, it will lead to confusion, disillusionment, disappointment, and worst of all, student failure. During this present transition stage, there is and will continue to be a proliferation of models. The naive adoption of such models without consideration of the many significant factors that must be considered will result in programs and related learning environments being rejected by the staff and/or community. In order to avoid such rejection and/or confusion, all educators must become knowledgeable in areas not generally considered to be their major responsibility. This book, therefore, is designed to provide a reader with an overview of the major signficant components that must be considered in developing and implementing programs and designing environments for students with special needs.

The book is not intended as a cookbook. The primary objectives of the book are (1) to familiarize the reader with the current state of affairs in regard to the education and learning environment of students with special needs, (2) to delineate current and potential learning/teaching problems, (3) to identify a variety of alternate designs of learning environments, and (4) to provide the methodology and process that will facilitate the development and implementation of viable programs. During this transition phase when all are seeking solutions, it will be necessary to proceed with caution. The approach recommended throughout this book, along with the content it contains, will be a valuable resource as it will prevent hasty and costly adoption of programs and learning environments not well suited to needs of local districts. Rather, it will provide the necessary rationale to assist in the selection and development of programs and learning environments that will best meet the needs of students in a specific local situation.

CONTENTS

Section IV: Research and Evaluation

DESIGNING LEARNING PROGRAMS AND ENVIRONMENTS FOR STUDENTS WITH SPECIAL LEARNING NEEDS

Section I

General Issues

CHAPTER 1

SPECIAL EDUCATION DELIVERY SYSTEM IN TRANSITION

LOUIS V. MESSINEO

I N recent years the changes in education have progressed at such a rate that traditional patterns embedded in past practices and conventional wisdom no longer provide an acceptable, consistent baseline for decision-making purposes or adequate guidance for educational practitioners. The most significant changes can be attributed to legislative and judicial action and have been predominantly directed to students at the tails of the distribution, i.e. students with special needs. The effects, however, impact on all students. The erosion of past standards and practices that heretofore gave a degree of stability and predictability in the day-to-day and year-to-year operation of the schools has given way to a more transient, less stable, and uncertain pattern.

Since its inception in this country, over a century ago, until the mid 1960s, special education has delivered services to handicapped populations predominantly through the structure of the self-contained classroom. During this time-span the primary emphasis was placed on differentiating and discriminating student populations through diagnostic procedures that reflected medical and mental testing categories. As special education expanded to meet the needs of an increased number of discrete populations with special needs, it produced an ad hoc patchwork of more and more quasi-autonomous classrooms and programs.

In time these practices began to be seriously questioned. Reviews of research over the past several decades have failed to demonstrate that these children achieve and/or adjust better than those who remained in regular classes. The validity of diagnostic instruments and classifications, and the relevance for educational programs have not been demonstrated. Some research indicates that the stigma attached to special education class placement may more than offset any advantage this type of program can offer. Finally, the raising of the issue regarding civil rights of children has led to serious questions regarding placements and procedures that have been common practice.

In response to these questions and challenges, educators, through federal grants, have expanded services to children with special needs and developed many innovative programs. These programs included the advice and recommendations from other professional disciplines, social agencies, and many local, state, and federal ad hoc committees. The advice and recommendations from these sources were, in most instances, subject to the review of local educational agencies, which had the responsibility and discretion to accept, modify, or reject them before plans were developed and implemented. Because of local control, changes made during this period needed to be interfaced with other programs so as not to be disproportionately disruptive to the overall school program. Changes that occurred during the late 1960s and through the mid-1970s were, for the most part, of a substantive nature related to new and refined programs, curriculum, diagnostic procedures, and conceptual theories and methodology.

The changes that occurred were apparently too slow and too minimal for many aroused groups, and by the mid-1970s the action of state and federal legislators became a significant force in the direction and practices of the educational enterprise.

With these new statutes and regulations there has been a dramatic shift from substantive issues to procedural ones. This is clearly reflected in the summary of PL 94-142:

> The regulations included provisions which are designed (1) to assure that all handicapped children have available to them free appropriate public education; (2) to assure that the rights of handicapped children and their parents are protected; (3) to assist States and localities to provide for the education of handicapped children; and (4) to assess and assure the effectiveness of efforts to educate such children.[2]

From an abstract and legal point of view, the classifications made by pupil placement teams appear to be based on firm criteria and guidelines. However, from a research and practical perspective, this view is not substantiated. Upon reflection and review, it turns out that the classifications are inconsistent and are based on presumptions from different contexts, which are unsystematically related to each other. Hollingshead, A.B., for example, has found that classifications of the same conditions were labeled differently depending on social status.[4]

The epidemeological study by Strole, L. et al., showed that the majority of residents in a community they studied had emotional problems.[9] From this it can be inferred that it would be difficult to establish a cause and effect relationship between emotionality and any specific problems such as a learning problem. In fact, one could hypothesize that if you were to determine the emotional status of learners and nonlearners there would probably be no difference. Most of the data to date seeks a relationship after the fact. Conclusions based on such data are difficult to validate. Therefore, until further studies are done indicating that emotional problems are related to learning difficulties, or that emotional difficulties are not related to learning difficulties, a cause and effect relationship between emotionality and learning problems should not be assumed.

A recent *Education, USA* article reviews the results of a study that indicated that 49 percent of 26,000 students placed in learning disability classes in the state of Colorado were not handicapped, and that 10 percent of the remaining students in this group were misdiagnosed.[3] David Kirp reports in a study that there were forty times more students labeled and classified as retarded than were students labeled and classified as emotionally disturbed.[5] These rates are dramatically different from those generally reported that show approximately equal percentages in these categories. The differences found in this study can be attributed to the preference of teams making the diagnostic and placement decisions and the availability of space and classes for retarded students. While some handicapping conditions such as orthopedic handicaps, and visual or hearing impairment, are easy to identify and classify, other conditions such as emotional disturbance, learning disability, and mental retardation are found to be ambiguous in their identifications, and except for extreme cases are difficult to delineate in an unequivocal manner. The problem of diagnostic classification is compounded further when such a classification as educationally disadvantaged is included as a separate category that must be provided with special programs. This type of ambiguity encourages the dubious practice of identifying the learning problem and then, after the fact, attaching one of several labels which meets the needs for an immediate placement.

The common practice of defining a remedial or handicapped student as one falling at or below a designated level of achievement is another area of interest because of the ambiguity it presents to practioners. Without relating achievement to other independent variables such as ability, students achieving below a specified level are automatically designated as needing special services to attain an average achievement. In a subtle way, use of this definition shifts the frame of reference from equality of opportunity to the equality of results. There is a hopeful assumption that allocations of resources will remove the condition with the magical result that students at the tail of the distribution will achieve in the average range. Use of this definition also encourages the practice of providing assistance to students who are already doing as well or better than expected, and not providing assistance to students who are achieving within the average range, but who, nonetheless, are several years below their expected level. The use of this first definition also places unrealistic responsibility and expectation on educators to assist students to reach levels of achievement that are clearly not possible at least within the constraints of our present knowledge.

Lipsky, M., reviews a study that is of particular interest as it illustrates some of the unresolved problems faced by professionals who have the responsibility for delivering social services. This study occurred at a time when tonsillectomies were popular. The study allows practitioners to view some aspects of the present condition from a somewhat different perspective and time. In this study a team of physicians examined 389 children and found that 174 would profit from a tonsillectomy. A second group of physicians examined the remaining 250 children and judged that 99 of the students would benefit from this operation. A third panel of examiners examined the remaining 116 children and recommended one-half for the operation. This study is instructive in that it points to three problem areas that are not being adequately addressed at the present time. The first problem relates to a tendency to overdiagnose when benefits are available. The second problem relates to the inconsistencies of classifications and decisions based on the judgment of clinical teams. The third problem is concerned with the risk and consequences of decisions to implement changes in cases where the change is questionable or not necessary. Upon reflection, it will be realized that decisions made by planning and placement teams are based on (1) the provisional judgment of ad hoc teams, rather than firm criteria; (2) students are often classified as handicapped in order to be eligible for services; and (3) information on the negative side effects of decisions is not available.

Another area that is currently not receiving much attention is a consideration of the social validity and consequences of each classification area. In the area of mental health, for example, it has been hypothesized that mental illness is a useful fiction that obscures interpersonal problems that are otherwise difficult to confront or resolve, and often shifts the responsibility from the source to other persons or agencies. Szasz, T.S., in addressing this issue stated:

> For it seems to be that — at least in our scientific theories of behavior — we have failed to accept the simple fact that human relations are inherently fraught with difficulties and that to make them even relatively harmonious requires much patience and hard work. I submit that the idea of mental illness is now being put to work to obscure certain difficulties which at present may be inherent — not that they need be unmodifiable — in social intercourse of persons. If this is true, the concept functions as a disguise; for instead of calling attention to conflicting human needs, aspirations, and values, the notion of mental illness provides an amoral and impersonal "thing" (an "illness") as an explanation for the problems of living.[10]

If there is any validity to this or other similar views, educators and other professionals will have to reconsider their positions, particularly with regard to treatment alternatives and individual responsibility. With the lack of clear definitions, along with alternative conceptualizations of the various classifications used inconsistently, it is not likely that services can be provided to students in an equitable manner. The unreliability of classifications can lead to inappropriate placements as well as allegations of malpractice. Remsburg, E.W., refers to possible legal and practical questions related directly or indirectly to the labeling process:

> First, there is a possibility that the process will result in over-restrictive classification. For example, a student who presents a discipline problem may be mistakenly classified as having a handicap requiring special education. . .
>
> Secondly, the classification process may result in the failure to identify the seriousness of the student's handicap. A student in a regular class may

have a handicap, but still be ignored if he is not a discipline problem. The teacher may simply consider him a poor student without any particular handicap. . .

Finally, even if a handicapped student is properly identified, he still may receive an improper classroom placement. Such a case could arise where a disagreement exists between the parents and school district over the extent to which the handicapped student is to be mainstreamed. . .

In each of these potential problem areas — misclassification of the exceptional child, or subsequent wrongful placement, the possibility of an educational malpractice claim exists. . .[8]

The lack of specifics in the statutes and regulations had the subtle effect of relegating the authority of making educational decisions to the courts. A review of court decisions establishes the fact that different interpretations of the statutes may be made by different courts. Levin, M.I., provides an example of such an occurrence:

In assuming the power of unilaterally determining the appropriateness of educational programs, the courts have adopted different standards, which are often in conflict with one another. In *Armstrong* v *Kline,* 476 F. Supp. 583 (E.D. Pa. 1979), the court held that a free appropriate education is one which maximizes educational benefits in the area of self-sufficiency and freedom from caretakers. In *Rowley,* on the other hand, the court rejected the maximization standards of *Armstrong* and held that an appropriate education is one which gives a handicapped child an opportunity to achieve his full potential commensurate with the opportunity provided to other children.

Contrary interpretations such as this, or court decisions that are so narrow as to raise more questions than they answer, are now part of the condition of special education. These difficulties, along with those discussed in the areas of classification and placement, have the effect of placing much of the emphasis on the political/social aspects of schooling rather than the more substantive ones of learning and achievement. Policies that emerge from political and/or social action do not guarantee a solution or even a better set of conditions for the educational practitioner and, therefore, the educational decision-maker.

Arthur E. Wise concludes that "Policies based on incorrect assumption probably will not work and may well have unintended (possible undesirable) consequences." He also provides a useful means-end analytical framework to assist in analyzing and determining if legislation is reasonable or irrational.

Concerning the weighting of means and ends, we shall say that rationalization occurs when the relationship between means and ends is known, when the ends are attainable, given the means, or when the means are reasonable given the ends. When the relationship between means and ends is not known and bureaucratic rationalization persists, we shall say that we are witnessing a phenomenon of hyperrationalization — this is, an effort to rationalize beyond the bounds of knowledge. This involves imposing means which do not result in the attainment of ends, or the setting of ends which cannot be attained, given the available means — imposing unproven techniques on the one hand, and setting unrealistic expectations on the other.

Ensuring that a practice conforms to norms requires replacing the exercise of administrative discretion either with procedures or rules. Rationalization occurs when procedures and regulations ensure conformity to norms and have the intended effects of fairness and equality. Hyperrationalization occurs when conformity to norms is not achieved by the procedures and rules imposed — when procedures are followed but the norm of fairness is not necessarily attained; when rules are obeyed, but the norm of equality is not necessarily attained.[11]

To rationalize "beyond the boundary of knowledge" is, admittedly, a risky venture, but one that must be undertaken in the face of the rapid change of such transition as education has experienced over the past two decades. To "hyperrationalize" in the face of logically inconsistent policies, procedures, and practices is quite another matter. It is demoralizing, particularly to those who, in good faith, adopt it unconsciously as a psychological defense one that, alas, has not proven to be effective against the oft-reported epidemic of "burnout."

This period of disorderly transition has proved unsettling to most. However, the solution being projected for the 80s seems even more alarming to many. The general mood of the country has, undoubtedly, become conservative. The "new federalism" portends a massive shift in responsibility from the federal government to local sources, entailing rather drastic cuts in federal aid to education, and a vigorous effort at deregulation and debureaucratization. The trend for the 80s is most clearly manifested by the increasingly popular demand for "back to basics," and the threatened dismantling of the only recently established cabinet status of the Department of Education.

It is not surprising that the initial reaction to this state of affairs should be one of depression and discouragement. It would seem, however, that the greater danger would be to succumb to a paralysis of despair and hopelessness. In order to avoid this, we must take a realistic look at what now is, and what is most likely to be in the foreseeable future. The present situation may surely be viewed as a crisis in special education. But as the Chinese symbol for crisis indicates, it is at the same time a danger and an opportunity. Clearly, the more productive view is to deliberately search out whatever opportunities may be afforded by the historical circumstances that present themselves. The rest of the chapter will, therefore, be devoted to an attempt to light some candles rather than continue to curse the darkness.

It would, perhaps, be helpful to view the attack by special education as being carried out on two fronts. On the broad front, we attempt to "educate the public" regarding the needs of education and the rights of students. On the narrower front, we must educate the students to meet their individual responsibilities. While educators must maintain their commitment to both fronts in waging its war against ignorance, it cannot always do so with equal effort. It seems almost certain that in the 80s we will see a shift in emphasis from the rights of students to be different to the obligation of students to take the responsibility for being different. On the assumption that the 80s will be dominated by this phase shift, it would seem that the expenditure of effort in searching out whatever might be good in this approach would not be wasted.

Destructuring the present system does not necessarily imply destruction: It is a necessary step to restructuring the system and it is the quality of the latter that will determine whether the outcome is more or less favorable. Thus, we can view deregulation and debureaucratization as providing us with an opportunity for looking anew at genuinely substantive issues unencumbered by the cumulative overlay of mandated procedures, which not infrequently operate at cross purposes to one another. Another positive effect would be the reduction in the educator's felt need to defend himself against the threat of noncompliance in the face of contradictory demands. The greater the number of demands, and the more remote the source of such demands, the greater the liability. Reversal of this trend would liberate any energy tied up in such counterproductive maneuvers as defensive documentation and, thereby, make this energy more available for reinvestment in more productive activities.

Even if only by default, one is now offered the option of regrouping whatever resources he/she has access to in terms of the unique demands of the local "pond ecology." This change in direction is more formally signalled by the recent enactment of Chapter 1 of the Education Consolidation and Improvement Act of 1981, the successor to Title I of the Elementary and Secondary Educational Act. The new legislation, contrary to the regulations of Title I, allows local education agencies to use federal funds to supplement local funds within the context of community school programs. This change provides local communities the required flexibility to meet the needs identified by legislators within a locally integrated program.

One might also hope for relief of a malady suffered by many practitioners who have been oppressed by the feeling that a plethora of statutes and regulations have been more a part of the problem than of the solution. They sometimes have appeared to have produced an iatrogenic effect, a circumstance wherein a doctor exacerbates the condition of the patient he would cure. The unwieldly system has unwittingly sustained the very condition it would remedy, creating a sort of "support system syndrome." Paradoxically, less rigorous "affirmative action" might work in the direction of resolving the dilemma covered by the description, "the solution is part of the problem."

Since our major resources currently are being committed to the "second front" of developing individual competencies and responsibilities, this is where we are most likely to see action during the 80s. As P. Coppelman has warned, "contemporary educators who reduce or eliminate standards out of concern for a child's self-esteem risk damaging the child far more seriously when they send him into the world poorly prepared to survive and function."[1]

Particularly in the case of our handicapped student, it is important that he/she develop a sense of self-esteem based on a realistically wide-ranging set of accommodative competencies. The fact that we live in a world of norms such as that of 20/20 vision is the result of no one's arbitrary decision: It is simply a stubborn fact of the world as given. It appears somewhat utopian to believe that the norms will ever be scaled down to meet the individual needs of a deviant minority over against those of the normal majority. Even in the case where norms are arrived at by social convention, the deviant child must be effectively prepared to deal with the pervasive pressures to conform to the norm. Just as a thermostat ought to be set for a value in favor of the common good and for no one in particular, so should a group norm be set impersonally to favor no one in particular. Thus, we face the challenging task of providing each child with the skills necessary to compensate his/her deviation from the norm within his/her expanding individual rights.

No matter what the 80s may bring, we shall surely be forced to acknowledge the truism that limits are permanent features of the human condition. No matter how successful a bureaucratic society may be in displacing these limits, we shall, nonetheless, have to live within them in turn. These remain the fronts where we are committed to do battle, as well as we are able, no matter what the decade.

REFERENCES

1. Coppelman, Paul. *The Literary Hoax.* New York: William Morrow and Company, Inc., 1978.
2. Education of Handicapped Children: Implementation of Part B of the Education of the Handicapped Act. *Federal Register, 42*; 163, 1977.
3. Half of Colorado LDs Said Mislabeled. *Education USA, 23*; 28, 1981.
4. Hollingshead, A.B., and Redlich, F.C. *Social Class and Mental Illness.* New York: Wiley, 1958.
5. Kirp, David. Schools as Sorters. The Constitutional and Policy Implications of Student Classification. *University of Pennsylvania Law Review, 12*; 4, 1973.
6. Levin, Michael I. Educational Placement of the Handicapped — Selected Issues. *Schools and the Laws of the Handicapped.* Washington, D.C.: National School Boards Association, 1981.
7. Lyssky, Michael. *Street-Level Bureaucracy.* New York: Russell Sage Foundation, 1980.
8. Remsburg, Edward W. Liability for Wrongful Identification, Evaluation or Placement — Is There Malpractice? *School and the Laws of the Handicapped.* Washington, D.C., National School Boards Association, 1981.
9. Strole, L., et al. *Mental Health in the Metropolis,* Manhattan Study, Vol. 1, New York: McGraw-Hill Book Company, Inc., 1962.
10. Szasz, Thomas S. The Myth of Mental Illness. *American Psychologist, 16*; 2, 1961.
11. Wise, Arthur E. *Legislated Learning.* California: University of California Press, 1979.

CHAPTER 2

DEVELOPMENT OF INSTRUCTIONAL TECHNOLOGY AND THE CHANGING LEARNING ENVIRONMENT

FARHAD SABA

ONE of the basic characteristics of the nature and essence of man's cultural evolution during the twentieth century has been the development of technology (Teich 1972, Freeman 1974, Bereano 1976). Technology has proliferated into almost all domains of human cultural activities including those that have traditionally derived and flourished from humanities. Industry, commerce and businesses are heavily dependent on technological developments. Industrial and technological developments are so closely related that the two concepts are indistinguishable at times. Technology constitutes the core of health care and hospital operations. Modern defense systems are inconceivable without technological systems and procedures. Artists and scholars of humanities are increasingly using technological processes and procedures to express themselves in novel and creative forms as well as in their research activities.

Technology could be defined in a parsimonious way as the use of scientific information (research results) in solving practical problems. Hence, instructional technology may be defined as application of scientific information to solve instructional and/or educational problems. Application of scientific information from a variety of disciplines to solve instructional problems including physics (optics, mechanics and electronics), behavioral sciences (psychology, sociology, management), communications and systems approach constitutes the core of instructional technology. Therefore, instructional technology is an interdisciplinary concept embracing a variety of theories, principles and methods in the process of instruction.

Technology and its impact on man has been scrutinized and criticized by many scholars, scientists and theoreticians. Criticism of

15

technology could be summarized in the following way:

1. Technology creates its own deterministic and universal culture, overwhelms human ethics and engulfs man's spirit in a limited environment characterized by the lack of freedom, creativity, and dignity.
2. Technology is neutral. It is a tool in the hands of man. The use of technology depends on the ethical and moral values of those who use it.
3. Technology is man's greatest cultural achievement in modern history. It has brought prosperity, education, greater freedom of movement, leisure and cultural enhancement to the masses in an unprecedented scale in human history.

It is the conviction of this author that the outcome of the use of technology depends on the moral and ethical values held by those who utilize technology for attainment of certain ends. Furthermore, introduction of technology in instruction has provided a unique opportunity for the scientific and academic community to incorporate human values in the use of technology and utilize the results of scientific research for attainment of desired educational ends based on highly regarded universal ethical and moral values. It is hypothesized that the union of technology and humanistic values is inherent in the use of technology for instruction. Technological development in the field of education, however, has been slower than in medicine, industry or defense (Willett, et al., 1979). Yet, proliferation of technology in instruction may prove to be the most rewarding and at the same time challenging and controversial use of technology. In instructional technology, human beings as learners are directly interacting with technology in an environment, which is not necessarily threatening (as in the use of technology in medicine or defense), therefore creating a unique opportunity for creative and humanistic use of technology.

It was mentioned that instructional technology is a multidisciplinary and interdisciplinary domain of knowledge. As the concept of instructional technology has evolved and grown, various analytical and inclusive definitions of the field were presented, which highlight these characteristics. Ely (1973) reviewed a number of definition statements. The following, according to Ely, is a widely accepted definition in the field.

Educational Technology is a systematic way of designing, carrying out, and evaluating the total process of learning and teaching in terms of specific objectives based on research in human learning and communication and employing a combination of human and non-human resources to bring about more effective instruction. This definition suggested by the presidential commission on Instructional Technology depicts educational technology as a practical field concerned with behaviorally oriented systematic instruction.

A definition emphasizing the management aspects of instructional technology could be found in Mitchell's (1977) article:

> Educational Technology is an area of study and practice (within) education concerned with all aspects of the organization of educational systems and procedures whereby resources are allocated to achieve specified and potentially replicable educational outcomes.

The word "study" in this definition also adds an epistemological aspect which is absent in the first definition cited here.

In his detailed and encyclopedic review of the field, Mitchell (1977) also presents a philosophical definition of the field.

"Educational Technology was seen as an intellectual and practical pursuit concerned with all aspects of the design and operational organization of educational systems and sub-systems and with the relation between their inputs and outputs, between desired outcomes and the allocation of resources to achieve them."

The use of the word "intellectual" adds a philosophical flavor to this definition. The definitions selected here at least suggest that instructional technology is a practical discipline concerned with enhancement of learning in a systematic fashion by utilization of scientific information. The discipline is also concerned with a study of its own nature, techniques and effects. It is also an intellectual pursuit looking into the philosophical roots and backgrounds of the discipline and future explanation and delineation of instructional technology as a branch of knowledge.

COMPONENTS OF INSTRUCTIONAL TECHNOLOGY

As implied in the definitions of instructional technology presented here the discipline draws from a variety of scientific basis to be incorporated in its processes and procedures. The most important scientific basis includes but is not limited to the following areas:

1. Systems theory
2. Learning psychology
3. Communication theory and media systems

One of the most common agreements among the practitioners and theoreticians of the field is that systems approach toward education is a distinguishing feature of instructional technology.

Systems approach to education provides at least two sets of different but related concepts to instructional technology. First and foremost, it provides a specific scientific outlook. Education, perceived through the system's looking glass, is consisted of a whole with interrelated parts. A whole (a system) that is greater than the sum total of its parts (subsystem); therefore, a systems approach is holistic towards education. Systems orientation approaches an educational entity in its entirety and tries to understand not only the parts (sub-systems) of the system but also the relationship between the parts (sub-systems). It is also concerned with the multiple, process, and output of an educational system and the effects of environment on an educational system in terms of feedback and delays.

Second, systems approach suggests a specific method towards education. The method consists of certain specific steps to insure adequate definition of goals and objectives based on needs analysis and other data, selection of appropriate teaching/learning strategies and evaluation procedures to insure quality control and a variety of information for cost-effective and efficient management of the system. Many relatively simple models have been developed and suggested on the basis of systems approach. More complex system models have also been developed and utilized for the study and modelling of a variety of social settings including educational institutions such as J.W. Forrester (1961) Systems Dynamics model. Systems approach to education remains to be the unifying and perhaps the most important element of instructional technology (Saetler, 1979).

THEORETICAL MODELS OF LEARNING

Instructional Technology as an academic and practical discipline is concerned with the process and conditions of learning. Therefore, it draws both theoretical and practical information from the body of knowledge that is known as learning theory. Different models of learning have contributed to the growth and development of the field of instructional technology.

Bloom in "Taxonomy of Educational Objectives" (1965) presented a relatively concise model for the analysis of educational outcomes in the cognitive area of remembering, thinking, and problem solving, based on the student's behavior representing the intended outcome of the educational process. The taxonomy was developed more than twenty years ago and, therefore, is both of historical and educational value. A major goal of the taxonomy was facilitating communication among educators by developing agreement on the nature and purpose of educational objectives through classification and definition of each category.

Skinner (1968) provided a behavioral model of human learning. The model ignores cognitive explanations of human behavior. Its emphasis is on external observable behavior of living organisms and provides certain schedules of reinforcement for shaping such behavior. Skinner's contribution has been invaluable in terms of arranging the environment to enhance learning. His principles of behavioral modification has found a number of practical applications in developing learning machines, programmed instruction and computer-assisted instruction. Attending only to observable behavior of living organisms to the expense of ignoring mental processes, however, limits Skinner's model in understanding human learning in its entirety. Other scholars have tried to provide cognitive as well as behavioral explanation of human learning. Some of these models that are more relevant to the growth of the discipline will be reviewed here.

Bourne, Ekstrand and Dominowski (1971) concentrated on the internal processes to the learner's external behavior. Similar to Bloom (1956), they presented a hierarchical model of thinking in which each lower level is a necessary precondition for the attainment of the higher level of intellectual skill. What this model appears to add to earlier works is that it identifies both the stimulus attributes and the response behavior as *conceptual* phenomena:

> All behavior is in a sense conceptual. We respond not to the uniqueness in our circumstances but to the regulations, the categories, the sequences and the functions of objects and events in the world.

In this view, the concept of behavior has been extended to include

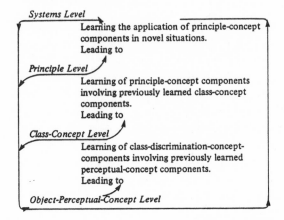

Figure 2-1.

knowledge, intellectual skills and intentions as the cognitive components of behavior.

> Knowledge, skills, and intentions are not non-behavioral mechanisms that produce performance (behavior), neither are they casual antecedent events or processes which effect (or affect) performance (behavior). They are rather part and parcel of behavior itself. Any discussion of real behavior will implicate each of them.

The development of thinking behavior, according to Bourne, et al., involves the development of conceptual components beginning at the lowest or "Object" level and proceeding step-by-step to the highest or "System" level of thinking, and the application (moving downward) of these learned behaviors in the solution of problems.

Gagné (1967) has been concerned with both hierarchical model of cognitive behavior *and* the external conditions that make successive levels of learning possible.

Gagné (1967) conceptualized learning as developing through eight different types that were differentiated, classified in a hierarchy, and described in terms of the conditions under which each is likely to occur. The notion that all learning is learned under the same conditions was rejected by Gagné. Each type is a precondition and a necessary factor for the acquisition of knowledge is a process in which every new capability builds on a foundation established by previously learned capability.

Similar to Bloom (1972), Gagné (1970) also refers to intellectual skills as an overall concept that includes discrimination, chaining, classifying, rule learning and problem solving. But he introduces a new concept in relation to the cognitive process of remembering these intellectual skills. Remembering is viewed as a general concept that includes two forms of recall and reinstatement. Recall involves simple verbalization of memorized materials, however, reinstatement of a concept involves "demonstrating its referential meaning rather than simply making a verbal statement."

THE EXTERNAL PRECONDITIONS FOR LEARNING. The acquisition and development of each different type of intellectual skill requires a particular set of internal and external prerequisite conditions.

In providing an overview of different cognitive views of learning, Hilgard and Bower (1948) have listed some central concerns about the preconditions of learning:

1. *The perceptual features*: the critical characteristics of what is to be learned should be sharp and clear in order to facilitate learning.

2. *The organization of knowledge*: information which is integrated and related to a central organizing theme is easier to learn than fragmented knowledge.

3. *Learning with understanding*: information which is learned in relationships to its meaning and value to the learner is acquired more quickly and retained longer.

4. *Cognitive feedback*: learning proceeds more rapidly when the learner has an opportunity to practice new knowledge and receive feedback information on results.

5. *Goal setting*: learning is more rapid and effective when the learner sets the goals, and the learning activities are directed towards these learner-goals.

6. *Divergent thinking*: cognitive psychologists are apt to focus on the conditions that facilitate divergent rather than convergent kinds of thinking.

Hilgard and Bower (1948) have also presented Bruner's cognitive development theory as it deals primarily with four specifications for a theory of instruction, and these can be viewed as guidelines for establishing the external conditions that are likely to lead to high levels of learning:

1. *Predisposition to learn*: provision of experiences and a context for learning that will lead the learners to be willing and eager to learn.
2. *Structure of knowledge*: presentation of a body of knowledge in a manner that emphasizes the structure that integrates that knowledge.
3. *Sequence*: presentation of learning materials in a sequence which moves from a simplified view of the whole structure to a complex view of the whole.
4. *Reinforcement*: specification of a schedule for reward contingencies moving from extrinsic reinforcement to intrinsic or self-controlled reinforcements.

COMMUNICATION THEORY AND MEDIA SYSTEMS

Application of principles derived from communication theory and utilization of media systems is an integral component of instructional technology. Delivery of instructional content to learners require encoding messages, sending messages through appropriate channels to the intended audience who will in turn decode the message. It is also expected that a corrective or supportive feedback be received by the sender of the message. Learners may be exposed to a variety of messages in the course of their daily activity. Peer group interaction, face-to-face communication with their teachers and parents are examples of situations in which learners are exposed to messages. Learners are also exposed to books, films, television, radio and other media. Messages received through these and other forms of media systems may be decoded and internalized by learners. This process also could lead to relatively permanent changes in the learners' cognitive, affective or motor behavior. The processes of communication as described here is an essential part of instructional technology.

Communication theory has evolved and developed on a more scientific basis since Shannon and Weaver proposed their mathematical model of communication in 1948. Since then, several other models of the complex and fascinating process of human communicating the external conditions that are likely to lead to high dynamic and detailed conceptualization of the process of communication. Some nonlinear models have also been proposed in recent years (Mortensen 1970). Efforts should be made to integrate the proposed theoretical models of communication to arrive at a more comprehensive yet parsimonious model, one that includes all of the complex contextual, cultural, linguistic, constructional and procedural elements involved in communication yet thorough enough to lend itself to rigorous scientific verification.

Rapid proliferation of media into the classroom has exposed the learners to a new set of learning experience derived from media attributes (Line, form, space, color, sound) and symbol systems. Such media characteristics have been under investigation by a number of researchers to understand their nature and their differential effect on learners in terms of knowledge acquisition and cultivation of mental skills. (Salomon, 1979) These investigations have yielded a set of principles:

All media have potential learning-teaching value for certain learners, under certain set of conditions.

Each medium possesses a set of unique characteristics that interact with learner's traits in a certain way to achieve a set of objectives.

Media materials provide differentiated learning experience for learners, each of whom are unique in their learning ability, style, and speech.

Media's ways of structuring and presenting information — that is, their symbol systems — are media's most important attributes when learning and cognition are considered and thus should serve as our focus of inquiry.

Symbol systems, the means by which messages are coded, address themselves to different aspects of content, and different symbol systems yield different meanings, when content is novel.

Symbol systems vary with respect to the kinds of mental transformations (or recoding) that they require, and they vary with respect to the kinds of mental skills they activate in the service of knowledge extraction. Thus, symbol systems in general, and coding elements in particular, vary as to the learners whose learning they facilitate.

The kinds of information one can, is required to, or chooses to extract from a coded message determines the coding elements one deals with ("top-down" processes) and the kinds of mental processes that are called upon ("bottom-up" processes).

The coding elements of a medium's blend of symbol systems can be made to cultivate the mastery of specific mental skills by either activating or overtly supplanting the skills, in interaction with a learner's skill-mastery levels.

Teachers as human beings provide a variety of functions, i.e. needs analysis, counseling tasks, evaluation, affective and supportive reinforcement. Hence, they are not comparable to media and certainly cannot be replaced by media systems.

As media assist the teachers to convey instructional content to learners, teachers may change their role from conveyers of information to instructional systems managers.

REFERENCES

Bereano, Phillip L. *Technology As a Social and Political Phenomenon.* New York: John Wiley & Sons, 1976.

Bloom, Benjamin S. (ed.). *Taxonomy of Educational Objectives* — Handbook I: Cognitive Domain, 17th ed. New York: David McKay Company, Inc. 1972.

Bourne, Lyle E. et al. *The Psychology of Thinking.* Englewood Cliffs: Prentice-Hall, 1971.

Ely, Donald P. "Defining the Field of Educational Technology." *Audio Visual Instruction,* March 1973.

Forrester, J.W. *Industrial Dynamics.* Cambridge, MA: MIT Press. 1961.

Freeman, David M. *Technology and Society: Issues in Assessment, Conflict and Choice.* Chicago: Rand McNally, 1974.

Gagné, Robert M. (ed.). *Learning and Individual Differences.* Columbus, Ohio: Charles E. Merrill Books, Inc, 1967.

Hilgard, Ernest; Gordon Bower. *Theories of Learning.* New York: Appleton-Century-Crofts, 1948.

Mitchell, David. "Educational Technology." Review copy. 1977.

Mortensen, David C. and Sereno, Kenneth K. *Foundations of Communication Theory.* New York: Harper & Row, 1970.

Saetler, Paul. *An Assessment of the Current Status of Educational Technology.* Syracuse: ERIC, 1979.

Salomon, Gavriel. *Interaction of Media, Cognition and Learning,* San Francisco, Jossey-Bass, Publishers, 1979.

Skinner, B.F. *The Technology of Teaching.* New York: Appleton-Century-Crofts, 1968.

Teich, Albert H. (ed). *Technology and Man's Future.* New York: St. Martin's Press, 1972.

Willett; Swanson; Nelson. *Modernizing the Little Red Schoolhouse.* Englewood Cliffs: Educational Technology Publications, 1979.

CHAPTER 3

THE REGULATIONS OF
SPECIAL EDUCATION: How the Law is
Affecting the Delivery of Special Education

Jeffrey C. Pingpank

T HE past ten years have seen a revolution in the legal rights of special education children and their parents. The first part of this period saw the establishment of some basic rights and responsibilities through both judicial decision and legislation. Most recently, courts, agencies and educational institutions have grappled with what the law really means and its effects. The first part of this article will briefly outline the establishment of these basic rights, while the second part will touch on its implications.

THE DEVELOPMENT OF THE LAW

Prior to the 1970s, the issue of special education was left largely to the individual states. This resulted in varying treatment of special education students and that treatment was often dismal. Handicapped children were often excluded from school, and often they were institutionalized. According to Senate testimony, when the Education for ALL Handicapped Children Act was passed in 1975, less than one-half of the nation's special education children had been adequately educated.

It was against this backdrop that the courts and then Congress acted. In the early 1970s there were several court cases that gave basic rights to special education children. These cases generally followed along two lines. In the due process cases, the most notable of which was *Penn. Assoc. for Retarded Citizens v. Penn.*, the courts established that a child had a right to a hearing before that child could be excluded from school or classified as in need of special education. In the equal protection cases, the courts established that special education students were entitled to the same sort of treatment

25

offered "regular" students.

In *Mills v. Board of Education,* 348 F. Supp 866, the court said:

"The defendants are required by the Constitution . . . to provide a publicly supported education for these "exceptional" children. The inadequacies of (the school system) . . . cannot be permitted to bear more heavily on the handicapped child than the "normal child.""

While these cases provided a broad outline of what special education children were entitled to, it remained up to Congress to fill in the details through legislation. Congress started, in 1973, when it passed §504 of the Rehabilitation Act, 29 U.S.C. §794. This section provided that no otherwise qualified handicapped individual could be excluded from participating in, or denied the benefits of, programs that receive federal funds. It is this section that has lead to, among others, building accessibility requirements.

EDUCATION FOR ALL HANDICAPPED CHILDREN ACT

The key ingredient for improving special education was the Education for All Handicapped Children Act, also known as P.L. 94-142 and 20 U.S.C. §1401-1461, which mandates a free appropriate public education for handicapped children. While the Act strives towards the substantive goal of an "appropriate education," it does so not through elaborate definitions of structured programs but rather through a system of procedural safeguards through which parents of special education children can participate in the development of their children's program, and appeal the results if unhappy with the decision. The only substantive requirements in the Act are that the education must be appropriate and, that if possible, and to the extent appropriate, the child should be "mainstreamed" — put in normal classrooms.

The Act sets up a number of procedural requirements. First, it requires that children in need of special education be identified. This can be done through any number and combination of means, including testing. When a child is identified as having special education needs, the Act's major provisions come into play, as the child's program is drawn up.

The program is drawn by the PPT, a planning and placement team. The PPT is comprised of the child's parents, the child's teacher, a representative of the school system and any others who either the system or parents deem desirable. The parent cannot stop the PPT from meeting and developing the program by refusing to appear, but the school system must make reasonable attempts to notify the parents of the meeting, and the meeting must be held at a mutually convenient time.

As it is the PPT that draws up the child's program, the real responsibility for defining what is an "appropriate education" rests with the team. Unless the team's program is challenged by the parents, its recommendations will stand.

The program that the PPT develops is called the IEP or individualized educational program. The IEP is an individualized, written statement for a given child, which is developed at a meeting of the PPT. It is important to note that the IEP is not developed beforehand and presented as a sort of fait accompli to the parents at the PPT meeting. Rather, it is developed at that meeting with input from all those present.

There are several requirements for an IEP. The IEP must contain a statement of the child's present level of performance, a statement of annual goals, including short-term instruction objectives, a statement of the specific special education program and related services to be provided to the child, and the extent the child will be able to be mainstreamed or put into the regular program. Lastly, the IEP should contain appropriate objective criteria to determine if the program objectives are being met.

In order to ensure that substantive justice, in the form of the creation of an appropriate education program, is done, the Act adds to the above procedures with additional safeguards for the parents and the creation of a right to appeal.

Prior to the PPT meeting, parents must be granted access to pertinent records and results of tests. Under appropriate circumstances, they can obtain an independent, outside evaluation at the expense of the school system. Parents must receive adequate notice of any meetings and the notices must be in the parents' native language. Parental consent must also be obtained before most actions involving the child take place. It is important to note that an IEP can be changed, and placements can be changed only through a PPT meeting.

If the parents are displeased with the results of the PPT, they can appeal. While the federal rules allow the states some leeway in designing appeals procedures, most states follow a basic three-step procedure. Most states provide for some form of review at the local level. If that fails to resolve the problem, the parents, or the school system, can ask for a hearing at the state level by an impartial hearing examiner. Finally, there can usually be an appeal to the courts. One additional procedure that is gaining in favor is the use of mediation prior to a hearing. Hearings tend to be adversarial, while mediation helps to lessen hostility and thus make conditions more favorable to settlement.

The Act has obviously created a great improvement in the delivery of special education services to handicapped children. The implemetation of the Act has, however, created tensions and raised serious legal and policy questions concerning some of its procedures. Certainly, this is to be expected in any major new law and social program, but the issues that have been raised over the past five to seven years deserve to be examined. The rest of this article will deal with some of these issues.

What is an Appropriate Education?

The requirement to provide a "free, appropriate public education" is only loosely defined as those special education and related services that are provided in conformity with the IEP. Thus, to a very real extent, the PPT defines what is appropriate. Unfortunately, there is very little legal guidance as to what is required to meet the mandate.

While some courts have held that a free, appropriate education is one that maximizes the educational benefits for a child, most courts have rejected such a stringent view. As one court said, (there is) "a standard which I conclude is more in keeping with the regulations, with the equal protection decisions . . . and with common sense. This standard would require that each handicapped child be given an opportunity to achieve his full potential commensurate with the opportunity provided to other children."

This is probably the appropriate measure. The law does not require that "most appropriate education" but merely an "appropriate education." Therefore, "appropriate" is defined, in part, by what is made available to regular children in a school system. This may cause some variations between what a given child might be offered in one school system as opposed to another, but as long as the program offered is appropriate, and as long as the program's type, range and quality can be analogized to the programs in the regular school, the program is likely to be found legal. In short, a "Cadillac" or "Lighthouse" school district should have Cadillac or Lighthouse special education programs; while a typical school district should have typical special education programs.

It will be interesting to watch what effect the school finance reform movement has on the delivery of special education services. As courts and legislatures require more equal educational opportunity between school districts, this should also affect the variety and range of special education programs offered in each district.

Should the PPT Define Appropriate?

There can be some serious questions raised about whether the burden of defining what is appropriate should be left to the PPT. On the one hand, each child is different and there can be an almost infinite variety of programs. To create stringent statutory requirements could very easily lead to inappropriate results. It seems to be one of Murphy's Laws that extensive regulation leads to bizzare results. A PPT, by having the flexibility it has, can avoid these results.

On the other hand, questions about the pressures on a PPT can be raised, along with questions as to whether there are appropriate checks and balances on the PPT. Most PPT's are dominated by school personnel. Critics have raised the question as to whether school personnel, who must balance the budget, always choose the appropriate program. There can be no denying that some special education placements are extremely expensive, and that placements can wreak havoc with a school district's budget. In the struggle to preserve limited funds are administrators unduly pressured to accept the least expensive alternative?

Coupled with this pressure is the concern that the checks on a PPT team are too few. In reality, only the parents are there to provide a check and balance. There is little other oversight. Is this an effective check when often the parents may be too poor (to afford their own advisors or advocates), uneducated, or too fearful or differential to school authority?

Mainstreaming

The Education for All Handicapped Children Act expresses a

preference for mainstreaming, for placing the child in the "least restrictive environment." This is a laudable goal and has some historic origins. Before the advent of these new special education laws, many handicapped children were placed in institutions. To break away from this isolation, the Act requires that to the maximum extent appropriate, handicapped children are to be educated with other children in the normal program; special classes, facilities or removal from the regular educational environment should occur only when regular classroom programming with supplementary aids and services is not satisfactory. The statute puts the burden of proof on whichever side, be it school or parent, which feels that mainstreaming is inappropriate.

With the budgetary pressures so great on local school districts, there is now a pressure to mainstream, to cut costs, even if that is not a truly appropriate placement. Mainstreaming can be achieved through many ways, be it through the standards a district uses in identifying a child, or in overambitious expectations for an in-school program.

Residential Placements

There can be little argument that the cost of residential placements can be exceedingly high. Residential placements can divert funds from regular programming or even for programs for less severely handicapped children. Since the cost burden in many states is initially the responsibility of local districts, local districts often attempt to restrict themselves to the payment of those costs that relate only to the educational component of the placement. There are some serious questions as to whether the Act allows such differentiation and it sometimes results in a child being held in limbo while the various agencies involved fight over who is responsible.

Related Services

Again, largely because of the costs involved, debates frequently arise over what is a related service. The Act has a paragraph of examples of related services, yet that detail has not ended the dispute. The Act defines related services to mean "transportation and such developmental, corrective and other supportive services . . . as may be required to assist a handicapped child to benefit from special education . . ."

Recent decisions have shown how broad the term can be, as music therapy, therapeutic recreation (including swimming) and sign language training for parents, have been held to be related services. In one instance, however, participation in a high school football team was not held to be a related service.

Cost and Benefit

Most of the above sections have raised issues that revolve around financial ability. The tensions between limited resources and extensive needs can neither be denied nor ignored. The resolution of these tensions has profound implications for the delivery of services to both special education children and those in regular programs. The available money can be stretched only so far, and there are many conflicting groups both in and out of education.

In the immediate future, it seems likely that the issues of cost and who is financially responsible for what treatment will influence the development of special education law as much, if not more than, issues involving more conceptual issues, such as, what is an "appropriate education." The cost of providing special education is causing school districts to make painful choices over the allocation of scarce resources. To the extent that the equal protection cases gave a boost to special education in the early '70s, it may provide some sort of limitation in the mid-or-late '80s, as the legal forces in special education pay greater attention to the cost and benefits of special education programs.

CHAPTER 4

THE CUMULATIVE EFFECTS OF ACADEMIC FAILURE

RONALD LOIACONO

I T is a stressful experience for many children to make the transition from the familiar environment of the home into the competitive setting of the classroom (White, 1964). The naive student ventures into the new arena of school with little knowledge of what to expect (Dreeban, 1968) and is quickly confronted with its challenging demands.

To participate in the educational experience, students are required to utilize their mental, physical, and social skills: each skill directly compared to the same skills of their peers. Through the years there is a growing awareness among students that the competitive atmosphere that exists mediates the rewards for success and the penalties for failure. Very often in the classroom situation, the success of one student is contingent upon the failure of another.

The competitive nature of the classroom may foster a fear of failure among students and, in conjunction with the emphasis on evaluation, can create pressure on all students to succeed. All students cannot be equally successful since performance standards are usually generated from group norms that place half of the students above the class average. Since each student possesses unique qualities and a wide range of variation exists among classmates and within a given individual, each student will experience success in some areas and failure in others. Furthermore, the below functioning student with special learning needs is particularly vulnerable to experiencing academic failure.

Previous researchers have extensively examined the debilitating effects of academic failure on elementary school students, Glidewell & Stringer, 1968; Kifer, 1973; Smith, 1971; Torshen, 1969. Chief among the most frequently observed effects of academic failure in school are counterproductive patterns of anxiety, maladaptive behavior patterns, and low self-esteem.

While the immediate experience of failure can have a negative effect on a student, Glidewell, Kanor, Smith, and Stringer (1966) address a more serious consequence, the cumulative effect of repeated school failure through the grades. These researchers propose a circular process in which school failure leads to inappropriate defense mechanisms. These reaction patterns bring about a reduction in the student's learning efficiency, which in turn, increases the probability of subsequent school failure. The interactive effects of school failure and inappropriate behavior steadily intensify through the grades in a circular, self-perpetuating process.

The failure cycle is summarized in the following diagram by the writer.

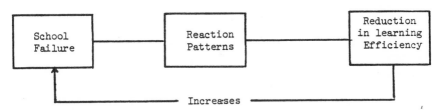

The state of objective self-awareness, as presented by Duval & Wicklund (1972), may shed light on how the unsuccessful student perceives the classroom environment. This state is produced when an individual's attention is self-focused and can occur in a social situation when an individual becomes aware of focused attention from others creating feelings of self-consciousness (Wicklund & Duval, 1971).

The theory posits that this state produces critical self-evaluation, and negative self-evaluation may be engendered by an individual's failure to meet external standards. The awareness of discrepant performance between actual and expected standards exacerbates the individual's perception of his/her deficiency and leads to negative regard of the self. These negative feelings are often reflected in a lowered self-esteem (Iches, W.; Wicklund, R.A.; & Ferris, C.B.; 1973) and motivate the individual toward reducing the dissonance (Festinger, 1957; Wicklund & Duval, 1971). If the discrepancy is not reduced, then the individual will engage in active avoidance tendencies (Gibbons & Wicklund, 1976).

The objective self-awareness model provides a framework with which to view the effects of academic failure in school through a new perspective. The student participates in a variety of activities requiring interactions with teachers and/or peers. Each time a student is called upon to answer a question, read aloud, or contribute information to the class, the opportunity for greater self-consciousness increases to an indeterminant extent. This state of objective self-awareness involves the student in critical self-evaluation. The unsuccessful student finds this condition uncomfortable and alienating since academic performance is discrepant with expectation. The student who is unable to reduce this discrepancy will be motivated to avoid this condition whenever possible.

The failure cycle can be further explicated by incorporating objective self-awareness into the model. School failure generates aversive objective awareness that leads to inappropriate patterns of classroom behavior and anxiety. These symptoms reduce the student's learning efficiency, which in turn, feed back increased probability of subsequent school failure. This cycle can be represented in the following diagram.

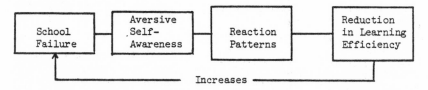

Various approaches have been recommended for dealing with the problem of failure in school. Glasser (1969) identified failure as the basis of almost all school-related problems and suggested educational reform. Mastery learning (Bloom, 1968) offers one approach to educators that attempts to provide successful experiences for almost all students. Nongraded schools (Goodlad, 1959) represent still another alternative designed to facilitate successful experiences in school.

While the importance of reducing classroom failure has long been recognized by educators, the phenomenon of failure appears to be inherent in the educational system, despite efforts to reduce it (French, 1965). The fact remains that students are compared against the norms implicitly, if not explicitly, of the different groups in which they find themselves members. Furthermore, learning to deal with the experience of failure is necessary and essential not only to the learning process, but to normal development.

The inability to overcome the failure cycle would result in the tragic consequences of steadily reducing the student's learning efficiency. A better understanding of the failure cycle would facilitate the development of more effective approaches toward helping students deal with this phenomenon. This is especially relevant to school district personnel who are involved with instructional programs and learning environments for the academically backward student with special learning needs.

Field research conducted by Loiacono (1978) reported findings that may shed further light on the failure cycle model. The purpose of the study was to assess the cumulative effects of academic failure on second, fourth, and sixth-grade students. The effects of failure on the student were explored along three dimensions: anxiety, acting-out behavior, and withdrawn behavior. The results revealed that the maladaptive behavior followed the predicted pattern of the failure cycle — they steadily intensified through the grades. However, the findings indicated by the anxiety variables did not cumulate through the grades but rather appeared to follow a curvilinear trend with an increase in anxiety occurring from second to fourth followed by a decrease in sixth.

The role of anxiety revealed by the results provided a convenient point of departure for fruitful speculation. In the light of this different perspective, a more comprehensive framework in which to understand the dynamic interaction of the failure cycle is possible. From the observed data, the anxiety variable appears to relate differently to the failure cycle model than the behavioral variables. The anxiety variable seems to relate more directly to academic failure with observed differences between successful and unsuccessful students emerging as early as the second grade. In contrast, the maladaptive behavioral variables seem to relate more indirectly (via anxiety) to academic failure, since observed differences in classroom behavior did not emerge until the sixth grade.

A tentative hypothesis that would offer an explanation for the observed relationship between anxiety and behavioral variables is that anxiety is a primary effect in the failure cycle, while the behavioral variables are secondary effects. From this new perspective, anxiety is viewed as an underlying variable in the failure cycle while the maladaptive behaviors are viewed as second order effects of cumulative anxiety. From this standpoint, it is possible to interpret the interaction between anxiety and maladaptive classroom behaviors in an educational setting.

The challenge of daily classroom activities, in many cases, produces expectations that create a certain amount of anxiety. Since the reduction of anxiety acts like a generalized motivator, anxiety can have a stimulatory effect, and cause the student to strive toward success (Pearson, 1954). The successful student is able to manage anxiety through accomplishing the associated learning tasks, and the mastery of anxiety leads to a definite feeling of well-being. The unsuccessful student, in contrast, is unable to control anxiety to the extent that the demands of the classroom exceed the student's academic skills. These students are thus deprived of the opportunity to reduce their anxiety through the required levels of academic achievement demanded of them. In this case, the unmastered anxiety stimulates maladaptive behavior, which secures escape from the aversive condition of having to learn in the face of repeated failure.

In the second grade, the unsuccessful students begin to show the primary effect of excessive anxiety. If academic failure continues through the fourth grade, these students appear to find relief by disengaging from the task-generated anxiety and by engaging in inappropriate behavior patterns. These behaviors interfere with the learning efficiency of the students and are therefore considered a counterproductive alternative to the academic management of anxiety.

This interpretation is consistent with the curvilinear relationship observed in the unsuccessful students' anxiety pattern. More specifically, the decrease in measured anxiety from fourth to sixth grade coincides with the emergence of the anxiety-reducing maladaptive behaviors.

In terms of the failure cycle model, the following diagram represents the shift in the role of anxiety.

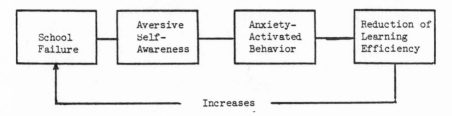

The aversive awareness of school failure generates a high level of anxiety. As these students' academic deficiencies accumulate through time, avoidance activities are employed. The maladaptive behavior patterns are presumably anxiety-reducing in nature. These symptom formations, high anxiety and maladaptive behavior patterns, lead to a reduction in learning efficiency which, in turn, feeds back increased probability of subsequent school failure, thus establishing a circular, self-perpetuating cycle.

The ideal solution to the problem of school failure would of course be to somehow eliminate it. This would prevent the student from entering the failure cycle in the first place. Reducing the degree of failure in school has been recognized as an important goal by many educators and various approaches have been recommended for dealing with the problem. To the extent that these approaches are successful, it would be expected that the student should be able to manage school task generated anxiety without the interfering, symptomatic side effects.

However, once the child has entered the failure cycle, academic intervention should be initiated as soon as possible. These children tend to experience a level of anxiety that exceeds their tolerance threshold with debilitating consequences. Not only does the anxiety associated with the aversive objective awareness of failure distract the student from learning, it may also encourage the formation of symptomatic behavior, having the double effect of disengaging the student from the anxiety-producing schoolwork and engaging the student in anxiety-reducing maladaptive classroom behavior.

What is needed to be done is to teach students how to cope with failure without suffering ego damage. This will be especially true for below functioning students with special learning needs, since repeated effects of failure can permanently damage their self-concept.

Since failure may be a very large part of these students' lives both in and out of school, it is important to help them discriminate between failure at a particular task and failure as a person. They must receive emotional support to help them face repeated failure experiences and still feel positive about themselves. They must learn to accept themselves whether or not they overcome their deficiencies. With the proper support and understanding, these students can learn to cope with higher levels of anxiety and be able to demobilize the defense reactions that interfere with learning — thus breaking the vicious cycle of failure.

REFERENCES

Bloom, B.S. Learning for Mastery. *Evalution Comment, 1,* No. 2, 1968.

Dreeban, R. *On What is Learned in School.* Reading Mass.: Addison-Wesley, 1968.

Festinger, L. *A Theory of Cognitive Dissonance,* Stanford, California: Stanford University Press, 1957.

French, L. How does it feel to fail? In E.P. Torrance and R.D. Strom (Eds.), *Mental Health and Achievement,* New York: John Wiley & Sons, Inc., 1965.

Gibbons, F.X. and R.A. Wicklund. Selective exposure to self. *Journal of Research in Personality, 10,* 98:106, 1976.

Glidewell, J.C. and J.A. Stringer. *Early detection of emotional illness in school children.* St. Louis County Health Department, Division of Research and Development, 1967. (unpublished)

Goodlad, J.I. and R.H. Anderson. *The Non-graded Elementary School.* New York: Harcourt, Brace and Company, 1959.

Iches, W.; R.A. Wicklund, C.B. Ferris. Objective self-awareness and self-esteem. *Journal of Experimental Social Psychology, 9,* 209:219, 1973.

Kifer, E. *The effects of school achievement on the affective traits of the learner.* Unpublished doctoral dissertation, University of Chicago, 1973.

Loiacono, R. *Differential response patterns of achievers and non-achievers as a function of locus of control.* Unpublished doctoral dissertation, Syracuse University, 1978.

Pearson, G. *Psychoanalysis and the Education of the Child.* New York, W.W. Norton and Company, Inc., 1954.

Smith, L.A. Five year follow-up study of high ability achieving and non-achieving college freshman. *Journal of Educational Research, 64,* 220:222, 1971.

Torshen, K. *The relationship of classroom evaluation to students' self-concepts and mental health.* Unpublished doctoral dissertation, Universtiy of Chicago, 1969.

White, R.W. *The Abnormal Personality.* (34th ed.). New York: The Ronald Press Company, 1964.

Wicklund, R.A. and S. Duval. Opinion change and performance as a result of objective self-awareness. *Journal of Experimental Social Psychology, 7,* 319:342, 1971.

Section II

Design of Instructional Programs and

Learning Environments

CHAPTER 5

ALTERNATIVE SPECIAL EDUCATION DELIVERY SYSTEMS

CHARLES C. D'AREZZO

WHERE ARE WE?

TECHNOLOGY has introduced many educational "tools" that could be used as alternatives in teaching the special education student. Some of these "tools" are the computer, video, slide projector, and multi-purpose audiotape machines.

A few years ago, educational technology was considered a gimmick for only the educational "handyman." Today, with home computers, cable TV, video disks, and other home video games, children, as well as their older brothers and sisters, are well versed in the utilization of these electronic marvels. Interestingly, many times their parents, who have purchased the electronic marvels, are timid in their use or are not interested.

A positive observation could then be made that educational technology may be a more appropriate learning tool in some learning situations than the traditional classroom approach.

We are in a generation of choice or preference; certainly education is no different. In the sixties and early seventies, we talked exclusively of either traditional classroom techniques or the use of instructional technology used separately. At this time, we are addressing learner preference. If this is true and this is an interest in the younger students learning via technology, why not provide that assistance via that mode?

Most educators suggest in their philosophical approach to learning that all students are special. They also suggest that we should provide the student with an opportunity to learn in any fashion he can. When students are considered to be atypical because of physical or learning disabilities, this ought to inspire educators to try alternatives to help these students learn.

The educational process, in the past, was thought to take place only in the traditional classroom. With the introduction of the satellite, telecommunications, home computers, video disks and other twenty-first century marvels, education can take place anywhere.

Most schools operate between 7 A.M. and 4 P.M., Monday through Friday, selected times of the year — observing holidays, teacher strikes, etc., etc. Through the use of educational technology and other delivery techniques such as satellites, home computers and video disks, students can learn anywhere and at any time.

The process of determining where the student is in the learning process is time-consuming, and many times it is not available for all students for some valid reasons. Through the use of small desk-top computers, diagnostics are readily available to any educator, with this same device supporting administrative tasks possible as well as assisting in teaching the student.

Students who have physical limitations can activate computers through voice commands; or, if there is no voice, a change in noise level would accomplish the same. The central thought is that no learner will be discriminated against in the use of any technological tool if we use our creativity and design a learning environment that best suits his needs.

As stated earlier, the learner ought not to be confined to an environment called a classroom, conforming to prescribed time. A student should be given an opportunity that is both physically and mentally convenient to him. In the early days of education, the better teachers called this "student readiness." The concept is most valid and should be considered as a central concern of any educator.

Because of physical needs of some of the population of special students, they are sometimes housed in residential centers. Residents sometimes spend most of their lives confined within these centers. Through the utilization of instructional technology, learning could occur any time a student wanted it. If there were a cluster of residential centers that served a geographic location or a state system, the equipment and software could be shared. As mentioned earlier, some of the hardware, such as the computer, could be used for multi-function activities within the center.

These activities could be administrative, establishing menus, keeping budgets, inventory control, and establishing repair schedules, to name a few. The same device could be used for recreational opportunities by providing computer games, both for individuals or groups. The above would be true for videotape players as well.

PHYSICAL CONSIDERATIONS

As mentioned earlier, there is no limitation of the educator's use of technology in assisting the learner. Some considerations should be made by the educator when considering physical accommodations for the equipment and the user of the equipment.

The following are only some of the considerations that should be considered. The involvement of a technocrat or consultant would be a prudent consideration by the educator who has limited technical experience. Consider the various personnel who make up the space experiments or other highly technological projects.

Most instructional technology utilizes electrical power. If a new building is being considered, flexibility is the key. Plan the power requirement for existing need, then add on an additional 25 percent for future growth. If conduits are used, be sure pull wires are drawn with the extra wires. Select receptical boxes that will allow expansion. Be very careful of grounds; make sure all of your electrical circuits are isolated and grounded. It is surprising how a typewriter or other device will introduce "hits" on a computer.

If an older building is being utilized and restored, similar considerations should be made as with a new building.

If a microwave disk is to be installed on a roof, consideration of wind, weight, and stress loads should be considered. If a disk is installed on the ground, a way to get the cable to the distribution system is a must. An underground system is preferred. Finally, if a tower is used to support a microwave disk, suitable pilings to support the tower and disk are important as well as guide wires to help with the wind loads.

Consideration should also be made of other objects in the line of transmission and/or receiving. If planes have flight plans that bring them near the line of transmission this might have to be discussed with the Federal Communications Commission as well.

The newer computers do not require as sensitive climate control as the "older generations." Consideration should be made of extreme heat or cold. Usually sixty-eight degrees to seventy-two degrees is preferred. Temperature is not only a consideration for hardware, but, also, for software. Video, computer disks, and film could be damaged by high humidity, smoke, or chemicals in the air.

In selecting furniture or having desks built for hardware, one should use the secretary's desk height when configuring. Consider shorter heights when dealing with smaller children and wider openings when accommodating students with wheelchairs.

Location of carrels, desks, or other teaching stations is critical when considering where natural light is coming from. When utilizing slide, film, video, or other projections where sunlight could "wipe out" the image, one has to be constantly aware of the problem and prepare for it. Location of equipment or suitable shades would be equal solutions.

Many times, furniture is selected because of the many drawers or storage areas built into the unit. Research has shown that drawers and storage areas are seldom used for what they have been designed for and are many times used for housing lunches and paper clips. It may be wise to spend money saved on simple desks or tables to accommodate the teaching machine to be used. The consideration on choosing the simple furniture could be applied to a professional distribution center for housing software and hardware.

One should consider color coding where software and hardware are stored to simplify utilization for the student. While suggesting color code for location of software and hardware, one should consider pictures and colors when giving instructions to the students who will be using the software and hardware.

Much is to be said about pictures located on the dashboard of a foreign automobile as well as the colors that complement a chain of events that have to be followed to operate the automobile. A similar approach would work with the above learning environment, whether it be carrel, classroom, or learning station.

When equipment will be disassembled to transport it from one location to another, a simple diagram would make it easier for the user to reconnect the proper wires or other attachments which make up the whole. Some prefer to place tape, with matching numbers, on parts of equipment which will be disassembled and reassembled many times. Color coding works out as well with the above.

A final word about equipment: The prudent user of instructional equipment will make provision for scheduled preventive and regular maintenance on his equipment. Nothing is more frustrating or detrimental to a project than having a student ready to use the instructional equipment and having it nonoperative.

Many times, staff can be trained to perform first echelon maintenance. This would include changing lamps, fuses, and broken belts and performing other simple tasks that one can learn without intense technical training.

The above suggestion can be accomplished by requesting a repair contract and training of staff when first purchasing the equipment. Additionally, a request should be made for replacement parts such as lamps, fuses, belts, etc., which the vendor suggests that the user ought to have on hand. One should also have all the technical specifications in the form of manuals and schematics that one can acquire when originally purchasing the equipment.

A good record-keeping system or log should also be kept on problems that occur to the equipment. This recorded information will help solve technical problems that are likely to happen repeatedly. All of the manuals, schematics, and logs should be well organized and kept separately, preferably in a file cabinet, and given the care of any important document.

SOME "NUTS AND BOLTS" OR "BITS AND BYTES"

Central to instructional technology is the software to be used by the student. Software is any material, whether it be film, video disk, computer disket, audio tubes, etc. One will quickly find out that the largest void in instruction technology is the software for the equipment.

When shopping for software, some considerations should be made: compatibility of format — does the format selected fit the equipment owned?; copyright — can you copy the material for multiuse within a similar school system or agency? Some thoughts would be to get written permission from the publishing or recording company before purchase. The vendor could be helpful with the above.

Because the software is expensive, many users suggest making copies of the original and placing the original in a safe place, continuing its use only as a master. Others will make several sub-masters and make copies only from the sub-masters. Whatever scheme you choose, utilizing the original only as a master is a good idea.

In selecting the software, one should also request a demonstration or preview to be sure the contents reflect the advertisement. There has been many a slick promotion of materials that were not educationally sound for teaching.

The readiness level at which the software was developed is important. This certainly will reflect upon the students who will be utilizing it. It will also have an effect on the time span of the students using the material. The reader may be concerned about what happens if he cannot find the software he is looking for. Most people prepare it themselves. Some of the better teaching software has been written, produced, and prepared by teachers. The central concern of any learning program or software is whether it does the job. If the student learns from the software, you, as the teacher, have been successful.

The only thing that the lay person cannot provide in the "homemade" software is some of the slickness of utilizing expensive equipment. In the case of computer software, your material will look exactly as the purchased software does. If you design and program your material to be a good Computer Assisted Instruction learning package, it will be. If you do not put the time into planning how the student will utilize it and learn from it, then it will be poor.

The above comments will be true of any learning material developed by the teacher. The analogy most always shared is the one pertaining to writing a good essay. If you do not have a good outline prepared, most likely the essay will ramble and be unclear to the reader.

If the teacher who is preparing his own software does a good job in writing his script or flow charting his computer program, the learning material will flow for the user. One cannot ignore good production or computer skills in enhancing the final learning package.

Some Last Thoughts

The focus of this chapter was to address: "learning environments to provide effective instruction and environments for the learner, i.e. residential center, special school, special class, resource room." The author has gone beyond that scope and has introduced other concerns that one has to consider along with good pedagogy. Some recent research indicates that technology will be used in an increased rate in the eighties.

The students who would best benefit from the flexibility of instructional technology could be those students who reside at residential centers, special schools, special classes, and resource rooms. Within the above you will find the gifted, slow, handicapped, or what we describe as the difficult to teach. Whatever the educational need, there is a way of providing for it through instructional technology.

Examine the techniques that industry, military, and other non-traditional schools are using to teach their students and you will find instructional technology central to that effort.

The perennial question is how do I get started, in addition to many other important ones. The answer is as different as there are different people who want to create an effective instructional environment. The central, common point is the desire to help the student. If that desire is strong enough, the rest is a matter of hard work.

To complete the project you select will require lots of hard work, learning of new skills, convincing people that your "new idea" will work as well as the old tried ones, and, finally, finding someone to fund the project. To think you will complete your project without adequate funding is a farce. One does not need a great deal of money, but the need is proportional to the scope of the sought-after project. The cry to get grant money is becoming fainter as federal and state moneys are drying up.

With all of the difficulties that one encounters, one wonders why one would take on an innovative project. The answer is a simple one: for the joy of observing a student learn and being happy, who might not have had the success if placed in a traditional classroom, which has been traditionally programmed to have atypical children fail or become discouraged.

CHAPTER 6

DESIGN OF ALTERNATE LEARNING ENVIRONMENTS

PATRICK R. PENLAND

A LEARNING environment is a set of conditions, an event or a happening within which an individual is led to so describe, analyze and structure personal experience that behavior patterns are modified, changed or redeveloped. Such learning conditions may be as programmed as a maze limited to one solution, expandable to a variety of branched advances or as open-ended and stimulus rich as the natural environment. Choice may be as severely limited as in rote memorization or the options may be openly confusing; but the product of the resulting processes becomes part of the individual or collective memory.

Interactive environments programmed especially for the purpose can serve as support systems for the development of human potential (Zalatino & Sleeman, 1975). Electronic networks can be employed to encourage and support the innumerable personal contacts so essential in human development; and data can be stored in digital form in order to provide on-line access and retrieval. But to depend upon them exclusively is to bypass and even escape from the interpersonal relations so essential to human development. The working together of people in a real time mode cannot be totally replaced by networks however interactive these may be.

An environmental approach to human learning suggests that the individual learns whenever the conditions are available for surpriseful encounter. These conditions occur so frequently in the transactions of everyday life that most individuals become experts in negotiating the encounters episodically as they occur. Individuals of varying information processing abilities are immersed in stimulus conditions that literally and continuously crowd in on their attention (Penland, 1982, p. 97):

> The environment may be real or contrived for the purpose of engendering meaning within one or more particular human entities. The environment may be formal or informal, knowledge classified or activity oriented, in-

stitutionally situated or interpersonal, group dominated or individually perceived. A learning environment can be as operationally simple as picking up the local directory whether the pages are yellow, blue or purple and making a phone call for assistance and guidance. Or, it may be as complex and threatening as walking out the front door of one's home, in order to get involved with one of the local neighborhood or community-based movements for change.

Life situations and settings such as these are convenient and offer an ambience for introducing the excitement of the new learning experiences. Although fascinated for various periods of time, the individual may tire of the promiscuity of happenings while attention shifts towards longer periods of engagement extended sequentially. But these too can become dull and commonplace unless there is provision for a variety of instructional methodologies and techniques. Adaptions in time, space and design are essential if interest in learning is to be sustained. Emphasis should be placed on the learning process through which information is conveyed; content on the other hand takes its cues from the learning needs and interests of both faculty and students.

HUMAN FACTORS

The concept of the alternate learning environment must extend considerably beyond the school. For example, among learning disabled children, who are soon to become adults, other elements are particularly important in the total planning such as motor training, psychotherapeutic support and language development. No one of these aspects can overly predominate but must be taken in an appropriate relationship with those facets of the environment such as family and other associates (Nihira et al., 1981).

It should also be noted that many distractions can exist in learning environments of various kinds. The majority of people are able to negatively adapt to those stimuli that are extraneous to the purpose at hand. Others however are not so fortunate whether through disabilities or missed opportunities in learning to concentrate. Theoretically, the learning environment should be able to adjust to the many degrees of hyperkinetic behavior or motor disinhibition that exists among the participants (Bradley & Caldwell, 1980).

Others who suffer from a perceptual processing deficit whether for psychological or educational reasons may become so involved with the parts of a perceptual pattern as to be unable to grasp the gestalt. This dissociation between the parts and the whole is closely related to sensory hyperactivity of a visual nature. The tremendous amount of stimuli which impinge online for such a person causes a reaction to things as if they were isolated from the whole and not as parts of a meaningful unit. In the course of events surrounding such a person, a variety of professional contacts are needed from good home planning to the services and skills of people from many professions.

Of considerable import in this regard is the mainstreaming of the learning disabled or handicapped individual that has to take methods into consideration for the successful involvement of parents, teachers and administrators in critical programming decisions. Alternate ways of bridging the gap between special and regular programs may include a learner-centered schedule of reinforcement where instructional materials in the self-contained classroom gradually parallel resources used in the regular classroom (Heron & Harris, 1982). As the learner gains ability in the three components of decisioning — values, information, strategy — that individual overcomes anxiety and regains self-confidence (Roloff, 1981).

There seems to be a direct ratio between mainstreaming and the availability of appropriate and efficient human role models. In other words, mainstreaming "demands" the participation of teaching teams as models because without them a normal environment can very well be the worst place for a perceptually impaired individual. Sparse, nonstimulus overloaded environments are less distracting to the person with short attention span, motor disinhibition, figure-background problems and a general attitude of defeated self-image and deflated self-esteem.

Controlled display environments may be as essential to some persons as stimulus-rich conditions are to others. Paying special individual attention to, or in coming into the lifespan of, and even touching that person physically can provide a conscious and deliberate reminder that there is a structure not only to the relationship of the two persons but also to the larger surroundings in which both live. At one moment, the model may be dominant and at others this dominance will give way as the individual learns to control and direct the self within the encompassing environment.

The surrounding conditions within which a person is involved such as noise level, crowding or color appear to have a considerable influence as perceptual interference. For example, by increasing the partitions and reducing the doors that are unnecessary in a room, interpersonal contact can be reduced as well as traffic flow with a subsequent lowering of personal space violation. The effect of crowding in an environment is produced as a function of the perceived or actual violation of an individual's personal space. The variables that produce these perceptions of crowding seem to reduce learning effectiveness (Weldon et al., 1981, p. 175.):

> Linear display of room dimensions appears to be extremely important in perceptions of crowding. If we make the tentative inference that this variable primarily affects perceived spaciousness of the room, then any room design variable that enhances perceived spaciousness of a room should reduce perceptions of crowding.

Other methods can be employed to focus the occupants' attention away from other individuals such as ample space for movement and exploration, small group locations and quiet areas. The type of activity can also have an effect on reducing the feeling of being crowded. For example, easily accessible materials, display and bulletin boards, individual carrels and listening facilities can help to mediate the competitive-cooperative dimensions of interpersonal behavior (Jones and McEwin, 1980).

The learning disabled person as a complex human entity is not necessarily physically or mentally disabled. Such a person may be an educational and psychological challenge, with problems that make it difficult for him to interact as effectively as others in interpersonal networks, but neither should that individual be permanently placed in a residential institution. That person has grown and continues to grow and develop in a total milieu that can be employed as the set of remedial circumstances. Such an environment must be sufficiently comprehensive with qualified personnel and administrative support as well as fully informed parental, family and peer-group cooperation.

Perceptual field inversion as in figure-background reversal is another characteristic of the learning disabled that has a significant effect in depressing the ability to learn. Those who are not able to see things because the background stimuli takes precedence over the foreground are characterized by reversal of field. The excitement aroused by the background impinges upon attention and the figure in the foreground is ignored. When this is combined with dissociation, individuals may constantly need to touch others and things not from sensual and sexual propensity but simply to orient the self to space relationships and to assure themselves that the figure or human actually exists.

Another perceptual processing deficit stems from the difficulty to turning off a stimulus response. Such dogged persistence cumulates in the inability to shift with ease from one mental activity to another. Whether from inertia or fixation, the individual finds it difficult and frequently impossible to move quickly from one to another. There is a prolonged aftereffect; the stimulus or subsequent activities leads to a preoccupation almost similar to a fixation over which the individual has little if any control. Such a person may repeat a word endlessly, continue writing one letter and coloring all over the page beyond the figure completed.

Any responsible and responsive learning environment will have to give adequate attention to the successful management of stress conditions for various persons. It is a frightening and debilitating thing to be under the pressure of knowing that an answer is expected, that others in the audience are waiting for a response that they already know and are vying with each other to give the expected answer. Under such conditions of stress, the individual becomes tense, forgets things that under other circumstances of less environmental stimuli might be recalled.

Individuals with learning disabilities as a whole are under almost constant tension and emotional stress and as a group have poor memories. Closely associated with the matter of memory is that of attention and attention span; the learning disabled individual is easily distracted by unessential and irrelevant stimuli whether internal or external. When a person is distracted by something the task assigned, or immediately at hand, is usually interrupted with unsettling consequences. Repetition has to be built into the instructional method, and redundance into the environment.

The perceptually handicapped individual frequently has a mutilated self-concept and body image. Such a person sees the self as one who cannot achieve and indeed has become a puzzle to the self, the family and the community probably since infancy (Cruickshank, 1977). In perceptually handicapped persons, the problem emerges as a psychological disorientation to the self and others. While such behavior may exhibit signs of neurological impairment, it appears rather that the poor conceptualization of the body with its parts and functions is interrelated with some aspects of the stimulus environment.

People with such perceptual processing deficiencies not only have difficulty remembering anything for any length of time but they also lack sufficient understanding of themselves and sufficient control to refrain from reacting to unessential stimuli that are everywhere a part of the environment. Hyperactivity may increase and attention span shorten under stimulus overload until things can go no further and an explosion or cop-out results. A failure experience has again been registered upon the person with a subsequent loss of self-esteem.

People with perceptual processing deficits are essentially controlled by and control themselves in terms of external stimuli and situations. Instead of being allowed to continue reacting to the external world and its contents, often in desperate and thoughtless ways, these individuals need help in controlling the world from within. These individuals react to stimuli whether experienced internally or externally induced in such a manner as to reduce the value (strength) and control the stimulus in order to protect the self. With a secure background, reasonably loving and understanding families and opportunities for experimentation, self-development can occur fairly well.

ENVIRONMENTAL ADVANCES

The notion of a diversity of learning environments is a concept that is highly consistent with the principles of a democratic society (Lipson, 1981). In a pluralistic culture, many voices continue to call for community involvment in education; and the need for institutional self-renewal in schools as well as local financial responsibility, accountability and even austerity (Raywid, 1981) is critical. Alternatives have helped to reduce the conformity required in those regular classrooms where there is a considerable emphasis on achievement, subject mastery, individual competition, and group-conditioned objectives, and especially where social acceptance is related to competition and performance within the group (Gallent, 1981).

The method of museum exhibit and display may constitute one basic model where information and learning experiences can be engendered. The discovery methods are more typical of those in the everyday environment where so many people seek information and share learnings from a coterie of informal sources such as peers and acquaintances. The museum is a social environment where people go to share with family and friends the audiovisual, movement and nonverbal stimuli that are typical of museum work as indicated by Kimche (1978, p. 270):

> Science centers provide a whole new field of self-motivating experiences in learning, through environmental exhibits that appeal to the senses, emotions, and intellect. They are among the most rapidly developing institutions of learning in contemporary society. They have been responsive to a growing public demand for knowledge and information. As more and more people visit them, the science centers have a unique opportunity to assist a large segment of the public to gain a greater understanding of the contemporary technological issues of society. The objects and exhibits can form the basis for other types of educational programs, not only within museums, but throughout the entire community.

Kimche goes on to point out that the rapidly increasing number and size of museums and science centers is a direct result of the rise in public demand. Few if any other institutions in the community are able to respond to those client-centered benefits that so effectively mirror the stimuli of everyday life. Visitors are attracted to museum exhibit and display in order to find meaning in newly perceived and interesting experiences. No conditions are placed on these happenings that are designed so that meaning is engendered by the same stimuli they have learned to process in the transactions of everyday negotiation.

Another approach to learning environments is represented by the alternate schools that have been employed as experimental laboratories for the field testing and validation of new educational concepts (Barr, 1981). In little more than a decade, the alternate school has changed from a radical idea to become a "magnet" component in the desegration of urban schools (Oliver, 1980). It has also made a significant contribution to resource conservation and redistribution (Case, 1981). Alternative schools have been credited with the effective mainstreaming of exceptional children (Wang, 1981) and with a considerable superiority in meeting student needs (Smith et al., 1981).

Within the mainstream of an alternate school, an individual approach to instruction can be considered as a viable method because of emphasis placed on adapting instruction to student differences. Thus, all children can be viewed as unique individuals who differ according to the nature of their learning needs. Of course, adequate instructional resources are necessary, both human and material; and these have to be combined within a well-designed discovery system (Lewis, 1982). When such an environment is planned and access scheduled within the available resources, learning needs of both exceptional and regular children can probably be met within the same classroom.

With the advances being made today, it is no longer possible to accept the improvisions of the past; the research and development of the past decade alone could revolutionize learning if applied to present learning environments (Toch, 1982). High-level technology is available for location in position and to replace such current "innovations" as the integrated library-media resource center. But if this technology is to succeed where earlier efforts floundered around built-in limitations, there must be a long-term effort to penetrate to the core of self-directed learning, that is the people themselves. Educators are expected to design the programming and "teach" its use to the people so that they can take over their own self-instruction (Stewart, 1975).

The computer and video communications technologies have been developing separately for decades. In the last five years, however the two have combined in the interactivity of media communication with the intelligent systems available in data base access, computer networking and teletext transmission. The data bases may be available commercially, educationally or produced and maintained in-house by the individual within his own electronic "cottage" or office. The programming of these interactive technologies could represent a shift from the mass education of new generations to the individual education of human persons. In any event, people whether adult or child must be helped to design and employ programming that makes these systems work in their own self-selected learning environments.

The organization of school libraries and documentation centers is being adapted so as to allow to take account of the changes that have occurred in recent decades, both within the school and in the surrounding world (Ford, 1979). At present, a library-media center is expected to perform the following functions:

- Collect together all the documentation of human endeavor whether stored in the school or not and regardless of its material basis, and make it available to the person using the center.

- Organize this documentation in such a way as to make it easily accessible and usable to the client-in-situation.
- Act as a method of self-instruction for independent educational activities as well as support service for the general activities of the school.
- Furnish the premises and arrange the equipment in a manner suited to the various functions of the center and to its educational action.
- Offer the facilities for producing both printed and audiovisual documents and the message design guidance for doing so.
- Facilitate the tasks of the consultants by providing them with the means of assisting pupils, guiding, evaluating and participating in their work.
- Provide case-load access to client-centered information consultants, learning advocates and communications mediators.

Increasing the control that people have over learning resources means providing a greater variety of media as well as the opportunity to communicate through many presentation forms. Media should not be viewed as competing forms but rather as complementary systems. Maximum effect can be achieved from information sources by involving individuals in the process of selecting, utilizing, experimenting, and producing as well as evaluating. The purpose of increased involvement is to help people grow as individuals (self-actualization) and contribute to society (acculturation) in a mutually rewarding manner.

Independence in individualized learning is presumed to be a function of open access where the individual's sense of personal space and self-control are supported by the physical, content and interpersonal arrangements of a mediated and interactive environment. A further consideration is the provision of a wide range of equipment for the production and reproduction of software by and for teachers and pupils: transparencies, films, sound recordings, slide-tape sequences, photocopying, photography, videotapes. The first step is to convert the classroom into a workshop so as to make it the method of self-instruction within which most students are naturally involved. In every unit of the system, teachers and students should have adequate facilities for this kind of work, no matter how "amateurish" the results may appear to be.

The second step during initiation involves the addition of a whole range of nonbook materials such as real-life and audiovisual software and hardware. These museum-like resources provide for individual or group listening and viewing activities. The chief purpose is to encourage and facilitate self-instruction, whether supervised or entirely independent. To this end, many schools provide facilities for individuals working on their own or in small groups ranging from two students to larger groups composed of several students. Under the combined impact of the development of the educational sciences and the advance of communication techniques, emphasis will have to be laid on self-instruction and learning.

The alternative environment for learning features the deemphasis of the role of teacher superiority, and the emergence of a team spirit and esprit de corps. The subsequent emphasis on participant involvement has been credited with that individual learning achievement which in some instances has been alternative to inner-city teenager disaster (Dunn, 1981). In regard to the successful development of these environments, the interactive modeling behavior of the professional staff cannot be overemphasized (Hamilton, 1981, p. 147).

> Staff members with interpersonal role orientation, in other words, contributed to the school's innovative quality, while those with organizational role orientations were most helpful in making the school stable. The role innovators, with ideological role orientations, were able to resolve the tension between innovation and stability by developing roles that embodied the school's unconventional goals and principles but also made it a stable organization.

Possibly the most powerful reason for the growing popularity of alternative schools may be that they provide local control for parents and students as well as for teachers and administrators at a time when the "new federalism" has begun to place emphasis on local initiatives and resources. Many such programs can be characterized by an informality rarely found in other schools. The development of interactive and intelligent centers such as those emerging prototypes to be found in library-media centers (Carter, 1982) can help to bridge transitional developments.

Concluding Remarks

Alternate learning environments constitute a system that evolves

from the following: what is known about how people process information and what they learn, the instructional process and the
learner's unique contribution to it, teacher skills and the performance competencies that guide instruction, the methods and techniques of instruction as well as how teachers and students communicate in verbal and nonverbal form. Not so well known at least
in application phases is how instructional presentations are designed
and created, which media are most effective for specific communications requirements, how learning spaces are designed and how a
mediated environment can help participants organize themselves for
learning.

Unfortunately, many of the learning environments of today such
as media, library and information centers have so many resources
invested in the goods and facilities of a physical infrastructure that it
is questionable whether an adjustment can be made to the revolu-
tions of the learning society quickly enough to be effective. The pace
of change itself has rapidly accelerated from the days when education was solely dependent on print literacy. Indeed while a third,
and even fourth generation of interactive media is already available
(Leveridge, 1979) within on-line electronic storage, many practitioners still debate whether films, slides and transparencies should
be included in the educational enterprise.

There are obvious differences between the curricula of the schools
and the everyday transactions of citizens "on the streets." One is
deliberate and systematically preplanned, while the other is an
elaborate evolution of happenings which emerge from a plethora of
individual negotiations. In the schools, the design of the system
rather consciously and deliberately reflects the goals of the designer
into which the development of the individual is retrofitted. On the
other hand, the usefulness of the transactional environment as a
multiplicity of subjective probabilities is a function of forecasting
neg-entropy.

Learning environments cannot be as effectively designed as by
the active involvement of the participants. In fact, instructional
responsibility can best be met as those persons become "consultants"
to the group. A responsive environment allows the participants to
freely explore opportunities and constraints at their own rates within
a developing awareness of the consequences of their own behavior
(Kline, 1982). In other words, the learning of content cannot be independent of the activities within the environmental setting; the mix

of stimulus elements is always a unique combination — too rich for some and too lean for others (Bradley, 1981).

The changes taking place today in society and in education — advances in communication techniques, curricula reform, new educational methods — are making it increasingly necessary to develop or set up learning environments in communities both to help improve the quality of education and to facilitate self-instruction and lifelong education. Alternate approaches and counterculture experiments attempt to deinstitutionalize the educational process and make it more democratic and humanistic such as community schools, nonschools, free schools, open schools, and experimental schools. Counterculture schools offer a more genuine alternative to traditional school systems because:

- Schools are only part of the learning total environment and the community is perceived as the environment programmed for learning.
- Secondary education is tending to become a cut-off point in educational development, a decisioning point for or against graduate education.
- Development of communication media and techniques has profoundly modified the thresholds of perception; children have become capable far earlier than previously of manipulating technical equipment and producing their own documents.
- Self-initiated and self-planned learning has begun to challenge the hierarchial position of the school in the educational enterprise.

The growing importance of informal education, the gradual disappearance of the notion of a communications elite, the exponential growth of knowledge and its increasingly scientific and technical character have led to an emergence of conditions requiring that the student's capacity for independent endeavor be developed while still at school. Henceforth each individual will have, to a greater extent, to assume responsibility for self-instruction in context of a lifelong education in which compulsory school attendance is no more than an elementary stage.

The situation has to be perceived as an interlocking set of components which engages the attention of the individual in an episode of awareness. The initial apprehension is almost like a compulsive leap and a grasping at understanding until differentiation occurs. As attention escapes and begins to diffuse inward from the surpriseful encounter, awareness spreads towards that cluster of behavior characteristics "dictated" by the initial apprehension. These conditions occur so frequently in the transactions of everyday life that most individuals become experts in negotiating these encounters episodically as they occur (Steinaker & Bell, 1979); or, they become overwhelmed with stimulus overload. In the latter instance, such persons as these engage in mental processes that in effect represent an escape to an external locus of control and to behavioral patterns which simply react to stimuli rather than in some exertion to control them.

The maturing learner is the center of activity and source of input serving as the organizer, the pacer and chief authority in the sequence of episodes. Concepts are compared and behavior is shaped as some activities are given more attention than others. The learner selects personal means for judging and guiding activities which appear to be consistent with the emerging overall direction of the learning project. Like the teacher, criterion sets for evaluating performance and completion are induced while working with the learning materials and resources. Unlike the teacher, the self-directed learning sequence is not communicated to others as a method for the external control of their own self-instruction.

REFERENCES

Barr, Robert D. Alternatives for the eighties: a second decade of development. *Phi Delta Kappan, 62*:570-73, April 1981.

Blessington, John. Implications of advances in television technology for higher education. *Educom Bulletin, 16(4)*:3-6, Winter 1981.

Bradley, Robert H. and Bettye M. Caldwell. Relation of home environment, cognitive competence and IQ among males and females. *Child Development, 51*:1140-48, December 1980.

Carter, William A. Serving handicapped students in the school media center. *The Journal, 9(2)*:47-49, February 1982.

Case, Barbara J. Lasting alternatives: a Lesson in survival. *Phi Delta Kappan, 62*:554-57, April 1981.

Cruickshank, William M. *Learning Disabilities in Home, School and Community.* Syracuse: Syracuse University Press, 1977.

Dunn, Kenneth. Madison Prep: alternative to teenage disaster. *Educational Leadership, 38*:386-7, February 1981.

Ford, Nigel. Toward a model of 'library learning' in educational systems. *Journal of Librarianship, 11(4)*:247-60, October 1979.

Gallagher, J. Children with developmental imbalances. In *The Teacher of Brain-Injured Children,* edited by William M. Cruickshank. Syracuse: Syracuse University Press, 1966.

Gallent, Barbara L. Out of the frying pan, into the fire: a teacher's view. *Clearing House, 54*:345-8, April 1981.

Hamilton, Stephen F. Alternative schools for the '80s: lessons from the past. *Urban Education, 16(2)*:131-48, July 1981.

Heron, Timothy E. and Kathleen C. Harris. *The Educational Consultant: Helping Professional, Parents and Mainstreamed Students.* Rockleigh, N.J.: Allyn & Bacon, 1982.

Jones, Robert S. and Kenneth C. McEwin. Creative learning environments for the middle school. *Childhood Education, 56*:146-50, January 1980.

Kimche, Lee. Science centers: a potential for learning. *Science, 199*:270-73, 20 January 1978.

Kline, Peter. Suggestopedia. *Instructional Innovator, 27(2)*:20-21, February 1982.

Leveridge, Leo L. Potential of interactive optical videodisc systems for continuing education. *Educational and Industrial Television, 11(4)*:35-38, April 1979.

Lewis, Angelo J. Making the public schools work: urban education in the '80s. *Focus No. 9.* Princeton, N.J.: *Educational Testing Service,* 1982.

Lipson, Joseph. Riding the wave of the new information technologies: the administrator's role. *Educom Bulletin, 16(4)*:7-11, Winter 1981.

Nihira, Kazuo et al. Relationship between home environment and school adjustment of TMR children. *American Journal of Mental Deficiency, 86(1)*:8-15, July 1981.

Oliver, John. Developmental process and outcome of an alternative school: a case study. *Journal of Negro Education, 59(2)*:154-64, Spring 1980.

Penland, Patrick R. Alternate learning environments. *International Journal of Instructional Media, 9(2)*:97-103, 1981-82.

Raywid, Mary Anne. The first decade of public school alternatives. *Phi Delta Kappan, 62*:551-54, April 1981.

Roloff, Michael. *Interpersonal Communication: Social Exchange Approach.* Beverly Hills, CA: Sage, 1981.

Smith, Gerald; Thomas B. Gregory, and Richard C. Pugh. Meeting students needs: evidence for the superiority of alternative schools. *Phi Delta Kappan, 62*: 561-64, April 1981.

Steinaker, N.W.; and R.W. Bell. *The Experiential Taxonomy: New Approach to Teaching and Learning.* New York: Academic Press, 1979.

Stewart, Don. *Instruction as a Humanizing Science* 3 vol. Fountain Valley, CA: Slate Services, 1975.

Toch, Thomas. Researchers ponder how to reach practitioners. *Education Week, 1(27)*:4, 31 March 1982.

Wang, Margaret C. Mainstreaming exceptional children: some instructional design and implementation conditions. *Elementary School Journal, 81(4)*:195-221, March 1981.

Weldon, David E. et al. Crowding and classroom learning. *Journal of Experimental Education, 49*:160-76, Spring 1981.

Zalatimo, S.D.; and P. Sleeman. *Systems Approach to Learning Environments.* Roselle, N.J.: MEDED Projects, 1975.

CHAPTER 7

MEDIA CENTERED LEARNING FOR STUDENTS WITH SPECIAL NEEDS

ALMA JEAN HARRINGTON

P ROGRAMS of instruction for students with special needs funded with designated monies, such as ESEA Title I or PS 94-142, have usually included some learning media in their instructional programs. Indications are that these programs employed more media than the regular classroom, also. Therefore, using media to help students with special needs learn is not new or different. The strategy which may be unfamiliar to educators is how to incorporate media in instructional designs based on learning styles and at the same time provide a program or environment which meets the learning needs of all students. In other words, this program would mainstream students with special needs.

Such a goal will take careful development and planning by educators, but it is possible to achieve. Thought and action must be given to (1) selecting and organizing learning materials, (2) instituting administrative procedures for media use and (3) developing instructional options. These three guidelines should be thoroughly thought through and delineated, whether the media program is one which will have a specially designated area for its use, or whether it will be enacted as part of the regular activities in the classroom.

SELECTING AND ORGANIZING LEARNING

The selection of materials should not begin until specific interests of the student population — who will use the materials — have been identified and summarized. This may be carried out by administering an interest inventory or questionnaire to the user population. This data-gathering instrument should contain specific items to elicit information about the student's feelings and use of media. This instrument should contain student's responses on the following topics:

newspapers, magazines, books, radio programs, television programs, video machines, hobbies, sports, games, pets, career or jobs, free time activities, favorite kinds of learning materials and favorite kinds of reading materials. It should also include items relative to: subjects which interest them, information which they would like to tell others and present learning habits. This will help the educators know more about his or her users and plan more effective programs.

Next, the educators should select the subject or subjects — such as life skills or language arts, reading and mathematics — which the students need to learn. Then the selected subject must be organized into types of categories of skills to be included. For example, vocabulary, comprehension, word attack and study skills might be the categories for reading. One may also want to delineate some of the competencies or specific skills to be included in each category. Having identified the interests of the users and the subject(s), the next step is to select the media materials or learning resources to be incorporated into the instruction.

Media for learning may be classified into nine basic types:
- audio (tape)
- audiovisual (tape and filmstrip; 8mm film and tape, movie; videotape; and machine)
- audiovisual-written (tape, filmstrip and response sheet; videotape recorder and workbook)
- audio-written (tape and response sheet)
- book
- book-written (book and response sheet)
- visual (filmstrip; 8mm film, computer program)
- visual-written (filmstrip and response sheet; film loop and response sheet)
- written (printed or dittoed response sheet)

Care should be taken to insure that at least one item is available for each type of media listed above. This will allow the program to meet all the varying learning styles of the students. Care should also be taken to include the types of media that the response data of the students indicates they prefer to use.

The approximate readability level of the learning material should also be ascertained. Reports and discussions on the topic of readability seem to say that no single formula or index can accurately pinpoint the reading level of material for every individual. It seems that factors such as interest of the student and format of the material as well as word difficulty and sentence length may also affect readability. The more feasible solution for this dilemma would seem to be to examine sentence length and word complexity of the contents, then compare them with those of the materials used to teach reading at the first through twelfth grades, next determine the approximate level of difficulty of the materials, then examine the concepts expressed in these materials to see if a reader of the designated grade level could comprehend these concepts, and assign the readability level to the material. This orders the materials in a developmental, hierarchichal sequence.

Next, using the materials you have gathered, classify each of them as to: type, approximate readability level, subject and skill areas and interest encompassed. For instance, one piece of learning material may be designated as: audiovisual-written; grade two; reading — vocabulary, comprehension; sports — basketball, career — coach, pro-player, referee. Having done that, an index to the materials listing subject and skill areas, type, readability level and interests, in that order, may be constructed. An index card or a notebook page would look similiar to

Written

Comprehension — Literal

Levels 4 - 6

Bowmar/Noble — NFL Football Reading Kit — Grade 4.0.
  Cards 41 - 45.
  Sports - basketball;
  Careers - pro-basketball player, referee, coach.

For those who have access to computer resources, this index information might be programmed into a computer terminal. Individual or group assignments for the students could then be made by entering specific descriptors.

Materials that the students will use should be shelved according to type rather than subject, subject category or skills. The reason for this is that many of the learning materials incorporate instruction for more than one skill area. Such an arrangement of the learning resources also starts the students thinking about the variety of media that may be used for learning, and it helps them match their mind set to the type of material that helps them learn most effectively.

STATING ADMINISTRATIVE PROCEDURES

After the materials are selected, specific administrative procedures for their use should be developed and designated. The manner in which the program will be enacted should be stated; then the forms needed to affect it should be developed. One such form might be a daily user report form. Another might be a user comment diary. These forms would give the educators up-to-date data on the students' reactions to materials and the program. These would provide the educators with important information that may also be included in periodic reports to the administration. An accession or inventory list and a materials replacement costs list would provide information for insurance and accounting purposes.

Administrative procedures for enacting instruction need to be instituted next. The students need to know the specific skills they have mastered or learned and those they still need to learn and practice individually. The students need to know, on an individual basis, what they may do to accomplish those skills, also. Therefore, initially, the students should be given a personal, written report on the specific skills they have mastered and those which they are expected to achieve in the given subject(s). This report should not be lengthy or wordy. In fact, if a standardized test is used, a graph of the stanine results may be one of the easiest ways for students to understand if their progress is below average, average or above average for specific skill areas. Such a report might be similar to the one in Figure 7-1.

A work form that allows the students to choose the various learning styles that he or she prefers that day is most effective and beneficial. Some of the reports on learning styles (Austin, 1978; Barbe, 1980; and Spache, 1976) indicate that the way an individual learns best may change from day to day because of a change in mind set or emotions, and it may also vary depending on the skill being learned. Allowing students to choose their learning materials gives the students a chance to make choices in how he or she will learn and the freedom to make decisions about the assigned task. The assignments should be based not only on the students' achievement

Designing Learning Programs and Environments

Stanford Diagnostic Reading Test, Brown Level, 1976

Name: _____ Grade: _____ Group: _____

T E S T S	Test 1	Test 2			Test 3	Test 4	Test 5
	Auditory Vocabulary	Literal Comprehension	Inferential Comprehension	Total Comprehension	Phonetic Analysis	Structural Analysis	Reading Rate
Raw Score							
S	9	9	9	9	9	9	9
T	8	8	8	8	8	8	8
A	7	7	7	7	7	7	7
N	6	6	6	6	6	6	6
I	5	5	5	5	5	5	5
N	4	4	4	4	4	4	4
E	3	3	3	3	3	3	3
S	2	2	2	2	2	2	2
	1	1	1	1	1	1	1
Perc.							

Figure 7-1.

level in the subject but also on his or her interests. This means that a variety of learning materials must be included on the work form for each skill category.

DEVELOPING INSTRUCTIONAL OPTIONS

Individualized instruction is being touted as the ultimate in teaching and learning style today. Yet, some reports seem to indicate that the format for instruction, such as whether it is individualized, small group or whole group, may not be as important as the amount of direct instruction given in a particular subject area (Good, 1981; Stallings; 1976). The amount of direct instruction students receive may be increased by combining teacher instruction and media instruction using materials which: (1) introduce and discuss a concept or skill, (2) give the student an opportunity to demonstrate his or her understanding of the skill or concept being learned and (3) tell the student what the correct response is and why any other response would be incorrect. Using media to assist in direct instruction may also mean that a small group may be receiving direct instruction using media, and the teacher may be giving direct instruction to one student or the rest of the group.

One of the most important aspects of using media effectively with students with special needs is that students be given the opportunity to choose, from a group of choices, what they want to use to learn needed skills or knowledge. At first, this concept may be frightening to some students who have been ingrained with the belief that they must execute assignments in the order stated. But, once the students begin to feel that it is acceptable to make such a decision, they will begin to choose their materials based on their feelings at the time they are to be learned. For instance, if a student is particularly sleepy, he or she may choose a tape and worksheet with quick-paced or lively instruction which forces him or her to concentrate on their task. On another day, the same student may choose to learn skills by reading a book.

The other aspect, which is as equally as important as free choice, is that media materials be based on the interests of the students using them. Ofttimes, students with special needs may fail to achieve or respond to subject area content because they cannot or do not relate what is to be learned to their lives. But, if the same skill or concept is taught using material of direct interest to them or if the students are helped to see how the skill or concept to be learned fits into their interests, the students will learn it more effectively and efficiently. Also, when material of direct interest is used for instruction, students seem to get the feeling that educators do care about them as people.

The instructional needs of students with special needs and average students may be accommodated by creating a learning center or area using individualized programs. Such an approach allows the students to select the media which suits their preferred learning style. The teacher or center director or manager would monitor their work and give direct instruction and add or delete media where necessary. Such an approach is highly motivational since it allows students to maintain their self-esteem and share their knowledge on a particular interest with one another while working at their own level on their own needs.

Teachers and administrators who are concerned about the achievement of students with special needs would do well to implement a wider variety of media into their instruction. Such an approach would result in improved instruction and produce more successful and satisfied learners.

REFERENCES

Books

Barbe, Walter B. and Raymond H. Swassing. Teaching Through Modality Strengths. Columbus: Zaner-Bloser, Inc., 1980.

Spache, George D. Investigating the Issues of Reading Difficulties. Boston: Allyn and Bacon, 1976.

Journal References

Good, Thomas L. Teacher Effectiveness in the Elementary School. *Journal of Teacher Education, 33*:52-63, 19 .

Stallings, J. How instructional processes relate to child outcomes in a national study of Follow Through. *Journal of Teacher Education, 27*:43-47, 19 .

Presentations

Austin, Mary C. and Margaret A. Donovan. Does Modality Preference Make a Difference? Paper presented at International Reading Association Conference, May, 1978, 12p.

CHAPTER 8

VARIABLES RELATED TO A MATCH
BETWEEN THE LEARNER
AND INSTRUCTION
Where Do We Stand?

KATHLEEN L. HAMMOND

THE idea of matching learner variables with instructional variables or the so-called individualization of instruction is not new to the last fifteen- to twenty-year period that has witnessed the growth of the field of instructional technology. Rather the idea of adapting instruction to the individual learner can be traced to at least the later years of the nineteenth century. In 1883 Lester Frank Ward wrote "the only thing that can be done is to equalize opportunities so as not only to enable the really exceptional man to demonstrate the fact but to make the avenues so numerous and so easy to travel that he will be sure to find the one to which he is best adapted by nature." Ward envisioned the need for alternative methods for teaching the same general truths to students possessing different mental abilities. Then in 1911 the monograph entitled "individuality" written by Thorndike was published. In 1958, Leona Tyler delivered a presidential address to the Western Psychological Association in Monterey, California, entitled, "Toward a Workable Psychology of Individuality" (Tyler, 1959). The list of individuals concerned with adapting instructional methods to individual differences no doubt could be continued. Yet despite a growing awareness on the part of the educators and parents of the need for individualizing instruction, the so-called selective model of education dominated most of our educational systems during the larger part of this century (Glaser, 1972;1976). Not until more recent times have adaptive models of education become the norm.

I shall describe these two models briefly for it is only within the framework of an adaptive model of education that we can discuss any meaningful match between learner and instructional variables. Selective models of education that have prevailed throughout a large part of this century have been characterized in the following way:

> Models which are selective have fixed instructional paths and fixed goals. Using intelligence tests and other tests of aptitude, educational outcomes are optimized by selecting students whose entering abilities as measured by such tests, indicate a high probability of attaining success in this relatively fixed instructional environment. The adaptive decision is either to accept or to reject individuals for an instructional program. Students whose test scores do not meet the entering criteria are further tested and diagnosed. They are then provided remedial instruction that will raise their level of initial competence so that they can eventually achieve in the fixed instructional environment (Paraphrased from Glaser, 1976, 1977, 1980).

This approach of testing general abilities that predict success in school and then permitting only those students whose test scores indicate that they are likely to succeed in this fixed path, fixed goal program has been described as the least adaptive model of education (Glaser, 1976).

After the 1930s growing dissatisfaction with the usefulness of tests of general abilities led us to an era in secondary education in particular, which was characterized by the belief that identification of specific aptitudes versus general abilities would help us to serve the special needs of individual learners. This period of so-called differential aptitude testing was not much of an improvement over the method of using tests of general ability to select students for the standard school program. The only difference was that now we had a number of selective programs, each with its own selection criteria (Glaser, 1972). These programs failed to adapt to individual differences in the sense that the methods used by teachers within a given program do in some way need to correspond to the past and present information available on a student.

There are two ways of adapting instruction. One method holds the goals or objectives of instruction constant and offers differing educational paths to these same goals. The second approach chooses different goals for different persons (Cronbach and Snow, 1977; Glaser, 1976). This later option may serve to foster the individual diversity that we cherish. However for purposes of this chapter, it is assumed that in areas like reading, listening, mathematics, writing and skills necessary for successful participation in society uniform objectives need to be identified and then attained in the greatest possible degree by all students. The adaptive model of education that serves this later purpose has been described in the following way:

> Students are tested to determine their entering levels of competence usually by means of achievement tests and/or criterion referenced mastery tests combined with teacher judgements. Instructional methods are then matched to whatever knowledge is available on each student. This matching is a continuous process. Each student's progress is reassessed at different points in time over the course of instruction. This new information is then used to decide how to further modify instruction so that student's gradually attain program goals. Instruction is aimed at not only accommodating differing initial abilities. In addition instruction is used to improve or modify initial entering abilities (paraphrased Glaser, 1976; 1980).

Within this type of adaptive model of education, the question for educators and for those individuals involved in the design of instruction is how we can best assess the learning characteristics and initial entering abilities of students on an individual basis and then adapt instructional treatments to these learner characteristics.

Historically our attempts to match learner variables and instructional variables can be grouped according to three broad categories of individual difference variables. The kinds of variables examined in each category are intrinsically related to the prevailing attitude toward intelligence tests and tests of aptitudes and mental abilities. The first attempts to match learner variables and instructional variables occurred as a result of growing disatisfaction with tests of intelligence and mental abilities. Because these tests were correlated with many kinds of academic achievement, they were not useful in making specific instructional decisions. What appeared to be needed instead were tests of specific mental abilities that could be used to guide instructional decisions regarding instructional treatments. This was the period of Guilford's monumental work *The Nature of Human Intelligence* in which he differentiated specific hierarchically arranged abilities. Many of the first learner variables that were examined as likely candidates with which we could match instruction consisted of these abilities and of aptitudes measures that had become popular during the differential aptitude testing era.

The success of this first wave of aptitude interaction research was extremely limited in its findings (Bracht, 1970). To a certain extent, these findings were flawed by inadequate statistical analyses and by the methods used to critique each study (Cronbach and Snow, 1977). Overall however, this early research on aptitude treatment interactions only substantiated the already growing awareness on the part of many individuals that aptitude tests and tests of ability that had been used to place students in educational programs were inappropriate tools for measuring individual differences that interacted with different methods of learning. This was because such tests were related only to the outcome of learning. They predicted those who were likely to succeed or fail but they were not useful in determining *how* individuals learned and then matching this information with specific treatments within a given educational program.

Following this initial period, there was a change in focus with respect to what variables might play an important role in our instructional decisions. This new focus developed during a conference on individual differences at the Learning Research and Development Center in 1965 (Gagne, 1967).

The central theme of this conference was that individual difference variables that affect performance and learning were best characterized as processes that intervene between stimuli and responses. However no unified process of learning or performance resulted from this conference. As a result a variety of different cognitive and noncognitive process variables that were related to individual differences in learning and performance were investigated during the period that followed this conference. The list of variables that could be mentioned is far too large so only a few of the more important examples follow.

Rosner's work (Rosner and Simon, 1972) which was concerned with perceptual processes that relate to reading skills of elementary students is one example from this period. Rosner was interested in auditory pattern perception. His work indicated that auditory processes involved in his phoneme synthesis and deletion task were differentially related to success in reading.

Witkin's research on field dependence as measured by scores on Embedded Figures tests represents still another attempt to identify learner characteristics that were related to how individuals learn. Subjects who can locate figures in a complex context are said to be analytic or field-independent. Subjects who have difficulty with this task are said to have a more global or field-dependent approach to tasks (Witkin, 1973).

Rohwer's work on mental elaboration is an example of a strategy variable that has been shown to differentiate students according to developmental levels and according to differing skill levels within certain age-groups (Rohwer, 1971). Mental elaboration refers to the way in which different individuals encode and transform the materials that they study.

Another noncognitive variable that relates to how individuals learn and that has been shown to have clear aptitude treatment interaction implications is an individual's modality preference — his visual, auditory or tactile preference. As will be mentioned in Chapter 17, this variable plays an important role matching instruction to the handicapped learner (Oaken, Wiener and Cromer, 1971).

The most important finding that has emerged from this period of research is the fact that those process variables which yielded significant interactions were highly correlated with and largely explained by measures of general abilities and intelligence. In the concluding chapter of their book *Aptitudes and Instructional Methods,* Cronbach and Snow state:

> Instead of finding general abilities irrelevant to school learning, we find nearly ubiquitous evidence that general measures predict the amount learned or rate of learning or both. Whereas we had expected to find specialized abilities rather than general abilities to account for interactions, the abilities that most frequently enter into interactions are general. Even those programs of research which started with specialized ability measures and found interactions with treatments, the data seem to warrent attributing most effects to generalized ability (Cronbach and Snow, 1977).

The somewhat circular trail of this entire discussion led us first away from intelligence tests and tests of general abilities and toward tests of more specific abilities and then eventually to processes that relate to how individuals might learn. Now it appears that we have been forced to once again examine measures of intelligence (Resnick, 1976). In most recent times, research efforts have been devoted to identifying what it is we mean by intelligent performance. Resnick and Glaser (1982) have stated that intelligence is simply "the ability to learn about one's environment in the absence of formal instruction." They suggest that "if we are to account for intelligence we must account for the processes involved as an individual makes the transition from one state of competence to another." We must account for both the differences which we find between experts and novices in various subject domains and we must account for the differences we find between individuals functioning within narrower ranges of performance.

Three main sources of individual differences seem to characterize these transitions in skill that lead from one level of competence to the next. These are differences in basic processes, differences in learned strategies and differences in the kinds of knowledge and the organization of that knowledge that appears to be involved in skill level transitions (Schuell, 1980).

Included under process differences are differences in channel capacity, differences in speed of accessing short-term memory and in memory scan — all of which are automatic processes. In addition, these processes seem to be relatively permanent individual characteristics (Hunt, 1976). These variables appear to characterize extreme differences in intellectual functioning such as that found between retardates and normals. In addition they may also differentiate between individuals of high and low verbal ability and high and low reading ability within a restricted range of ability such as that found in a college student population (Hunt, 1975; Hunt, 1976, Hunt, 1980).

Strategy variables are individual difference variables that are presumably learned by individuals in varying degrees. Strategy variables include being able to detect problems, scan for features, set goals (Resnick and Glaser, 1982), categorize (Rosch, 1978), and perform various kinds of mental elaboration (Rohwer, 1970). These variables and others that relate to differences in the manner in which individuals encode, rehearse, organize, store and retrieve information are what we call strategy variables. In addition to these, certain personality or cognitive style variables could be included as strategy variables (Kagan and Kogan, 1970). Frequently strategy variables interact with process variables. For example use of encoding strategies can appear to affect channel capacity owing to the increased size in the chunks of information that are manipulated.

Knowledge differences that are relevant to a given instructional task are a third important source of individual differences. Expertise in an area be it reading, math or a game like chess cannot develop without a large store of accessible knowledge. Furthermore there appear to be differences in the kind and organization of knowledge that individuals differing in skill level seem to have available. In highly skilled individuals, the store of knowledge appears to be better organized for retrieval (Simon, 1976).

The process, strategy and knowledge variables are all sources of individual differences that affect the transitions from one level of competence to another on instructional tasks. Yet it should be evident that a large amount of work remains if we are to identify specific learner profiles that can be valuable in helping individual students achieve instructional goals in various subject areas and through various instructional delivery systems. Our students differ greatly with respect to these processes, strategy and knowledge variables that lead to competent performance. More detailed intraindividual taxonomies of the relationships among these variables will have to be developed.

In the meantime we must take what we can from research such as that mentioned above and integrate this information with some of the less sensitive measures that are used in public schools today. Eventually new tests will need to be developed (Glaser, 1981). In addition more global models of instructional systems which match population characteristics and curriculum treatments will need to be established and then modified as research progresses (Glaser, 1980). The "Non-Textbook Instructional Model" discussed in Chapter 17 of this volume is one such model.

REFERENCES

Bracht, G.G. The relationship of treatment tasks, personological variables and dependent variables to aptitude treatment interactions. *Review of Educational Research*, 1970, 40, 627-745.

Cronbach, Lee J. and Richard E. Snow. *Aptitudes and Instructional Methods*. New York: Halstead Press, 1977.

Gagne, R.M. (ed.). *Learning and Individual Differences*. Columbus, Ohio: Merrill, 1967.

Glaser, R. *Adaptive Education: Individual Diversity and Learning*. New York: Holt, Rinehart & Winston, 1977.

Glaser, R. The future of testing: A research agenda for cognitive psychology and psychometrics. *American Psychologist*, 1981, 36, 923-936.

Glaser, R. General discussion. In R.E. Snow, P.A. Federico and W.P. Montague (eds.), *Aptitude, Learning and Instruction: Cognitive Processes Analyses of Aptitude,* Hillsdale, New Jersey: Erlbaum, 1980.

Glaser, R. Individuals and learning: the new aptitudes. *Educational Researcher,* 1972, 1, 5-12.

Glaser, R. In L.B. Resnick (ed.), *The Nature of Intelligence,* Hillsdale, New Jersey: Erlbaum, 1977.

Hunt, E. Varieties of cognitive power. In L.B. Resnick (ed.), *The Nature of Intelligence,* Hillsdale, New Jersey: Erlbaum, 1977.

Hunt, E. and M. Lansman. Cognitive theory applied to individual differences. In W.K. Estes (ed.), *Handbook of Learning and Cognitive Processes* (Vol. 1). Hillsdale, New Jersey: Erlbaum, 1975.

Kagan, J. and N. Kogan. Individual variation in cognitive processes. In P.H. Mussen (ed.), *Carmichael's Manual of Child Psychology* (Vol. 1), New York: Wiley, 1970.

Melton, A.W. Individual differences variables and theoretical process variables. In R.M. Gagne (ed.), *Learning and Individual Differences.* Columbus, Ohio: Merrill, 1967.

Oaken, R., M. Wiener, and W. Cromer, Identification, organization and comprehension for good and poor readers. *Journal of Educational Psychology,* 1971, 62, 71-78.

Resnick, L.B. *The Nature of Intelligence.* Hillsdale, New Jersey: Erlbaum, 1976.

Resnick, L.B. and R. Glaser. Problem solving and intelligence.

Rohwer, J.W. Mental elaboration and proficient learning. In J.P. Hill (ed.), *Minnesota Symposia on Child Psychology,* 1970, 4, 220-260.

Rosch, Eleanor. Principles of categorization. In Eleanor Rosch and Barbara B. Lloyd (eds.), *Cognition and Categorization.* Hillsdale, New Jersey: Erlbaum, 1978

Rose, Andrew M. Information processing abilities. In *Aptitude, Learning and Instruction: Cognitive Process Analyses of Aptitude,* Hillsdale, New Jersey: Erlbaum, 1980.

Rosner, Jerome and Dorthea P. Simon, *The Auditory Analysis Test: An Initial Report,* Learning Research and Development Center, University of Pittsburgh, Pittsburgh, Pa., 1970.

Schuell, Thomas J. Learning theory, instructional theory and adaptation. In R.E. Snow, P.A. Federico, and W.E. Montague (eds.), *Aptitude, Learning and Instruction: Cognitive Process Analyses of Aptitude* (Vol. 2). Hillsdale, New Jersey: Erlbaum, 1980.

Simon, H.A. Identifying basic abilities underlying intelligent performance of complex tasks. In L.B. Resnick (ed.), *The Nature of Intelligence,* Hillsdale, New Jersey: Erlbaum, 1976.

Tyler, Leona. Toward a workable psychology of individuality. *American Psychologist,* 1959.

Ward, I.F. *Applied Sociology.* New York: MacMillian, 1906.

Witken, H.A. In Lee J. Cronbach and Richard E. Snow, *Aptitudes and Instructional Methods.* New York: Halstead Press, 1977.

CHAPTER 9

MICROCOMPUTER EDUCATION EVOLUTION — REVOLUTION

DAVID L. WILSON

HISTORICAL PERSPECTIVE

TECHNOLOGY has always been an important element in how and what people think and how they communicate. In the *Republic* Plato spoke of the effects of the development of writing on memory and other training skills associated with the oral tradition. The invention of movable type put the Bible within the reach of the common man and permanently altered the religious views of Europe.

During the last few years the effects of the electronics revolution on society has impacted education to the same degree that print and movable type changed the religious views of the people of Europe. This revolution, which is destined to have long-term consequences, parallels to some degree the evolution of developmental theories as to how students learn, the forces that motivate them to learn and the effects of external stimuli on memory and cognition.

It was not until the mid 1950s and early 60s, however, before attention turned to classroom application of learning theories. Although Pressey experimented with a test response device in the 1920s, the real resurgence of the programmed instruction movement in the United States is generally credited to B.F. Skinner of Harvard University. After a relatively brief flurry of development of both simple and complicated teaching machines, the field moved from a concern with the hardware to more intense concern with the way in which information is structured for the individual learner.

Earlier "teaching machines" appeared to be a compromise between a scroll and a textbook and offered students little more than linear programs of instruction housed in a machine with lessons for students to manipulate as they progressed through the unit of instruction. As machines and programs became more sophisticated students were able to acquire information independently through carefully selected, sequential and systematic steps. During its evolutionary stages, the "teaching machine" and programmed instruction helped advance the theory that individualized and systematic programming could be productive and efficient.

Although considerable progress was made during the 1960s toward developing individual and tutorial instruction, tradition prevailed and teachers continued to lecture, and to use the chalkboard. The textbook continued to serve the core curriculum.

It was not until the beginning of the 1970s that the school environment began to change. As the school environment changed, so did the educational environment. As new technologies began to emerge and as computers increased our ability to manipulate information, the "little red school house" became as nostalgic and as outdated as the slate board and the slate pencil.

A NEW LEARNING ERA

During the economic boom years of the early 1970s, American teachers had access to a wealth of communication media at a level unattainable during the 1960s. New and improved overhead and opaque projectors, automatic and random access slide projectors, self-contained film-strip projectors, audio cassette tape recorders, video recorders and cameras all seemed to be standard equipment in most school systems during the 1970s. Efforts were made during this era to use the new technologies to individualize programs and to provide for remedial instruction in both elementary and secondary schools across the country.

The Face of the Future

The 1970s ended in a recession and school budgets suffered from enrollment declines and escalated fuel prices. School boards closed some schools and consolidated others. Media Centers and libraries were integrated and there was strong community effort to force schools to return to the basics.

Despite the current recessionary trends, the evolution of new technologies and new system of instruction will impact education during the 1980s as never before. Most analysts say the long range trend is set — more and new instructional technology is inevitable.

The Impact of Microelectronics

The electronic revolution represents one of the greatest intellectual achievements of mankind and is destined to have significant and long-term consequences, especially in education, business and industry.

The impact of electronic technologies is already having a pervasive effect on education outside the classroom. Examples are the tremendous increase in the number of manufacturers and distributors of inexpensive hand-held calculators including the Little Professor® a derivative of the electronic calculator. An electronic game, Speak and Spell®, teaches correct pronunciation and spelling and is advertised as a "revolutionary product with electronic voice and brain — and not a single moving part."

The hand-held calculator has already substantially altered the character of the traditional "problem sets" in science and engineering and before long the slide rule and multiplication table will be replaced by a thin and lightweight pocket-size calculator. The development of microelectronics and the computer chip has already reduced large technologies to miniature level, and as a result the school system will be forced to change the ground rules under which they have operated in the past.

The Big Magic Box

In the good-ole fashioned school days,
Days of the Golden rule,
Teacher said "Good morning class,"
And so she started school.
Alas! how different things are now
The school day can't begin
Till someone finds the socket
And plugs the teacher in

Lilyn Carlton

The "plug in" teacher was conceived during the 1960s when people were intrigued with computer application to prescriptive and corrective learning. Probably the most successful example of such a system is PLATO (Programmed Logic for Automatic Teaching

Operations). Developed in the 1960s by the University of Illinois and Control Data Corportation, PLATO is cited as an exemplary mechanical teacher containing more than 8,000 hours of course ware, much of it in a continuous curriculum. This means that if a student responds incorrectly to an item in PLATO's data bank, PLATO will search its memory bank and review the major points again. During its heyday, PLATO offered the student both the challenge and reward that comes with learning.

For instructional and remedial purposes, PLATO and other mainframe systems are extremely expensive since they require open lines to the central computer. Large mainframe systems can also slow down or stop at peak times during the day. Most users do not care why a computer slows down. The fact that it does is what matters. Simply put, systems slow down or stop when more and more computing and information are demanded by users, and as a result people wait longer to get answers. Most proponents of microcomputer instruction would not support the concept of PLATO since the system is expensive, is prone to backing up, and the system does not always lend itself readily to what is the most intellectually demanding use of the computer: learning how to program it.

The Small Magic Box

The first successful attempts at finding a solution to big and expensive mainframe computers came from the smaller companies headed for the most part by a younger generation of computer experts who refused to believe in the "bigger-faster" maxim. Many of the firms flourished, and today they are leaders in the manufacturing and distribution of both microcomputer hardware, software and courseware.

Because of the expense and time constraints placed on mainframe computers, many experts believe that the 1980s will be the decade of serious applications of inexpensive, easy to operate, easy to maintain microcomputers. The current trend in computer sales to schools seems to support that notion. During 1980, for example, there were 52,000 computers available to students for education and training purposes, and 40,000 additional units made their way into schools during 1981. According to various industry studies, there may be from 300,000 to 650,000 computers in the schools by 1985.

The trend is apt to continue.

Schools that are using microcomputers find that they are effective in presenting routine drill and practice exercises, but most educators are more impressed with the computer's potential for simulating complex and difficult cognitive processes, especially in physics, biology, earth sciences and mathematics. A computer simulation is an extension of a student's ability to apply basic concepts of math and logic to programming and modeling. Through simulations, students are able to walk through a program in steps, correcting their own errors, and generally becoming more independent in their own work.

As students work independently or in groups, some of the most important changes in attitudes and abilities may go comparatively unnoticed as students work together teaching each other and developing one another's programs. The development of social and interpersonal skills may rank among the affective objectives in a future generation of cognitive-based programs.

A Gain for the Disabled

The handicapped and disabled student can also benefit from microcomputer training systems. At the American School for the Deaf (ASD) in West Harford, Connecticut, computer-assisted instruction is available for tenth, eleventh and twelfth graders who are either deaf or have impaired hearing. Students learn not only grade level math skills but also they develop basic skills in computer programming.

The American School for the Deaf is only one of an increasing number of schools to use computers with the handicapped or disabled. Two schools that use microcomputers, The Mill Neck School for the Deaf, Long Island, New York and The Schneiler Communication Unit in Syracuse, New York, both report positive gains by students in academic achievement and in the development of positive attitudes toward self and others.

The microcomputer, when used as an extension of a student's genetic communication network, can be a positive force in equalizing educational opportunities for the handicapped and disabled. With assistance from the National Science Foundation many disabled people now own personal computers and software; and even without financial assistance, many homebound students are finding ways to purchase their own equipment and materials.

How Schools Use Computers

Instructor, a magazine for elementary school teachers, recently conducted a survey among readers to find out how many schools were using computers and for what purposes. The responses, from more than 4,000 teachers, librarians and school administrators, disclosed a high interest in computers among all three groups. "It's one thing everyone in our school district agrees on," wrote Judy Harris, of St. Paul, Minn.

The survey findings appeared to refute the notion that teachers feared displacement by a "teaching machine" and so were reluctant to use computers. Likewise, it challenged the myth that elementary level students will be unable to benefit from computers.

"Math and science teachers at the secondary level had a head start in computer use, but, thanks to the microcomputer, we've seen a dramatic reversal of that trend in Houston," said Patricia Sturdivant, assistant superintendent of technology for the Houston Independent School District.

How are computers being used by schools that have them? Tables 9-I and 9-II summarize the findings.

TABLE 9-I

PURPOSES

Drill and practice	68%
Enrichment	62%
Games	62%
Computer literacy	47%
Computer programming	45%
Remedial work	43%
Tutorial	37%
Problem solving	32%
Record keeping	22%
Testing	12%
Managing instruction	9%

TABLE 9-II

SUBJECT AREAS

Math 86%
Language arts 45%
Reading 43%
Social studies 27%
Science 25%
Special education 3%
Business 3%
Computer science 2%
Art and music 1%

Source: *Instructor Magazine* (5)

Integrated-Interactive Micros

Tell me - I forget
Show me - I remember
Involve me - I understand

Ancient Chinese Proverb

Perhaps the most significant advantage of micro applications to learning is the programmatic potential of the computer to engage students to think in new and different ways. Learning "with" computers forces students to analyze data more critically than before.

Organizational skills are developed when students are provided information and data and are forced to bring the data into a coherent functional relationship. The interaction of the student with the computer is similar in many ways to the tutorial interaction of a student-teacher relationship. The exception of course, is the tolerance and patience of a computer when a student displays a total lack of understanding of the steps involved in solving a problem.

Endowing a computer with genuine intelligence and humanistic characteristics would merely resurrect a bygone fad. The computer program is the heart and the brain of the interactive system, and the variables involved in designing an effective computer interactive system are almost endless. Programming is not a single process, nor is it a simple process — it is an ongoing, systematic and a student-learning process.

Integrating Technologies

In today's technological world, it is easy to lose sight of the importance of the development process in program design. Microcomputer course ware, as any program material, must be designed to optimize learning efficiency while maintaining a balance between a mechanistic and a humanistic curriculum.

The microcomputer is not the only technology on which we can program and provide for interactive learning experiences. Many school systems can develop additional program flexibility by integrating (or interfacing) microcomputers with either video cassettes or video discs. The rewards of integrated technologies are greater than if one system were used separately. Floyd points out the value of integrated interactive learning by stating:

> Well designed interactive programs combine many of the advantages of a number of different types of instruction with none of the compromises. . . Using a computer with a videorecorder provides the flexibility and accessibility of a book, with the impact of motion and immediacy of video, as well as the feedback and documentation that we generally associate with live instruction. Well designed lessons can actually increase the feedback. . . while reducing the delivery cost. . .

Industry sources predict that during the 1980s and beyond, the greatest impact of technology on education and training will not come from a single technology, but from the combination of different technologies. This "integrated" electronic approach will become the conduit for a comprehensive self-contained communications network that will connect many different types of individually designed electronic work stations.

The integration of microcomputers with other communication systems offers a great many advantages over earlier attempts to provide Tutorial Instruction via machines of various sorts where information was the same with students simply progressing through the steps at different times and at different speeds.

The electronics revolution is changing our society so rapidly that it is difficult to predict what the future holds. One thing seems to be certain, however, the classroom environment is far different today than it was yesterday, and we have not yet witnessed the limits of what is possible in changing the system as we know it today.

REFERENCES

Fiske, Edward R. Schools Enter the Computer Age: An Analysis, *The New York Times*, Section 12, April 25, 19 .

Floyd, Steve. Designing Interactive Video Programs, *Training & Development Journal*, December. 1980.

Grinstein, Louise, and Rina J. Yarmish. The Computer in Education: MYTH and Reality, *Educational Horizons*, Vol. 59, No. 4, 1981.

Hitchens, Howard. The Evolutions of Audio Visual Education in the USA Since 1945, *Educational Media International*, No. 3, p. 6, 1979.

Time, Magazine, Computer Generation — A New Breed of Whiz Kids, p. 54.

CHAPTER 10

INTERFACING MICROPROCESSORS/ COMPUTERS WITH VIDEODISCS

James G. Buterbaugh

URING the past decade, few technologies that have been introduced have caused as much speculation, interest and excitement as the interactive videodisc. Literally, hundreds of new opportunities are emerging with the combined promise of computer intelligence interfaced with video presentation modalities. This combined promise of interfacing computer technology with new
videodisc systems is exciting educators, instructional developers,
producers and publishers. Destined to become one of the fastest
developing communication systems, the interactive videodisc is a
potentially revolutionary instructional medium.

Computer technology coupled with videodisc systems provides a
flexible means for quickly and accurately locating and combining the
instructional features of various learning resources. For example,
books, microforms, slides, filmstrips, motion film and video, audio
formats and digital/analog data are stored and retrieved inexpen-
sively. Containing extremely high resolution imagery, multi-
channel audio signals and digital coding, the videodisc is a non-
volatile storage medium which resembles a long-play (LP) conventional phonograph record without visible grooves. Videodisc
technology is being refined to provide both home consumer and the
educational/industrial markets with an inexpensive, easily accessible
microprocessor/computer interfacable source for conventional audio
and video learning resources. Present videodisc units have user
playback capabilities; however on the near horizon, desired eras-
ing/rerecording accommodations are emerging that will far surpass
the resolution qualities of the present state-of-the-art videotape unit
standards.

The amalgamation of videodiscs with microprocessors/computers
is being interfaced into a unified instructional technology called "in-

telligent videodiscs." This coupling permits the interactive and graphic/text generating capabilities of microcomputers to compliment the videodisc's comprehensive contents. A combination of printed text, audio, film and video imagery and the computer can enable the efficient and effective information transfer, whereby systematically prescribed instruction is stipulated. This computer interfacing capability with videodisc technology extends a random access "menu" selection approach for the learner to choose from an extensive range of curricula offerings. Appropriate learning sequences, as determined by the individual learner's interests or aptitudes, can be programmed by this "menu" composition technique.

INSTRUCTIONAL VIDEODISC APPLICATIONS

Conventional audiovisual formats can be viewed or reviewed in a variety of programming methods by a learner who is using videodisc systems. Learning resource consolidation is a major advantageous feature of videodisc technology and extends ultra material access convenience for user retrieval.

Comprehensive collections of existing resource materials have been replicated in the videodisc format. In the main, the "linear" playback method is a straightforward, traditional sequence, which (relating a story or conveying a lesson, one point at a time) utilizes the videodisc's most rudimentary function.

The "nonlinear" playback method permits varied access from one point to another with omission or repetition of selected sections. Main features of this format extend the juxtaposition of still frames with motion sequences or "branching" techniques to the varied videodisc contents, depending upon the learner's commands. With the support of appropriately placed "menus" or tables of contents, the learner is able to manually enter frame "addresses," which correspond to available videodisc contents. In turn, the learner can then select desired presentation modes, levels of difficulty or personal interest sequences. Manual selection access can extend the learner's ability to process the videodisc's contents by skipping forward or reversing, scanning at high speed, freeze framing, advancing in slow motion or repeating significant and more difficult sequences.

Three levels of learning resource application have been identified for instructional videodisc applications:

EXISTING ENTERTAINMENT OR EDUCATIONAL MATERIALS. Videodisc distributors license feature films, television programs, documentary and educational films for replication. A sampling of a videodisc distributor's catalog lists classic feature films, Walt Disney Productions®, television movies, nonfeature home films, sporting events, informational and educational films produced generally for linear playback uses.

EXCLUSIVELY PRODUCED INSTRUCTIONAL VIDEODISCS WITH INTERACTIVE FEATURES. This type of instructional programming is relatively expensive and generally produced for special interest markets. Development of these resources has been limited; however, educators are beginning to recognize the potential of this medium. This originally produced material can be utilized in either the linear or nonlinear formats. For optimum instructional benefits, the format should be programmed for nonlinear applications for specific audiences or individual learners. This instructional application introduces a development strategy that prescribes selected learning sequences that may be determined by the individual student's responses to diagnostic testing elements.

VIDEODISC PROGRAMMING CONTROLLED BY A MICROPROCESSOR/COMPUTER. Selected microprocessor/computer applications (intelligent videodiscs) can prescribe, issue and control sophisticated learning strategies. The creation of "intelligent videodiscs" can involve the use of a text editor to design or "author" the program, an assembler and a videodisc player with a microprocessor controlling unit. The "authoring" is the design and creation of computer-enhanced materials for translating a common communication bond between the learner and the instructional developers. Within the memory capacities of a microprocessor, the videodisc system can be automatically programmed to deliver all random access features. The microprocessor can control "branching" frames and direct normal play, slow motion, freeze frame and other system features. The connection of an external microcomputer with a videodisc unit provides features that are available with a microprocessor as well as capabilities that significantly expand the "intelligent videodisc's" instructional potentialities. This advantage not only extends graphic provisions, operational commands and freeze frame "addresses," but it also provides capacities to store and analyze extensive instructional programs and prescriptive results of the learner response data. The evaluation, analysis and prescriptive results of the learner response data exemplify the significant contributions a system of this design can provide the instructional development process. The microcomputer's full-logic capabilities permit ultra-sophisticated "branching" techniques. Interactive simulations enable a learner to manipulate the various aspects of a model and to immediately ascertain the consequences of the input data.

Simulation opportunities with "intelligent videodisc" technology open far-reaching ranges of instructional applications and are advancing the science identified as "engineered or artificial intelligence." The use of computer programs and programming techniques to cast additional light on the principles of human intelligence, and thought in particular, is the area of greatest unexplored potential of combining the technologies of videodisc and ancillary computerization in the future.

DESIGNING VIDEODISC INTERACTIVITY APPLICATIONS

The Sony Video Product Communications Group in their *Videodisc Program Production Manual* has exemplified a design to utilize computer intelligence to execute interactive playback options:

1. Start the program with a still frame to give the learner a choice of proceeding through the appropriate path for her or his background or go directly to a particular segment.

2. Ask the learner what her or his background includes and then select the appropriate playback path.

3. Stop during or after a segment to test the learner's comprehension. If correct, the learner can proceed. If incorrect, return the learner to the segment for repetitive viewing or extend a different segment that explains the concept differently.

4. At any time, provide access to the table of contents or other support segments.

5. Provide the learner with the ongoing test response scores.

6. Present freeze frames (slides) with a predetermined amount of time allotted for each still.

7. Change audio tracks from one to the other or turn one on and then off.

8. Instruct the learner to put a "bookmark" in a certain point and then return to it later in the program.

9. Ask the learner if he or she wishes to view a particular segment before it is presented; if not, skip it.

10. Show a sequence in normal speed, then replay it in slow motion.

11. Direct the learner to simulate a series of actions by branching among several choices at each step.

12. Ascertain the number of certain responses (such as incorrect responses) and design a branch to a certain segment when the total reaches a predetermined level.

13. Provide a still frame for a specific period of time and then remove it.

The Sony Model LDP-1000® Videodisc microprocessor unit can execute the following interactive provisions:

- Search for a particular segment or still frame
- Set the appropriate audio channels for either stereo or single channel (either one) playback
- Play in either normal, fast (3 × normal), slow (1/5 normal) or step (automatic frame by frame) mode in a forward direction.
- Hold a still frame on the screen for a predetermined period of time.
- Accept an input from the learner and process it as an instruction for subsequent playback.
- Keep data of how many times a particular action has occurred.
- Memorize the addresses of segments and still frames.
- Know which control instructions to consult after a particular action has occurred.

Based on this limited number of interactive techniques, an instructional developer has an almost infinite choice of programming options.

INTERACTIVE LEARNING OBJECTIVES

An instructional rationale should be predetermined before interactive strategies are to be designed and implemented into any videodisc learning program. Five distinctive instructional designing

Figure 10-1.

elements include: comprehension verification, information retrieval, simulation, diagnostics and guided presentations.

COMPREHENSION VERIFICATION. To evaluate a learner's comprehension of content viewed before program continuation is termed "comprehension verification." If the learner's comprehension is confirmed, he or she proceeds; however, if the test reveals incorrect responses, a repetitive loop through the viewed material or a branch into different resource contents are instructional design programming options. The instructional design strategies should be determined by the analysis of the program's specific objectives, the specific audience and the specific learning environment.

INFORMATION RETRIEVAL. A learner's ability to select any desired videodisc segment and then to have the system locate it instantly is called "information retrieval." The provision of a table of contents (menu) at the program beginning will extend an initial summary for the learner to review the videodisc's segments and then to select desired contents. Another indexing option would identify the videodisc's segments in an alphabetical sequence in addition to the order-of-presentation table.

SIMULATION. Another interactive pattern allows for simulations of complex activities. A learner is presented several choices of alternative actions for selection response. The apparent consequences for this response are shown and another set of options is proposed. Simulations have proven to be extremely effective in training applications for potentially hazardous activities provide vivid reality in a safe learning environment. By exposing a learner to the results of adverse judgement, simulation activities can reinforce the seriousness of the training exercise and condition the learner hypothetically to the elements of reality. Once the learner has experienced a critical situation with simulation, she or he may be less prone to panic should that situation occur in actual circumstances.

DIAGNOSTICS. Complex engineering systems that require sophisticated maintenance and repair techniques may utilize the diagnostic videodisc programming for technician training purposes. Rather than storing several shelves of service manuals, a single videodisc can accumulate the same amount of information on still frames. The microprocessor can direct a preprogrammed routine through this extensive material, guiding the learner in the proper approach. The initial frame in a diagnostic routine would specify a measurement or observation to be conducted. Possible conditions would be the learner's input choices. Based on the condition input, the next instruction would continue along the proper diagnostic path. In some cases, these diagnostic routines must be stored on microcomputers rather than self-contained microprocessors in order to accomodate the program's massive volume.

GUIDED PRESENTATIONS. This interactive pattern is similar to both the straight information retrieval and the diagnostic techniques. This guided presentation pattern involves learner query routines that are designed to elicit information from the student in order to initiate an automatic search for the appropriate material. In many cases, the learner will not know what information should be accessed to make a decision.

Another type of guided presentation utilizes an external computer to gather input data from sensors and then searches feedback segments. The American Heart Association has designed a manikin for Cardiopulmonary Resuscitation (CPR) training which interfaces an Apple microcomputer with a Sony Videodisc unit. The learner practices resuscitation on the manikin, which has sensors providing data into the computer. The computer selects appropriate feedback from the videodisc in tutoring the learner.

These five interactive categories are not all-inclusive, but rather exemplify possible patterns.

DESIGNING THE INTERACTIVE VIDEODISC

The Sony Video Production Communications Group has extended an instructional development model for planning a successful, interactive videodisc. Their VIDEODISC PROGRAM PRODUCTION MANUAL relates the following steps:

Step One is to fully *determine* the various *objectives* of the program, and to *prioritize* them as program topics.

Step Two is to use these objectives to *clarify* each separate *audience* we expect for the program.

Step Three is to *conduct* an *audience needs analysis,* whereby we determine exactly what each audience needs to know about each topic.

Step Four is to *map out* the *program* as a series of segments designed to match each audience's information needs.

Step Five is to *design* various *support segments* made possible by an interactive, optical videodisc system.

Step Six is to *design* the *interactivity* that will allow the viewer to direct the program's presentation paths.

Step Seven is to *create* a *flowchart* that will let us put all of the above steps onto paper so we know exactly what we are doing.

Step Eight is to *write* the *computer control instructions* which will drive the videodisc during playback.

These steps have been suggested as discrete tasks to be performed in a certain order by the Sony Product Communications Group.

FUTURE VIDEODISC TECHNOLOGY TRENDS

Videodisc technology has the potential of storing and retrieving an entire universe of information and instructional principles. Future videodisc technology developments will include a greater content storage density, decreased access time and ultra-high resolution clarity. A number of videodisc manufacturers are involved with perfecting self-contained units that will enable "local" system recording capabilities. Philips Laboratories has satisfactorily demonstrated their *DRAW* (Direct Read-After-Write) system. The Quixote Corporation of Chicago has developed a videodisc recording medium that facilitates fast "local" disc processing.

Sony is perfecting a high-resolution video monitor that incorporates 1,100 horizontal lines, as opposed to the current 525 line standard. This increased video image resolution quality will rival present 35mm photo standards and will be highly competitive with conventional photography clarity. Technical research indicates that a videodisc containing double the resolution standards in both the horizontal and vertical directions will be introduced in the mid-1990s.

Technical advances are occurring at such an increasing rate that the continuing challenge for educators will be to master and implement these emerging technologies to create an efficient instructional environment to meet the learning needs of the special student.

William H. Fields, publisher of *Videodisc News* has written:

> Efficient and effective information transfer is the lifeblood of any organization. In fact, the transfer of information between individuals and organizations forms the very foundation upon which civilization is built. Videodisc technology is the world's first *Total Information Transfer System*. It combines all the features of the book, the phonograph record, the motion picture/television and the computer. Such a combination endows this medium with awesome communication powers. Mankind for 8,000 years maintained an agrarian culture. With the coming of the "Industrial Revolution" only 300 years ago, mankind learned to lever his muscles with evermore sophisticated machines and created the modern industrialized world of today. Now with the total information transfer capabilities inherent in videodisc technology, mankind is about to lever his mind. Future historians will mark this event as the embarkation point from which mankind truly became victorious over his most dangerous foe, ignorance.

REFERENCES

Buterbaugh, James G. *Alternative Media Storage/Retrieval Systems: A Futuristics Forecast for Educational Technologists.* Pullman, WA: Information Futures, 1980.

Fields, William H. Videodisc Perspective. *Videodisc News 3(5):*16, 1982.

Mokhoff, Nicolas. A Step Toward Perfect Resolution. *IEEE Spectrum 18(7):*56-7, 1981.

O'Donnell, Dan Harris, and Ted Sato. *Videodisc Program Production Manual.* New York: Sony Video Product Communications Group, 1981.

Schneider, Edward W., and Junius L. Bennion. *Videodiscs.* Englewood Cliffs: Educational Technology Publications, Inc., 1981, pp. 1-117.

Sigel, Efrem, Mark Schubin, and Paul Merrill. *Video Discs: The Technology, the Applications and the Future.* White Plains, N.Y.: Knowledge Industry Publication, Inc., 1980, pp. 1-183.

Sippl, Charles J. and Fred Dahl. *Video/Computers.* Englewood Cliffs: Prentice-Hall, 1981, pp. 1-246.

Winslow Ken. Videodiscs at National Audio Visual Association. *The Videoplay Report 11(3):* pp. 1-8, 1981.

CHAPTER 11

DESIGNING A COMMUNICATION STRATEGY: THE ULTIMATE AUDIO TECHNOLOGY

ROBB RUSSON

N EW instruments for communicating and transmitting information are the most conspicuous aspects of instructional technology for the decade. Videodisc, microcomputers, cable/communication satellite linkage, two-way television, digital audiodisc; all have significant implications for education in an era of pressured change in delivery modes and method. Those who have a developmental and operative responsibilities for this technology — educators, communicators, media producers, instructional developers, administrators — must grope and feel their way through a bewildering forest of technical specifications, must receive special training in application and operation, and still, perhaps, feel hesitant when it comes to using high technology face-to-face.

"Hardware" training and use is an integral part of any up-to-date methodology of instruction. In many cases such hardware has dictated new teaching strategies and even new languages such as "Pilot," "Pascal," and "Fortran." Those who plan for instruction must remember, however, that technology is but one of many routes to successful learning.

A West coast university, in 1981, decided to give its graduate program in educational technology a "success-in-the-marketplace" focus in an effort to make the department's curriculum more useful to those who enrolled in its courses. The faculty and advisors sent a brief questionnaire to institutions, businesses and industries in the region. Twenty-six skills were identified by the survey as those most required on the job training situations, and respondents were asked to rate each skill on a scale of 10 (most important) to 0 (not at all important).

For those whose task it is to design instructional programs or create a successful learning environment for students who need special instruction, the results of the survey were interesting to say the least. One would tend to think that the influence of high technology and new delivery systems would be a central concern of those whose task it is to train, teach and produce materials for instruction. This is not so. The skill category seen as most desirable by the respondents was, surprisingly, not computer programming, not television production, not even slide-tape or audio skills. Of the twenty-six, the skill ranked number one was "interpersonal communications."

While the results of one survey on a regional basis are not by any means conclusive, the direction it points is worthy of consideration. Those skills receiving the lowest priority on the survey were, in almost every case, related to "hardware technology:" computer programming, multi-image production, still photography, media storage and retrieval, and graphics skills. While this is no attempt to denigrate those aspects of instructional technology, the survey indicated an importance for an often-neglected piece of equipment universally available to any learning program. This equipment, with a minimum outlay of additional resources, can be used with great effect in any learning environment. Its adaptability is facile and ready but, somehow, its development is ignored as a matter of course in most universities. In an effort to bridge this gap, the following User Manual for the ultimate in audio technology is offered.

THE UPRIGHT HUMAN BODY —
A SYSTEM USER MANUAL

(A preliminary version of this system was developed "in the beginning" and, after extensive testing became operational. Subsequent revisions, for some reason, have not been found to be necessary.) Note: Much of the following text assumes the reader has a minimal grasp of terminology and a feeling for the structure of the unit.

Installation and Handling

Most units exhibit some evidence of a phenomenon known as

"fright" when exposed to conditions such as performance in front of audiences. This is normal with most models and should not worry you. A scientific study was conducted some years ago in which over one thousand well-adjusted models of this unit were studied. Ninety-four percent of these units were operating with evidence of fear and worry. Those fears exhibited most frequently were:

1. Too self-conscious, too sensitive, too worried about what others thought of them.
2. Fear of criticism by others.
3. Fear of the opinion of others.
4. Lack of confidence in their ability.
5. Lack of ability to speak in public.

If your unit has these problems, especially the last one, what do you do? Emerson (a great mechanic for these units) says this: "Do the thing that you fear to do, and death of fear is absolutely certain."

Getting Started

Good. You have decided to use the unit for speaking purposes in front of others. Now, let's talk about *how*. Start-up involves two parts: first *how* to speak: second, the state of adjustment known as "relaxation."

Let's start with how to speak. You may assume that speaking means the use of only the voice output of the unit. But it is more than that. Speaking means also the use of the total unit known as the "body." First, stand the body in such a way that it inspires confidence in it as a speaker. Of course, there are some situations where informality is the rule. The unit could be placed around a table with other units or may half sit on a desk with certain accessories, such as a hand, placed in a pocket. But let's assume that the unit is to be used before a group.

In this situation, it is best to place the unit erect, with the hands hanging loosely at the sides. This is the best way to begin. The hands are free to use for gestures and the unit *looks* relaxed — an important factor. Place the accessory feet with one a little ahead of the other and with the weight of the unit on the back foot. In this position the unit is free to move a little when changing from one part of the delivery to another. This slight change of position becomes a nonverbal punctuation.

Remember, even though the unit looks relaxed it need not actually *be* relaxed. However, you will find that the adjustment known as "relaxation" will be present if you combine physical ease with an inner programming in the unit known as the "don't care attitude." This state is reached through the following information cycle: "O.K., so I'm a flop on this speech. It isn't the end of the world. I'll just do the best I can and forget it." You will find that the unit will respond to this information and *will* relax a little and speak much better than if the information fed it were something such as, "I succeed with this or I die."

Every time the unit is fed the information, "I *have* to speak well for this is life or death," you can be sure that it will do poorly. When the input is, "I have to be perfect," the automatic tensing function (ATF) will activate (put there when the unit was in development) and ATF is death to effective speaking.

Operation

234410

Now that you have started up the unit by learning to use the total body and how to adjust for relaxation you will be ready for the operative mode. During the operative phase of the presentation you will need to initiate another accessory available on the unit: the eyes. The particular use-state for this accessory is known as "eye contact." You will have proper usage of this accessory if eye contact is maintained with each part of the audience from time to time. Proper adjustment means that the eye is in direct line with some particular unit in the audience — in the center, perhaps, and then at others nearby — not at the back wall or ceiling.

After a few minutes, the adjustment is altered to the left or the right and contact is made with other units on that side. Again, keep the alignment on this spot for a while, taking in three or four units in that general vicinity. Don't leave any area out. If you do, the phenomena known as "audience neglect" will result.

A second operative element is closely tied with relaxation. If the unit is not relaxed it will exhibit certain aberrations known widely as: *"nervous mannerisms."* Even if your unit cannot be entirely adjusted for complete relaxation you can avoid nervous mannerism aberrations. Adjust the accessories to exclude putting the hands in and out of the pockets, jingling keys in the pocket, pushing hair back from the face, clasping and unclasping hands, unmeaningful foot movement, and any form of fingers to the face. These actions inhibit effective operational mode.

During the operative mode the unit will display one accessory more than any other: the *voice*. Correct adjustments of the control board for the voice accessory will ensure proper operation of the unit. The control board has five modifiers: pitch, volume, projection, articulation, and resonance.

First, *pitch*: Many units are set at a higher pitch than they should be. The best setting for your unit should be four tones above the lowest possible setting for that model.

Volume is the amount of force put into the voice. Don't think about volume too much, but do vary the force according to the importance of what is being said. Changes in volume make what is being said more vital and interesting. Remember to keep the adjustment up, particularly at the end of sentences. Punch the last word or phrase to give the sentence life.

Projection will allow the unit to throw the voice to the farthest corner of the room. When speaking to a small group when all are sitting close together, there is no need for projection adjustments; but if the unit is used for large audiences, adjustment should be made for the last row.

Articulation will allow each word distinct pronunciation. As Shakespeare said (a master at programming these units), "trippingly on the tongue." Your unit may be worn to the point of slurring words, or running them together. It may omit word endings. To correct these faults, adjust the articulation control to slightly exaggerate the consonants in the words and say each word ending crisply. This adjustment can be made in private and the unit should be ready for public demonstration after some practice.

The *resonance* control will adjust the breathing and throat opening together. When this is done properly the unit will produce sound from the solar plexis, rather than from the chest, which produces thin sounds. Adjust the throat by inducing the unit to yawn and speak at the same time as practice. Notice how the voice sounds. Positive feedback can be produced by cupping the ears with the hand accessories and listening to how the unit sounds to others.

A Word About Maintenance

During prolongled operation the unit will sometimes develop a tendency to interject "er," "uh," and "um" into the programmed material. This condition is brought on by a loosening of the inner fiber during operation and can be controlled by the manual pause lever. Usually, there is a slight hesitation just before one of these three symptoms is noticed. At this point, merely pull the manual pause lever which causes a conscious pause and allows the unit to produce the correct word wanted and then go on. The manual pause lever can also be useful now and then to keep the unit under control, since most tend to operate a little too fast for easy understanding. Do not be hesitant to use the manual pause; it is far superior to "uh" and "er."

It is hoped that this user's manual has been helpful. These units are the common denominator in high technology. There is no substitute for them even though sometimes they receive a low priority in the budget. A comforting thought, however, is that these units *can* be modified. Last year's model is not out of date and can be used effectively with the most modern and sophisticated hardware in use today. Practice in their use can only bring greater rewards and undreamed-of benefits wherever they are used.

CHAPTER 12

PROVIDING SPECIAL ENVIRONMENTS FOR THE PARTIALLY SEEING LEARNER

JOHN LEACH

TO identify the children who are unable, because of visual difficulties to take advantage of the educational facilities provided for the normally seeing is of the utmost importance; but little is accomplished for their well-being unless definite steps are taken to make available to them the special environments that will enable them to develop their capabilities to the fullest extent.

The American Foundation for the Blind indicates that there are approximately 32,000 partially seeing children in the school systems of the United States. It further states that approximately 37,000 visually impaired are under the age of eighteen.

Naturally, most of the special environments for partially seeing children have been in the larger urban areas. Now, however, small communities and rural areas are successfully providing adequate services for partially seeing children. It is possible for special environments to become a part of all school programs in large and small urban areas and in rural communities only when adequate state legislative appropriation is made for this purpose, and there is a state department of special education with personnel adequately prepared to help formulate and guide the operation of a local program. Because communities vary in their needs as well as in their facilities, state legislation providing for special education services should be flexible enough for each community to choose the type of program best suited to its needs.

SPECIAL ENVIRONMENTS

It is well known that efforts to provide special environments for partially seeing children resulted in the establishments of two types of special classes: (1) a segregated class in which the partially seeing undertook schoolwork requiring close use of the eyes in a specially equipped classroom, but participated with their normally seeing companions in the regular grades in all other activities considered desirable for them to undertake. The first, or segregated class, marked a decided advance by making available in public schools educational environments suited to the needs of the partially seeing, who heretofore had received little if any attention. There was however, the great disadvantage of having these children deprived of contact with their normally seeing companions for all school activities, thus setting them apart as a special group and emphasizing their disabilities rather than stressing their capabilities.

The second, or cooperative class, was a decided step forward since it made available the advantages of special learning environments needed by the partially seeing and, at the same time, provided them with the opportunity to participate with normally seeing companions of their own age in many activities, thus adding to their incentive for success. Berthold Lowenfeld (1973) states that the partially seeing child whose visual capability is neither recognized nor used is liable to become a frustrated and disturbed individual.

CHANGES IN EDUCATIONAL PROCEDURES

During the years that have passed since the establishment of these two classes, ideas regarding educational procedures for all children have undergone many radical changes. One of the most pronounced of these changes indicates that any type of unnecessary segregation tends to limit the development of the whole child.

Nowhere is this change more apparent than in the attitude of society toward exceptional children. Although the mental and physical disabilities of some children are so marked that segregation may be necessary for their safety and development, such a course does not apply to those children whose deviation from the generally accepted norm requires for their general well-being only the special learning environments suited to their needs.

In order that education of partially seeing children might accord with the modern concept of avoiding unnecessary segregation, in many places programs are being successfully carried out that do not minimize the advantages of special learning environments but, rather, add to them opportunities for general well-being and social development. The most significant change is that instead of being registered in special classes established for the partially seeing, such children are enrolled in regular grades where they participate in as many activities as are considered desirable for them to undertake. To meet their needs for special learning environments a resource room in the school building is provided with the necessary physical equipment and educational materials that will enable partially seeing children, with the instruction and guidance of an adequately prepared teacher, to engage in those activities that cannot or should not be included in the schedule of the regular classroom teacher.

At first thought, this procedure may seem merely a reversal in form, but there is the much deeper significance of considering the children as members of the regular grade rather than as members of a special class. Thus their interests and general well-being are continually integrated with those of the other pupils in the grade.

Such an arrangement does not necessarily increase or decrease the responsibility of either the regular grade teacher or the special teacher. It tends, rather, to encourage a spirit of understanding, cooperation and helpfulness for the best interests of the partially seeing child. Where such a program is being carried out successfully it has favorable effects on the child, on classmates, and on parents who often object to the placement of their partially seeing child in a special class and who welcome a plan that recognizes the child as a member of the regular grade without the deprivation of the opportunity for needed special learning environments.

Many communities are providing an even broader program for keeping partially seeing children in a normal school situation through the establishment of the itinerant teacher plan. This arranges for the child to remain in the home school and provides the special help that is needed through the services of the itinerant teacher who visits the child regularly for counseling, teaching and the providing of special materials and equipment. This plan carries the need for the same cooperation with regular school personnel as do the other plans, and assumes that the special teacher will be one with the same special training required by the resource or special room teacher.

PROVISION FOR SPECIAL ENVIRONMENT
ON ALL SCHOOL LEVELS

Whatever program is decided upon by the administrative authorities, it is evident that it should consistently provide the necessary special environments on all school levels from the kindergarten through the high school.

Finding the visually handicapped child early is the first responsibility of the school if partially seeing children are to be given the kind of help they need to succeed from the very first moment of their school career. Frank Bowe (1980) indicates that early intervention can dramatically alleviate the effects of a disability.

It is generally recognized that the earlier needed environments are made available for partially seeing children, the greater is the hope of success educationally, psychologically, and socially. It has also been found that partially seeing children develop more successfully when they can spend most of their school day in the regular kindergarten or first grade room. Thus, early recognition of the handicap and explanation of it to the child's regular teacher are of paramount importance. It is here that the special teacher can be of greatest service to the partially seeing children in interpreting their limitations and needs to the regular teacher. In this phase of their school careers, their needs are apt to involve such simple modifications as proper seating and lighting, and permissive attitude in freedom of moving about the room. Joyce Mitchell (1980) feels that the student should be allowed to move around the room in order to see demonstrations, the blackboard and films.

In most situations print size at this early stage will not be a matter for much concern. As the child grows and develops in social and academic skills, he or she learns to use whatever modifications in materials and procedures are necessary to move into more complicated modifications easily. The child also learns to deal with such things as texts printed in larger size type. The regular classroom teacher, through cooperative work and planning with the special teacher, develops an awareness of the importance of vision and learns to provide for differences. By the time the partially seeing child reaches the high school level, having been brought up in such an atmosphere, he or she is usually ready to accept the responsibilities of each grade and can adapt to meet visual limitations. Unfortunately, in many places there have been no well-developed programs for identifying a child who may be visually handicapped; therefore, such a child may struggle unknowingly until he or she is discovered accidentally. Not having had the advantage of early help, such a child will require much more attention, time and effort to adjust to any aids necessary for success. Other children may, through disease or accident, suddenly be faced with a visual handicap that will necessitate similar adjustment.

Older children may be even more sensitive to feelings of difference than the younger ones are. Their need for acceptance by their companions and teachers must be met for their security. The special teacher, with understanding of the visual problem and the psychological factors involved, can best help the older child and other teachers through careful interpretation and planning. The special teacher must be able to provide for the child's needs in the most unobtrusive manner while making it possible for him to take advantage of the tools and equipment to be used. The special teacher can be of great help in program planning through conferences with administrators, teachers, counselors, and other school personnel. Perhaps a simple change in schedule can make the deciding difference in the partially seeing child's success or failure. Such planning must of course take place before the opening of school so that there is complete understanding by everyone. Advance planning will help to avert changes and disruptions in the pupil's daily schedule and the consequent upsets they may cause. Through the special teacher's conferences with the school staff, an understanding of the problem is arrived at and also an assurance of the child's ability to follow the prescribed plans. The special teacher is also a valuable resource person to whom all of the teachers can turn for extra help for children with temporary and less severe visual problems.

VOCATIONAL OPPORTUNITIES

Often the partially seeing child is ignored in vocational guidance because of a visual problem. It is here that the special teacher should take the initiative in arranging conferences to plan for a program geared to meet the child's vocational desires. The special teacher is best able to emphasize the capabilities of the pupil, and to stress the fact that limitations should be concerned only insofar as they may interfere with the successful carrying out of a desired program or with the child's physical well-being.

REFERENCES

American Foundation for the Blind, Inc. Facts About Blindness and Visual Impairment, *Pamphlet #2 Blind,* New York, New York, 19 .

Bowe, Frank. *Rehabilitating America,* New York: Harper & Row, 1980.

Lowenfeld, Berthold, ed. *The Visually Handicapped Child in School,* New York: The John Day Company, 1973.

Mitchell, Joyce. *See Me More Clearly,* New York: Harcourt Brace Jovanovich, 1980.

CHAPTER 13

THE DESIGN OF MEDIA FACILITIES FOR INSTRUCTIONAL PURPOSES

RICHARD L. GORHAM

THE controversy is as old as education itself: who should design the space where instruction, and more importantly learning, takes place? What factors should influence the function as well as the aesthetic appeal of space? Finally, how will teachers and their students be affected by their physical environments?

The answers to the above questions are not simple. The complexity of the decision-making process is most evident when one begins to apply logic to the design of space for media utilization. This complexity is multiplied tenfold when the learners are other than *normal* as defined by the educational/political leadership.

This chapter will focus on the principles inherent to intelligent design of available space for media usage, by teachers and students who work daily with mainstreaming programs. It will not address the ideal — fifty acres, a 90 million dollar building fund, and unlimited input to the design process by practitioners and users.

Suppose, rather, that you have X^5, Y^5 space, already designated as your AV resource room (or another innocuous title); a capital equipment budget of $10,000, a few hundred dollars for remodeling the existing space, and a direct order from above to prepare your "facilities" for use in the fall term by many (number N) eager learners.

Logic would suggest that the scenerio presented is, at best, absurd, and/or unduly sarcastic. In fact, it is probably closer to the truth than many media/special education practitioners would care to admit. A review of literature (1) suggests that while a great deal of writing has focused on the design of space (its applicability for media and learners use), little assistance is provided that covers the worst-case situation. Unfortunately, worst-case becomes the norm in too many instances.

The author suggests a basic logic to the design of functional space for media utilization — media defined as print and nonprint mediums (software), appropriate equipment and delivery systems (hardware), and facilities (the marrying of hardware/software in a pleasant, functional environment).

Let us begin with several key design principles that should lead to a basic understanding:

1. Allow the users (teachers and supervisors) to design their working space. At the least, seek their input from day one to completion of a remodeling effort or a new building.
2. Ask one question and repeat it often: who is the beneficiary of design decisions? Conversely, who will suffer when poor design occurs?
   Answer: Multiple choice:
   a. learner   b. learner   c. learner   d. all of the above
3. Common sense, when combined with expertise, will out over blind ambition, dedication and good intentions.

The above three points are not viewed technically as "design principles," but they are the next best thing.

Clearly, certain elements must be incorporated into the functional design of space for media use. They include the following:

- Adequate outlets and proper amperage to them (suggested: two 20 amp lines in a 20 × 40 ft space: outlets in the front, back, sides and middle of the room).
- Darkening capabilities that will allow natural light when desired and vice versa.
- Noise level control, whether through carpeting or other accoustical means.
- Projection, lighting and audio control from the front and back of the room and/or key locations.
- Proper heating/cooling and ventilation control (air is for breathing!).

The above points are predicated, to be repetitive, on the desires, goals and expected outcomes of the learner and his/her teacher. Critical decisions will be reached when the following basic questions are answered thoroughly: *What will the allocated space be used for; what is the instructional strategy(ies); will the space allocated for media affect learning in a positive manner; how will I (we) know?*

The latter question is, in effect, the most critical to the functional design of space for media application. By constantly asking this question, and seeking it's answer, quality design becomes second nature. More importantly, the ambience of functional space becomes clearly evident to all its users.

In closing, the reader should thoroughly review the reference listings that follow this chapter. It is important to seek all available input from fellow practitioners and others whose professional training and careers are devoted to this subject. However, the application of common sense, and the absence of mental blocks (I can't do it, hire a consultant) will serve well in time of need.

The challenges are not new; rather, new thinking and new ideas must continue to be applied. The process of designing space for media utilization by "special learners," indeed special people, requires input by the practitioner. It truly is exciting.

REFERENCES

The following references were prepared by: Bibliographic Retrieval Services, Inc. Latham, New York. Keywords: Classroom Design: Special Education 1966-82

Berkell, Arthur. Computerized classroom. *Progressive Architecture, 49*:8, 132-134, August 1968.

Chun, Sherlyn, and others. *Learning Center and Study Carrels: A Comparative Study.* Technical Report #18, 1974.

Cohen, Uriel et al. "Mainstreaming Handicapped Children: Beyond Barrier-Free Design," 1979.

Cooke, Gary. Open up your classroom and use learning centers. *Teacher Education, 9*:3, 22-6, Spring 1974.

Coons, Maggie, Ed. and Margaret Milner, Ed. *Creating an Accessible Campus,* 1978.

Dahnke, Harold L. et al. Academic Support Facilities. *Higher Education Facilities Planning and Management Manual Four.* 1971, Revised.

Kessler, John. *A Peek at Primary Learning Centers,* 1978.

Lifchez, Raymond. Teaching a social perspective to architecture students. *Journal of Architectural Students, 31*:3, 11-5, 1978.

Media Center Facility Design for Maryland Schools, 1975.

Media classroom works two ways. *American School and University, 53*:12, 48, August 1981.

Patterson, Clyde A. Multi-Media Space for Young Multi-Handicapped: Decision, Design, Delivery. *Integration of Related Disciplines.* First Chance Project Space — Interdisciplinary Program, 1977.

Smith, Lynn M. *The College Student with a Disability: A Faculty Handbook,* 1980.

What Went Wrong *Maintenance and Operation Errors to Avoid in Educational Facility Planning,* 1968.

Section III

Program Implementation

CHAPTER 14

THE SCHOOL PRINCIPALSHIP: A CRITICAL ROLE

Gerard Rowe-Minaya

The school principal has the opportunity to make it all work — or not.

Roland S. Barth (1980)

THAT the role of the school principal is critical to what happens in our schools is well documented and agreed upon. Barth's observation cryptically catches the essence of what Sarason (1982), Comer (1981), Roe and Drake (1980) and Sergiovanni (1981), among many others have confirmed. In effect, the successful school is associated with successful leadership; but it works both ways. The school principal is usually the most influential leader in the building for better or worse. And of course that influence extends to those students with special learning needs. Just as attitudes and programs for exceptional children have changed profoundly in the last twenty years, so the role of the principal in the United States (likely society itself) has undergone significant changes. Principals through most of the 1960s and well into the 1970s were often little affected by special education. Among the reasons:

1. the special classes for handicapped populations, e.g. the mentally emotionally disturbed retarded or the physically handicapped, were usually in a few selected school buildings in each school system;
2. in those buildings where one or more classes for the handicapped were located, the principal and other staff were often minimally involved in testing, screening, placement, instruction, etc. The classes tended to be self-contained and were often located in a remote part of the building.

By 1980, principals in the Northeastern United States were reporting that on the average from one to two full days of each

week's work were devoted to Special Education matters brought
about by the impact of Public Law 94-142, with inner city principals
generally reporting the greatest special education workload as associated with students who were predominantly black and Hispanic
(often from families living below the poverty level).

The author and several colleagues recently worked with all of the
elementary and middle school principals in a large New England
city. On one memorable day in April in 1979, I participated in a
process which illustrates the increasing and changing role of the
principal in several areas including special education:

> Seventeen principals sat either at the conference table or with their
> backs to the walls on three sides of the room, which was overheated as
> usual. The District Director, Dr. Berry, presided. "We have several guests
> today — why don't we get right to them."
>
> First came the bad news regarding teacher evaluation. The State
> Department of Education had mandated in 1975 that each school system
> develop a comprehensive plan for the evaluation of all professional staff. "I
> realize it's April but here are the lists of those staff members who must be
> formally evaluated before the end of the school year (in late June)."
>
> Then it was my turn. "The Superintendent has given as his highest
> priority, your development of instructional plans for your staff in order to
> overcome low test scores on a standardized nationally normal achievement
> tests." (They rolled their eyes — they weren't even bitching any more.)
>
> The Director of Special Education was last. As surely as planting the
> last straw on the camel's back — he advised the principals that the State
> Department of Education was insisting that all children now in special
> education classes must have Planning and Placement Team Meetings
> (PPTs) in order to assess the effect of the 1978-79 school placement and,
> modify their individual education plans for the 1979-80 school year. *And
> these PPTs had to be accomplished before the end of the school year!* The principals
> didn't blink an eye. I think they were numb with disbelief.

There is little reason to believe that these principals from New
England are unique. More and more demands are being made upon
principals in many areas, but this chapter will concentrate on thinking about several frames of reference related to special education:
the self-fulfilling prophecy; the need for autonomy; the importance
of understanding as much as possible about each child *and* his or her
environment.

The Self-Fulfilling Prophecy

Andy Serio started his teaching career in 1953, and when I interviewed him in 1976, he was in his third year as a principal. We sat on tiny chairs built for six-year-olds in an abandoned boys' bathroom on the third floor of the school. Before the formal interviews began, he was telling me about the town, an economically depressed area in Eastern Connecticut that seemed never to be able to regain its vitality once the textile mill had closed a number of years earlier. "We get the dregs (referring to the students) — we don't expect much."

Just then, we were interrupted by the school secretary who knocked on the door with the message that a state police officer wanted to speak with him. I stood waiting in the hallway, drinking a cup of coffee, and coincidentally, Mr. Serio and the police officer walked by me to a classroom fifteen feet away.

The policeman stayed out in the hall while Mr. Serio went in. A minute later the principal returned with a boy I judged to be about ten years old. "Keith, this is Officer Smith — he is a very nice man." I could hear the conversation clearly. It seemed that Keith and several other youths had broken into a school building in town and had done a certain amount of vandalism. I watched and listened as the interview progressed. I thought that Keith was conducting himself with poise and was reasonably articulate considering the traumatic circumstances. It developed that his mother had no telephone. The policeman took Keith with him to see Keith's mother.

Mr. Serio returned with me to get started on the interview. I wanted to ask him to tell me more about the incident, but I didn't have to. The principal explained that Keith has been in trouble before and that "He is in the special class." To myself I thought that perhaps Keith was in a class for "emotionally disturbed" youth. But I was incredulous when he went on to say, "Keith is mentally retarded."

We went through the whole interview — not returning again to the subject of Keith. As we walked down the stairs, Mr. Serio said, "The parents in this town are terrifically supportive of me and of the teachers. If I have to spank a child, they will often call and say they would have done the same thing themselves."

Two weeks later, I was sitting in my office at Yale, and I couldn't get Keith out of my mind. I just couldn't accept the idea that he was an educable mentally retarded boy. I called the principal and asked him more about Keith — the testing, etc. Mr. Serio pulled Keith's personal file and came back to the phone. He was tested on the Stanford-Binet (individually administered I.Q. test) and scored 79. And then later was tested on the W.I.S.C. (Weschler Intelligence Scale for Children) and received exactly the same score. (If he had scored 80 or higher, he probably wouldn't have been in that class).[*]

I went to see a professor of psychology in an office nearby. He listened to my story and to my request. Did he know of any test that might be more appropriate for Keith? (After all, the score of 79, even if accurate and meaningful, was but a tantalizing point or two away from the lowest reaches of normal. "Damn the pseudo-scientificism of the whole process, anyway," I thought). My friend, Professor R., was very helpful and gave me the names of people I might contact for further ideas.

But before I did any other investigating *vis-à-vis* I.Q. testing, I talked with my friend and mentor, Seymour Sarason, also a professor of psychology with a special-

---

[*]In 1982, in many states, the I.Q. score necessary for judgements about placement may be lower. Also a second measure, scores on achievement or aptitude tests would also be used.

ity and expertise not only in mental retardation, but in social systems, especially schools. He listened patiently at first and then grew more restless as I neared the end of the account of my discussion with Professor R. He said, "Jerry, there isn't any test that's going to help Keith. It's the social system, including the school, that is the problem."

I thought back to the day in Keith's school. Here was a boy, in a class with other "mentally retarded" children, in a school in which the principal regarded *all* of the children as the dregs of the town. And then I recalled how supportive the parents reportedly were of this principal and his staff. In effect, they turn the children over to the "professionals" — because they "know best." And I realized with a defeated feeling exactly what Seymour Sarason meant. The problem was the system — the school.

After telling this story to a group of prospective principals, I suggested that perhaps the proper role for the principal *vis-à-vis* special education students or prospective students is an *advocate* for the child. This group was very much upset by my suggestion and one of the persons replied, "Are you kidding? We'd be fired. Our responsibiltiy is to the school system."

Questions: Who is the advocate for the student?

How do the principal, the teachers and staff, parents, and interested others regard students, individually and collectively? From what sources do these perceptions spring? Can the positive forces of the self-fulfilling prophecy be harnessed?

How do these perceptions get translated into school curriculum and/or individually tailored curriculum and instructional strategies?

HOW MUCH AUTONOMY DOES THE PRINCIPAL HAVE?

Shouldn't instructional strategies and curriculums be developed as close to the learner as possible? Local control is an important educational and organizational concept, although it often seems to be given away. Principals need to assess carefully how much authority they have, where that authority comes from, and then, of course, how to use it.

Seymour Sarason's views are useful when examining autonomy (Sarason, 1982 p. 172). He states:

[(We have been interested in)] "the degree to which principals feel that they are *as individuals* because of forces external to them in contrast to those perceived as internal. That is to say, there are principals who act as if *they* are primarily in control of their destiny, and there are those who act as if what they have been, are, and will be (is) largely a function of external condition over which they have had or will have little control."

But the principal is not alone in running the intricate affairs of special education. Instead of unilateral decisions made by one or a few persons, P.L. 94-142 has caused a revolution in teamwork among central office and building personnel. Now teamwork is more apparent. Is this a blessing, providing the wisest possible learning environment for each child or is it a potentially damaging shift in decision-making?

Teamwork can have a positive effect on staff. Olson says:

> Participating as a team promotes task execution. More and more employees suffer from anomie, a term coined by the French sociologist and philosopher, Emile Durkheim. It refers to a feeling of isolation and aloneness created by the size of institutions, burgeoning urbanization, increased specialization, and greater emphasis on complex technologies. Employees don't usually see the end result of their contributions, nor the consequences of their work. Involvement promotes a sense of belonging, a team spirit.

But the values of teamwork alone do not answer the question. There is the question of the products of team decision making and execution of tasks. McDermott sees a collusion among policy makers and school personnel, which is emerging. He says:

> Children not learning in school are not so much broken or different as they are made to appear that way. Competition is endemic to our society, and the search for inherent skills effectively organizes the school day and its children around the issue of successful and unsuccessful competence displays. School failure is constantly looked for, noticed, hidden, studied and remediated; it is a fetish that we bring to life with most of the actions we call educative.

The amount of autonomy a principal has and the way that she or he uses it is intertwined with the culture of the school.

UNDERSTANDING THE CULTURE OF EACH SCHOOL

How can a principal be sure about the successes and failures of the changes in organizational structure that have been associated with special education legislation? And with the increase in decisions to be made in special education, has the *quality* of these decisions been of a uniformly high standard? Someone needs to look at the whole of the school to understand the connections.

I knew a contractor who would sit on the grass and stare at a house and think of all the numerous connections between the specialists and the general picture of a healthy building pushing up into its environment. Who will play the role of the contractor in a school setting? If the principal (as the contractor) could or would take the time, that might be the logical choice. The ability to stand back and view the whole of the operation of the school is essential, albeit difficult. It may take help from others.

It is common to find a school psychologist as a full-time member of large school staffs, with smaller schools having the services of a psychologist in proportion to need. These services are taken for granted in 1982 as essential to the needs of students in a general sense and most especially to the proper functioning of students with special needs. However, most psychologists are trained to and function in a way that examines each client more or less as an entity distinct from the context of the school, of the classroom, and from the family.

Why this happens is complicated and not always as clear-cut as I am stating it. But psychologists usually put boundaries around their work just as electricians have a specialty that usually keeps them from installing the plumbing or shingling the roof.

How about paying an anthropologist to offer a naturalistic view in order to provide a context for the more experimental, individualistic work of the psychologist?*

Thanks to our emphasis on school psychology we are left with a better view of the *personalities* of selected clients than we are of the *culture* of the institution. Tests are selected and given, labels are affixed, assignments are made, expectations are held, treatment is administered in the form of a dose of curriculum and given five times a week by the teacher. And often, these diagnoses and treatments are quite valuable to the students. But some uncertain areas remain. Consider the culture of schools in which programs for gifted and talented often turn out to be for white students. Contrast this with programs for mentally retarded students in which blacks and Hispanics are selected disproportionately to what might be expected. Let us examine each of these briefly.

---

*It's not that there are not some persons who are capable of providing psychological anthropology or anthropological psychology (see Spindler, 1978). But unfortunately these people are rare.

The idea that gifted and talented students might also be handicapped in the context of the general school curriculum and teaching-learning styles was not recognized by the federal government until 1972. Some states, however, were actively funding such programs earlier than that. Evolving from an earlier emphasis on I.Q. test scores has been the work of Renzulli (1978) who contends that a gifted student must have equal proportions of above-average abilities, creativity, and task commitment applied to any performance area.

The principal might want to consider the idea that if there are to be resource rooms in the school building that such rooms have multiple use. That is, that gifted children, learning disabled children, as well as those who have no labels will all be welcomed from time to time just as a school library is open to all. Since judgements about who belongs in what grouping are not made with absolute certainty this would at least avoid some of the effects of labelling. Mislabelling is a particular problem with poverty-affected children and is especially evident among blacks and Hispanics. For example, Jones and Wilderson (1976) in examining Mercer's data (1973) found that ten times as many Mexican American children and seven times as many black children were placed in special classes (especially those classes for the mentally retarded) as might be expected.

In discussing this phenomenon with the director of psychological services in a large Eastern United States city recently, I was told of the unwritten policy to identify the largest possible number of mentally retarded students in order to attract lucrative state and federal monies.

Questions

How is it that males outnumber females in mentally retarded and emotionally disturbed classes? Why do we find more black and Hispanic youngsters with similar labels? Is the "Learning Disability" label one which is applied more often to white middle class children than to the poor? Do we find it irresistible to fill our various special classes, gifted, L.D., EMR, etc. in order to receive state or federal monies?

But if much of the school-related teaching and learning takes place in classrooms, then a clear understanding of what is going on is necessary. Behavior outside of the classroom context, usually thought of as satisfactory may often become unsatisfactory to the teacher in the classroom. Let us consider the "emotionally disturbed" (E.D.) child.

Are emotionally disturbed youngesters "disturbed" at home; on the playground, in church, in clubs and other social settings? Or are E.D.'s best seen in school settings? Is it possible that the E.D. student is one of the most sensitive barometers of what is going on in a classroom? Don't we need to see the context in order to understand these individuals? Or, does the removal of the E.D. student add to a complacency that starts with the premise that the special needs of these students are often best met in some out-of-the-way room with only the most cautious mainstreaming of E.D.'s. The main point is that problem may be the climate of the regular class; that the easier route has been to remove one or two students rather than deal with the milieu of the classroom.

Mainstreaming

The professed goal of P.L. 94-142 is to provide for the least restrictive environment of all youngsters with special educational needs. And this has been translated into the goal of returning all children who have been taught, in part, in ways and or places separate or distinct from normal classmates, to the regular classroom for as much time as judged to be appropriate. But this strategy, without adequate understanding on the part of the classroom teacher can be less than satisfactory. Sokoloff observes:

> In some mainstreamed classes, disabled students seem quite stimulated and in others they seem to be unstimulated. Sometimes the educational background of a disabled student can provide some insight into a student's academic and social involvement. Many disabled students have been in special education classes where they were not pushed to achieve academically. A number of teachers, regretably, do not know what the disabled students are capable of accomplishing or how to assist them in doing and progressing further. Often teachers are locked, mind and body, into set curricula.

Summary

Learning programs and environments for those members of our

society with special learning needs have come a long way in the past quarter century. And this has been accompanied by long sustained interest by individuals and groups. Intense political pressure has changed the functioning of our public schools in many revolutionary ways. These changes have impacted on the role of the school principal with many principals reporting that they spend the equivalent of one to two days per week on special education related work.

This chapter dealt with (1) the phenomenon of the self-fulfilling prophecy and though the example given was of low expectations, this phenomenon has another side — the values of high expectations; (2) a case was made for autonomy for the school principal, in part because specific decisions about curriculum and instructional strategies should be made as close to the student as possible; (3) a look at the rise of the influence and the contribution of school psychologists was followed by a call for understanding the culture of each school. Perhaps we should have school anthropologists. The next best thing may be to train the principals as well as other members of staff in some of the techniques of educational anthropological research.

REFERENCES

Barth, R.S. *Run School Run*. Cambridge, Massachusetts: Harvard University Press, 1980, p. xvi.

Jones, R.L., and Wilderson, F.B. Mainstreaming and the minority child: An overview of issues and a perspective. In R.C. Jones (Ed.). *Mainstreaming and the Minority Child*. Reston, Va.: The Council for Exceptional Children, 1976.

McDermott, R.P. "Stages in the Ethnography of School Failure 1960-1980: From the Rhetoric of Schooling Through the Problems of Our Children to a Confrontation with the System." Presented to the Third Annual Ethnography in Educational Research Forum, University of Pennsylvania, Philadelphia, March 18, 1982.

Mercer, J.R. *Labelling the Mentally Retarded*. Berkeley: University of California Press, 1973.

Olson, R.F. Performance Appraisal: *A Guide of Greater Productivity*. New York: John Wiley & Sons, Inc., 1981.

Renzulli, J.S. "What Makes Giftedness?" Re-examining a definition. *Phi Delta Kappan*, Nov. 1978, pp. 180-185.

Roe, W.H. and Drake T.L. *The Principalship*, Second Edition. New York: Macmillan Publishing Co., Inc.

Sarason, S.B. *The Culture of the School and the Problem of Change*, Second Edition. Boston: Allyn & Bacon, Inc., 1982.

Sergiovanni, T.J. (In the Foreword) of Smith, S.C., Mazzarella, J.A., and Piele, P.K., (Editors): School Leadership: *Handbook for Survival.* Eugene, Oregon: Clearinghouse on Educational Management, 1981, p. xiii.

Sokoloff, M.W. *Teacher/Student Interactions in Mainstreamed Settings: A Qualitative Study. A Paper Presented to the Third Annual Ethnography in Education Research Forum, University of Pennsylvania, March 18-21, 1982.*

Spindler, G.D. (Editor). *The Making of Psychological Anthropology.* Berkeley: University of California Press, 1978.

Spindler, G.D. (Editor). *Doing the Ethnography of Schooling: Educational Anthropology in Action.* New York: Holt, Rinehart & Winston, 1982.

CHAPTER 15

TOWARDS A FUNCTIONAL ANALYSIS OF THE IEP

STEPHEN LAWRENCE

THE implementation of P.L. 94-142 in the late 1970s caused a series of major changes in the basic conceptual framework of special education in the United States. This legislation had the effect of mandating that each public educational agency endorse the following goals: The provision of a free, appropriate public education for all students in need of special education; and, full participation of parents in the process of planning and evaluating their children's special education programs (Dep't. of HEW, 1977). While the implementation of this law provided for a number of procedural safeguards, on the individual, state, and federal level, to ensure that these goals are carried out, these safeguards function in an *a posteriori* manner — they come into effect only after an educational action has been taken. By evaluating the adequacy of the educational process, these safeguards provide a remedy for those occasions on which the desired goals have not been met.

On a prospective, or *a priori*, basis, a tool was needed to ensure that free, appropriate public education with full parental participation was provided on a day-to-day basis. The tool developed to be used "on the front lines," in the schools where the children are, not in a review, appeal, or retrospective situation, was the Individualized Education Program (IEP).

Each child who needs special education must have an IEP written and in effect before any special education instruction or related services are provided. The nature of the IEP and the process specified for its development have resulted in significant modifications in the placement, instructional planning, and communication processes of special education. With the IEP as a central management and planning tool, effective, high-quality special instruction can be provided; but changes of the magnitude demanded by P.L. 94-142 have resulted in anxiety, concern, and apprehension among those responsible for implementing the law — teachers and administrators alike. Unfortunately, after a number of years of working with IEPs, they have come to be seen by some as exercises in educational jargon, by others as lesson plans which should be the province of the teacher and which are shared only grudgingly with parents and other staff, while others may regard the IEP only as bureaucratic paperwork designed to meet the requirements of an increasingly intrusive regulatory system. A functional analysis of the IEP, however, reveals that it serves a number of important purposes in the educational setting. It is helpful, then, to review some of the things that an IEP is, and is not.

An Individualized Educational Program is a written statement concerning a child who requires special education. It must contain several components mandated by the federal regulations (Dep't. of HEW, 1977) and must be written according to a procedure spelled out in detail in these regulations. The federal mandates, it should be remembered, are minimum requirements, and many states have enacted statutes and regulations which require considerably more.

The IEP is a program plan that contains at least the following components:

(a) A statement of the child's present levels of educational performance;

(b) A statement of annual goals, including short-term instructional objectives;

(c) A statement of the specific special education and related services to be provided to the child, and the extent to which the child will be able to participate in regular educational programs;

(d) The projected dates for initiation of services and the anticipated duration of the services; and

(e) Appropriate objective criteria and evaluation procedures and schedules for determining, on at least an annual basis, whether the short-term instructional objectives are being achieved (Dep't. of HEW, 1977, Sect. 121a.346).

In addition to meeting the requirements of content represented by these five required components, the IEP must be written during the course of a meeting which must include the following persons: (1) The child's teacher; (2) Another representative of the school, other than the teacher, who is qualified to provide special education or to supervise the provision of special education (in actual practice, this person is generally an administrator); (3) One or both parents.

The third basic requirement of an IEP is that it must be timely: the IEP must be less than twelve months old. It must be reviewed, by a planning committee, at least once each year, and rewritten appropriately.

An IEP is *not* a lesson plan, or a series of such plans. There is no statement in either the law or the regulations that would require the specificity needed to develop daily or even weekly instructional plans; rather, the IEP contains annual goals for educational development, which have been agreed upon by the planning committee. It also contains short-term instructional objectives that are intermediate steps between the student's current level of achievement and the annual goals for that student. These short-term objectives must be evaluated at least annually; many school systems evaluate them at the time of each report card, which means three or four times each year. Daily and weekly lesson plans can be drawn up to teach specific lessons and skills in order to reach the short-term instructional objectives, but lesson plans are not required by the federal law and are a matter of local option.

If a program plan is written about a child in need of special instruction, and if this plan contains all of the components listed above and is written in a meeting of a planning committee constituted according to the P.L. 94-142 regulations, then by definition this program plan will be an IEP. While this document is not a performance contract which would specify results, it is a commitment to provide specific services.

The IEP is a statement of process rather than outcome; it states what will be taught, and how, and even states what the student is expected to learn; but it does not guarantee that the student will learn as expected:

> Each public agency must provide special education and related services to a handicapped child in accordance with an individualized education program. However, Part B of the Act does not require that any agency, teacher, or other person be held accountable if a child does not achieve the growth projected in the annual goals and objectives (Dep't. of HEW, 1977, Sect. 121a.349).

But can the school system be held accountable for providing the educational services specified in the IEP? The question has arisen whether the IEP is simply a recommendation that services be provided, a recommendation that the superintendent of schools or other adminstrator might be free to veto. The federal Office of Special Education has provided the following to interpret this area:

> Is the IEP a commitment to provide services — i.e. must a public agency provide the services listed?

Yes. Each handicapped child's IEP must include all services necessary to meet his/her identified special education and related services needs; and all services in the IEP must be provided in order for the agency to be in compliance with the Act. One of the purposes of the IEP is to set forth in writing a commitment of resources necessary to enable a handicapped child to receive special education and related services (Office of Special Education, 1980, p. 25).

The end-product of the planning committee's work, the written Individualized Education Program, is a valuable tool for planning and evaluating special education programs. When properly written and followed, the IEP provides a framework for effective, prescriptive teaching (Peter, 1965), including diagnosis and assessment, intervention, and evaluation. The design and evaluation of appropriate goals and objectives, and ensuring that they are correctly designed for the individual student, is outside the scope of this chapter (though in a broad sense it is the topic of this book as a whole). The balance of this chapter will focus not on the outcome of the planning committee's work (the IEP), but on one function which the committee must fulfill: communication between those involved with students in need of special education.

COMMUNICATING WITH PARENTS

In order to write an IEP, the school system must arrange for a meeting to which the parents are invited; in fact, the school must take a series of positive steps to encourage parents to attend. These steps include scheduling the meeting at a time and place which is agreeable to both school and parents, and following up with letters and phone calls if the parent has not agreed to come. If the parent does not attend, the school is required to attempt to gain the parent's participation by phone calls, letters, and visits in person. A simple note informing the parent of a meeting to which he or she is welcome is not enough; an active attempt must be made to ensure that the parent has an opportunity to participate. These attempts to maintain communication between school and parents (which in many cases may be attempts to open communication for the first time) are not optional, but are required by the regulations. School personnel cannot simply accept the fact that parents have not responded to a written notice, or have not shown up at the meeting time selected by the school; educators are required to make active, documented efforts to reach out to parents so that the parents can be involved in this process.

Other Required Participants

But staff-parent communication is only one part of the interactions encouraged by the mandate to develop an IEP. The conference must include the child's teacher and another person, representing the school, who can provide or supervise special education. This allows states or local schools the options to decide (a) Which teacher is to be considered "the child's teacher" if the child has more than one; and (b) Who shall the third person be?

In many areas, the building principal, or a representive of a system-wide special education office, fills the third-person role. This has the effect of establishing a consultative role, providing additional opinions which can be valuable when making the decisions needed to complete the IEP. Alternatively, this may mean that there is a supervisory role, such as when a building principal has the opportunity to observe teachers in a face-to-face, intensive setting which demands a high degree of skill in human relations. The third-person requirement ensures that parents will have some contact with personnel other than the child's teacher, and this can be sued to maintain effective and productive communication channels between administrative or supervisory personnel and parents.

When the third person is the building principal, this requirement often has the effect of helping the administrator to understand the demands of the special education teacher's job. All too often, there is a special education department administered out of a central school office, which bypasses the building administrator's supervisory function. When this is the case, the principal may feel that the "special ed people" are not part of the building staff but work for someone else and keep to themselves. Without frequent contact with the special education personnel, the principal may unwittingly encourage the rest of the building staff to perceive special education personnel in the same way, causing problems of isolation and distrust that are counterproductive and that eventually lead to inefficient educational relationships for staff and students alike. If the principal participates in the IEP planning conferences, and assumes the responsibility for implementing the administrative aspects of the decisions agreed upon at these conferences, a feeling of being a responsible part of the system is more likely to develop.

Goldstein et al. (1980) observed fourteen IEP planning conferences and found that nine meetings (64%) were not legally constituted because of the absence of this school representative. In their sample, only 43 percent of the conferences were attended by a regular classroom teacher (resource room teachers attended 100 percent of the conferences). The legal attendance requirement may not be violated by the failure to have a classroom teacher present, but unless the child being discussed is in a completely self-contained setting, the communications function of the IEP planning meeting is certainly being overlooked when this is the case.

While the law and regulations require only three persons to be at the planning committee meeting, it is not unusual, in many school systems, for a parent to arrive at school to find the following persons in attendance:

Local building administrator
Central office administrator, i.e. Director of Special Services
School psychologist
Guidance Counselor
Five major subject teachers
One or more "special" subject teachers
Special education teacher
Nurse
Speech and hearing teacher

The effect on the parent of having to participate in a meeting with this group of professionals has not been adequately investigated. Goldstein et al. (1980) found that in the meetings they observed, where the mean number of participants was 3.7, parents spoke less than half as many times as the resource teachers did. How much participation, then, should be expected from parents in meetings that are considerably larger?

This problem has developed because of a basic misconception of the role of the IEP planning conference. This is not intended to be a review of every aspect of the child's school program, but only of those aspects that are relevant to the child's special education program. Similarly, normal childhood behavior may be a relevant topic for discussion, but if this is not germane to the development or review of an individualized education program, then it should be discussed in some other forum such as parent-teacher conferences, report cards, or phone calls. The IEP planning committee meeting has a certain set of tasks to accomplish and this meeting should be run in such a way as to ensure that parents have a reasonable chance for full participation in the review and development of the IEP; intimidating parents by a preponderance of staff does not allow for full participation.

The federal Office of Special Education has commented:

> Generally, the number of participants at IEP meetings should be small. Holding small meetings has several advantages over large ones. For example, they (1) allow for more open, active, parent involvement, (2) are less costly, (3) are easier to arrange and conduct, and (4) are usually more productive (Office of Special Education, 1980, p. 13).

COMMUNICATION ABOUT GOALS

The greater the number of staff attending the planning meeting, the more important it becomes for the staff (and parents) to be well-trained in the function of the meeting and the goals of the planning committee. Fenton et al. (1979) studied the perceived goals of 1,478 members of 230 different placement teams. The team members were given a list of eleven possible goals that could be the responsibility of a placement team. For each goal, each team member indicated whether the team should offer a suggestion, make a decision, or do nothing (because this goal was not the responsibility of the team). In actuality, each of the eleven goals was a specified responsibility of the planning team according to federal and state regulations. The results clearly showed a need for intensive training in the planning team process: only 37 percent of the planning teams had at least a three-fourths majority of their members who knew that the team had a responsibility to formulate long-term goals; only 22 percent of the teams had such a majority of members who knew that the team had a responsibility to set a review date; only 11 percent of the teams had a three-fourths majority who knew that the team should determine criteria for reviewing a child's program. None of the goals was recognized as appropriate by more than 37 percent of the teams (using the three-fourths majority as the criterion for recognition). Administrators, support personnel, and special education teachers were most accurate in their perceptions of appropriate goals; regular classroom teachers were least accurate. Furthermore, the greatest amount of error occurred in relation to those goals concerned with implementing programs, such as developing specific programs and evaluating them. Fenton et al. state

> If all programming responsibility is relinquished by default to the teacher or teachers who received the exceptional student, then what safeguard does the system provide to ensure the appropriateness of the program? . . . Agreed upon standards provide the placement team with a basis for making decisions about the continuation of a student's program. Further, school-parent communication is improved by using these stated criteria as a common basis for evaluating the child's progress and the program's continued appropriateness. (p. 643)

COMMUNICATING ABOUT ROLES

The problem of ensuring that IEP planning meetings are appropriately designed so as to ensure full parental participation in the process of designing and implementing special programs is highlighted by the work of Yoshida et al. (1978) who studied the perceptions of planning team members as they related to the parent's role in the planning meeting. Twenty-four activities, which were all selected by Connecticut Education Department personnel and local school administrators and support staff as being appropriate for parental participation, were presented to planning team members. The members were asked to indicate which of these activities were appropriate for parental participation. Fifty percent or more of the team members considered that parents should be involved in (a) Presenting information relevant to the case, and (b) Gathering information relevant to the case. All other activities were selected as appropriate for parental involvement by less than half of the team members. While some of the activities may not be clearly defined in the regulations as parental responsibilities, many of them are clearly stated to be a function of the planning team in which parents are to have full participation. For example, the activity of setting evaluation criteria for the student's academic performance in the special education program is a clear responsibility of the team, yet only 6.2 percent of the team members questioned agreed that parents should have a part in this function.

The results of Gilliam's (1979) study indicate that there may be significant discrepancies between the goals of teamwork, and full parental participation, espoused in P.L. 94-142, and the reality of planning meetings. Planning committee members were asked to rank the importance of fifteen different roles to the educational planning process; the rankings were carried out before and after educational planning meetings. There were significant differences between the expected importance of some roles and the *post hoc* perceived importance. While special education teachers were expected to have the most importance in this process, and were perceived after the meeting as having actually had the most importance, the role of building principal was found to drop from seventh in expected importance to twelfth in postmeeting perceived importance. Similarly, parents were expected to be third in importance and were rated, postmeeting, as ninth in importance. While this study should only be regarded as suggestive (due to the failure to control for prior history of the planning team participants), it does indicate that the goal of parental participation as a full member of the team has not yet been reached. Gilliam suggests, as has been mentioned above, that intimidation of parents by professional personnel might help to explain the low perceived ratings of parents in his study.

When designing an agenda for the IEP planning meeting, these results could be used to suggest modifications in the typical activities that generally take up most of the committee's time (Goldstein et al., 1980). Information can be circulated in written form prior to the meeting so that little time needs to be spent in listening to one teacher read extensive comments from other teachers; more time can be spent on discussion of the goals of the meeting, and of the IEP (Gilliam, 1979).

In addition, circulating suggestions for the content of the IEP to be developed, in particular, supplying the regular classroom teacher *and the parent* with written suggestions from the special education teacher as to the specific academic areas to be addressed by the IEP, so that participants can be familiar with them and can prepare their own comments and suggestions for presentation at the meeting, could help to avoid the tendency for IEP planning meetings to develop into presentations by the special education teacher. Goldstein et al., (1980) found that the overwhelming majority of IEPs are developed prior to the meeting and are simply presented to the parent and other staff at the meeting. If any aspect of the IEP is not agreed upon, the document must be revised; and special education teachers, who spend a tremendous amount of time developing IEPs (Price and Goodman, 1980), should welcome a way to avoiding these revisions. If teachers could be encouraged to follow the mandated procedures and to refrain from developing IEPs beforehand, but to be careful to develop suggestions, and tentative goals and objectives which can be easily revised, then parental input and the ideas of regular classroom teachers could be incorporated into the IEP with much less work. The actual participation of parents might be increased if they felt that their contributions to the IEP were welcomed; it seems to be appropriate to communicate to parents about the goal of full parental participation, during the process of IEP development.

Each member of the educational planning team has a role to play, and if each one fully utilizes the opportunity to participate in the planning process, the document that emerges will have a good deal of value. The finished IEP will represent a commitment of educational services which parents and educators have agreed upon; it will represent coordinated planning and evaluation, which will result in appropriate learning experiences; and it will represent a communications process which encourages the full and efficient participation of all those concerned with the child's education. An intelligent use of the IEP process results in more than a document mandated by the law; it can also generate valuable and productive relationships between educators, parents, and students, which can benefit all three groups.

REFERENCES

Department of Health, Education and Welfare. Education of handicapped children — implementation of Part B of the Education of the Handicapped Act. *Federal Register*, 42 (No. 163), 42474-42518, August 23, 1977.

Fenton, K.S., R.K. Yoshida, J.P. Maxwell, & M.J. Kaufman. Recognition of team goals: An essential step toward rational decision making. *Exceptional Children, 45,* 638-644, 1979.

Gilliam, J.E. Contributions and status rankings of educational planning committee participants. *Exceptional Children, 45,* 466-468, 1979.

Goldstein, S., B. Strickland, A.P. Turnbull, & L. Curry. An observational analysis of the IEP conference. *Exceptional Children, 46,* 278-286, 1980.

Office of Special Education. "Individualized Education Programs (IEPs)." (OSE Policy Paper). May 23, 1980. Available from U.S. Education Department, Assistant Secretary for Special Education and Rehabilitation Services, Office of Special Education.

Peter, L.J. *Prescriptive Teaching.* New York: McGraw-Hill, 1965.

Price, M., & L. Goodman. Individualized education programs: A cost study. *Exceptional Children, 45,* 446-454, 1980.

Yoshida, R.K., K.S. Fenton, M.J. Kaufman, & J.P. Maxwell. Parental involvement in the special education pupil planning process: The school's perspective. *Exceptional Children, 44:* 531-534, 1978.

CHAPTER 16

A NONTEXTBOOK INSTRUCTIONAL MODEL FOR CHILDREN WITH SIGNIFICANT READING PROBLEMS

KATHLEEN L. HAMMOND

INTRODUCTION

DURING the later part of the 1970s social pressures combined with state and federal legislation required school systems to focus major amounts of attention upon those students with special learning needs. This chapter provides a rationale and an approach for providing content area instruction for certain middle and high school students with significant reading problems. Until the third grade and beyond when increasingly larger demands are placed upon students to read in order to acquire meaningful information in specific content areas, the affects of reading deficiencies are not detrimental to cognitive development. However as children with significant reading problems advance chronologically, their need for knowledge that facilitates learning becomes more important and at the same time their access to this knowledge is diminished owing to their reading problems. As a result of these two factors many students develop feelings of helplessness, alienation and frequently they become academically retarded. Remedial reading instruction is not the major focus of this article. Rather the chapter is about techniques and procedures to permit those students who have specific reading deficits but who have average intelligence and listening comprehension abilities to acquire knowledge in content areas like science, math and social studies.

This chapter will provide a description of a nontextbook instructional model based in large part on the author's experience with Project Non-print Curriculum. This project, a part of the Tolland, Connecticut Public Schools, was supported by a P.L. 93-380 Title IV Federal Grant through the Connecticut State Department of Education in the years 1978-1980. The project is an ongoing instructional systems approach to providing appropriate instruction to specified target populations by matching a student's unique information processing abilities to instructional events (Messineo and Loiacono, 1979). The components of the model include:

1. curriculum objectives
2. identification of student learning characteristics
3. design and delivery of instructional messages
4. storage and retrieval of instructional materials
5. evaluation

Each of these components will be addressed in the remainder of this chapter.

COMPONENTS OF THE INSTRUCTIONAL MODEL

Curriculum Objectives

An instructional systems approach to education demands that the content of the curriculum be specified and sequenced in terms of measurable learner outcomes. We can think of the curriculum as a series of content units arranged hierarchically such that the learning of each unit occurs readily provided that the knowledge and skills needed to master prior units in the curriculum have been mastered by the student (Gagne, 1967).

According to Gagne each content unit should be expressed as a series of specific learner outcomes or curriculum objectives corresponding to a given unit. In addition, careful analysis must be made of both the declarative knowledge structures and the cognitive strategies and procedural knowledge that are utilized during an instructional event and which are necessary if the student is to attain each of the objectives. These objectives are instrumental in helping teachers and those specialists involved in the design of instruction to plan a sequence of activities that will help the learner to aquire a specific body of knowledge and skills. In addition these objectives provide at least a partial standard against which the effectiveness of the curriculum and the students' progress within the curriculum can be monitored.

Identification of Student Learning Characteristics

Matching learner and instructional variables enhances the probability that a larger number of students will be successful in learning. The first step is to identify certain learner variables. As indicated in an earlier chapter in this volume, this is no simple task. Three basic kinds of information might be used to begin determining learner characteristics. This information includes:

1. Information processing abilities of students
2. Entry achievement levels of students
3. Anticipated goal level for each student

INFORMATION PROCESSING ABILITIES. Information processing typically refers to the way in which an individual takes in information, processes it, and produces output. Many different models have been proposed (Atkinson and Shiffren, 1968).

For purposes here, Osgood's (1957, 1976) generalized model of communication will be used as a framework for conceptualizing the gross level information processing profiles of students. This model delineates three interacting dimensions. These dimensions are:

1. Levels of mental organization consisting of
   a. Representational or meaningful information
   b. Integrative or nonmeaningful information
2. Three levels of language transmission processes
   a. Receptive
   b. Organizing
   c. Expressive
3. Channel or modality of the communication

The model differentiates between those dimensions of the communication process in which the student merely demonstrates perceptual and integrative skills (such as recognizing letters, words and other skills involved in the mapping of one's knowledge of spoken language onto print), and dimensions requiring meaning or comprehension of material.

The reciprocal influence between perceptual and integrative processes and representational or integrative processes as these affect comprehension has been discussed by individuals involved in the study of learning disabilities (Wepman, 1967; Berko, 1966) and cognitive psychologists (Perfetti and Lesgold, 1979). Berko refers to levels of organization by distinguishing between the effects on learning of conceptual reasoning ability (propositionality) and perceptual integration (automatized) behavior.

We have defined the level of propositionality, inferentially at least, in terms of the level of cortical integration at which a given act is organized. Nonpropositional or "automatized" behaviors are relatively reflexive in terms of organizational or integrative levels. As propositionality is increased progressively higher levels of cortical integration are called into play, and the greater is the conscious ego involved in the performance of the act. Here we see the development of a "vicious circle" for the child: His nervous system is so organized that there is relatively little automatization of behavior. Thus he is forced to function at relatively high propositional levels most of the time. (Berko, 1966, p. 155)

Skills necessary to aquire the code vehicle used to transmit a message are associated with perceptual abilities while skills necessary to deal with the meaning of the message are associated with representational abilities. Cognitive psychologists have termed the reciprocal nature of these two types of abilities the "bottleneck problem" (Anderson and Bower, 1973; Perfetti and Lesgold, 1979). According to Perfetti and Lesgold:

The capacity for reading comprehension is limited by momentary data handling requirements. Working memory is thus a potential bottleneck in reading comprehension. Working memory is particularly taxed if it must keep track of partial solutions for heuristic processes that "home in" on decisions in an iterative manner. On the other hand, if some of the components of the reading process are ballistic (i.e. not requiring attention once they are initiated), there will be less working memory congestion. . . . When print maps automatically to phonologically referenced words, the decoding requires no monitoring and hence does not waste limited working memory. This is a good example of two conceptually independent components that are functionally intertwined. Because decoding leads to meaning, affecting the efficiency of print decoding affects the efficiency of meaning access.

Needless to say, any realistic assessment of a learning disabled child requires attention to process, modality or channel and organizational or knowledge level skills. Furthermore it is important to consider these two dimensions separately when designing and delivering instructional messages to these students.

A procedure that separately assesses the student's ability to deal with the meaning of the message (content) and the code vehicle carrying the message is described as follows: The student's ability to process messages through the different modalities is defined as the student's Relative Accessibility Pattern or his RAP Index. Once the RAP Index is determined, valid entry behaviors in each of the content areas can be properly assessed and instructional techniques can be specified (Messineo, 1975).

The RAP Index requires a measure of the student's ability to obtain information from the reading modality, the listening modality and the nonlanguage (experiential) modality. This information can be obtained by using the results from a standarized reading test, a listening test, and a nonverbal intelligence test. The three measures provide educators information concerning individual variation in the learner's ability to process information. The first measure of the RAP Index reflects the learner's ability to comprehend material communicated through spoken language; the second measure reflects the learner's ability to comprehend material via the written modality; and the third measure represents the degree to which a learner can comprehend through field experience. While the first two measures of the RAP index are language dependent, the third measure is language independent.

The following three RAP indices selected from a sixth grade population illustrate different RAP Index profiles. The data analysis of the first student revealed a flat RAP of 6.1- 6.3 -6.2 indicating a sixth grade level ability to receive messages through the printed, listening and experiential modalities. The second student analysis revealed a RAP index of 3-7-7 indicating an above-grade placement level to receive messages in the listening and experiential modes with significant deficiencies in the reading modality. The final example, a RAP of 4-4-6, illustrates a student with receptive difficulties in both language dependent modalities, without any deficiencies in the experiential channel. Once the information of the RAP index is available on a given student, it is possible to establish the appropriate administration procedures for measuring a student's achievement entry levels in content area subjects. These same procedures can also be used to determine how we should administer criterion-referenced mastery tests that assess specific student performances throughout the year. The student with a flat RAP can be properly assessed by following standardized testing procedures. Students with deficiences in only the first index, reading, should be assessed in the content area subjects via the listening modality, while students with channel deficiencies in both the print and the listening modes require more diagnostic testing and the use of informal techniques.

ENTRY ACHIEVEMENT LEVELS. In order to know where to place a student we must know the initial state of the learner's knowledge and skills. It would be ideal to have teachers sit and work through a variety of instructional tasks in every content area with each student. Practically, though, we must rely at least initially and in part on certain standardized achievement test scores, criterion-referenced mastery tests and diagnostic measures. It is not the purpose of this Chapter to debate the pros and cons of these tests. As has been pointed out by others, the economy and the management aspects of the achievement test approach have contributed to their widespread use.

Nevertheless critics of the approach have brought attention to the fact that these tests are unfair; they penalize a student not because he or she lacks the knowledge or general ability but rather because certain students are unable to comprehend the questions due to inability to decode and encode the message. As mentioned above, for those students who are good listeners but poor readers, it is especially important to assure that results of testing reflect each child's level of functioning and not simply his decoding deficits. It is important for teachers to make differing judgements as to the student's ability to function at higher cognitive levels — his abilities to conceptualize and his ability to read given his deficit.

Modified achievement testing requires the teacher to make two judgements. First the teacher must decide what level achievement test is best used to assess the students' reading comprehension abilities. Second the teacher must decide what level of achievement test is best used to assess the students' level of listening comprehension and content area subject knowledge such as science, math concepts and social studies. Then in those cases where students have significant reading problems, these later subtests need to be presented verbally or via a taped presentation.

Attention to this relationship between comprehension, skill in different modalities and modality of testing was investigated by Messineo (1975). He reports:

> The subjects in this study were upper elementary grade students spanning grades four through eight with diagnosed reading problems. Two alternative forms of a standardized reading comprehension test were administered. The students were required to read one form of the test themselves while the other form was read to them. The results of both tests

were then correlated with their intelligence to determine the students abilities to demonstrate their potential as a function of code vehicle. The analysis of the data demonstrated that comprehension through the written code accounted for 25% of their measured intellectual ability, while comprehension via the spoken code accounted for 58%.

The study demonstrated the importance of considering their code deficiencies in assessing their level of cognitive ability.

ANTICIPATED GOAL LEVELS. The preceding discussion of learner information processing profiles and assessment of entry achievement levels should have alerted the reader to the fact that such test profiles are primarily to indicate the students potential level of development regardless of his handicap. A major assumption in our entire identification of learner characteristics framework is that the learning that takes place in content areas should be at a level that challenges each student's potential to learn. Traditional achievement testing by contrast is frequently used to group students in a spirit which suggests that performance on these tests sets the upper limit on the level of instruction with which the learner can cope. Furthermore, in the case of certain students this limit is set far too low when we use traditional achievement testing.

For example, compare the two graphs in Figure 16-1. The "G" on the vertical axis of each graph tells us that based on this student's full IQ, his "goal" level achievement is grade 8.8. The norm level for a student with this IQ is 7.9. In graph A, the student's total achievement level is grade 5.2 (the point where the floating "X" axis intersects the vertical axis of the graph). This student's total achievement level as measured by traditionally administered achievement testing is far lower than both the norm or goal level anticipated for a student with this level of intelligence. By capitalizing on his ability to listen and modifying achievement test administration, a totally different profile of what the student knows emerges. This can be seen in graph B.

Examine the two graphs. Notice the floating axis (the broken horizontal line which represents the student's total level of achievement) and its relationship to both the norm and goal levels on the vertical axis. Notice also the differences in achievement levels for the various subtests presented via tapes — language, math concepts and application, social studies and science. It should be clear that had we relied on the results of traditionally administered achievement

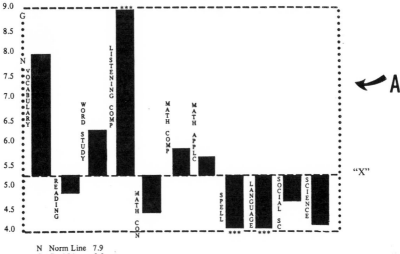

N Norm Line 7.9
G Goal Line 8.8
*** Achievement Score Beyond Scale

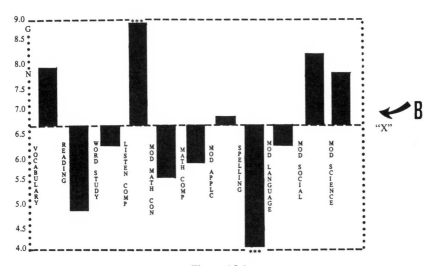

Figure 16-1.

testing to plan entry level instruction, we would be limiting the student's potential and not challenging him to learn (Messineo et al., 1975).

The two graphs allow us to view this student's potential to develop in several ways. First the difference between this student's reading and listening subtests scores provides an indication of what amount of improvement in reading ability that we should anticipate if the student receives remedial reading instruction (Sticht, 1979). Given the high intercorrelations between reading, listening and IQ scores (Vineyard and Bailey, 1960), the difference between the student's listening level and the "G" or goal level based on his IQ can be viewed as another area for potential development. In the case illustrated, this student's listening score is already at a level commensurate with his goal achievement level based on his IQ. Had this not been true, then further analysis of the component skills of listening and evaluation of the student's performance on these components could be used to increase his ability to listen.

The graphs that have been illustrated represent one type of student profile. However, once we have established each student's RAP Index, we can examine the effects of his/her RAP Index on overall achievement as measured by the total achievement test battery score.

To understand the relationship between RAP and achievement, the RAP indices can be collapsed into homogeneous groups by applying a statistical method called hierarchical cluster analyses (Anderberg, 1975). Five distinct subgroups typically emerge from this kind of analysis. These groups are shown in Table 16-I.

TABLE 16-I

CLUSTER ANALYSIS OF RAP WITH TOTAL ACHIEVEMENT

Group	N	Reading RAP	Listening RAP	Performance RAP	Total Achievement
1	12	High	High	High	High
2	26	Avg	Avg	Avg	Avg
3	5	Low	Low	Low	Low
4	7	Low	Avg	Avg	Low
5	6	Low	Low	High	Low

For purposes of identifying students in terms of RAP and achievement, a high, medium and low coding scheme has been used. Group one, with above-average RAP indices in all three channels, performed above-average on the Stanford Achievement Test. The average RAP indices of group two was commensurate with their performance on the achievement test. For either group one or two, delivering instructional messages at their cognitive ability level could occur equally well through any modality.

The flat low RAP index of group three represents 9 percent of the population studied and indicates to educators that all three modalities are below average. Since this group's ability to process information is limited, it would be an obvious mistake to require them to maintain the "normal" ten months progress per academic year. These students can learn, but they may require more instructional time and a more careful diagnosis of their processing deficits and performances on various instructional tasks if they are to attain the curriculum objectives.

Students in group four represent 12.5 percent of the population studied. All were males. The graphs illustrating traditional versus modified achievement results were taken from a student within this group. This group's RAP pattern indicates difficulties in encoding/decoding print materials. Although these students have intelligence, their below average traditional achievement test performance was presumably caused by their code vehicle deficit in reading. The instructional format that would match these student's processing profiles would include taped lessons, sound filmstrips, movies, discussions, field experiences, etc. These are students who can achieve in regular content area classrooms provided that the instruction is altered to match their RAP. At the same time these students should receive special reading and language arts instruction.

Students who are members of group five represent about 10 percent of the population studied and shown an uneven RAP index with deficits in both language dependent modalities. Conventional classroom instruction will not be effective with these students. More time and effort must be given to mastery of language dependent activities.

DESIGN AND DELIVERY OF INSTRUCTIONAL MESSAGES

The major assumption of the model presented in this chapter is that students achieve better when information and instructional tasks in content area subjects are presented to them in a format matching their RAP. This section will describe an approach that has been used in order to design instructional materials for students in group 4 discussed in the preceding section.

By using the RAP index to identify this type of student, we are advocating the procedure of utilizing the student's strongest sensory modality in order to permit students to achieve in content area subjects while remediation continues in special reading and language arts classrooms. Use of this approach is based upon one of the clearer findings in the aptitude treatment interaction literature (Oaken, Wiener and Cromer, 1971). It is hoped that besides permitting these students to aquire knowledge that will further their cognitive development and school achievement, this approach will eventually foster transfer of tasks like identifying, inferring, applying information from listening modality to the reading modality as decoding problems are remediated.

There is some evidence that listening instruction might result in improvement in reading comprehension (Dumbie, 1968). While the empirical evidence on the transfer of skills and knowledge is admittedly mixed, we do have an idea about what conditions might make transfer possible. We know for example that transfer from listening to reading requires that some of the processes or knowledge used in reading need to be essentially identical to those learned while developing skill in listening. Furthermore learners need to be made explicitly aware of these skills (Woodworth and Schlosberg, 1954). In order to maximize the possibility that such improvements might occur, it is necessary to choose an approach to delivering instructional messages via tapes that focus the student's attention on comprehension-related tasks common to both listening and reading. One method that has proven successful in creating taped lessons in content area subjects is based upon the pedagogical considerations presented by Harold Herber in his book *Teaching Reading in Content Areas* (Herber, 1975; Hammond and Messineo, 1979). This approach is based upon what Herber calls "functional teaching of reading — teaching the processes the students need if they are to understand what it is you want them to read, as they read it." Within this context reading is taught functionally when:

1. skills being taught are those which must be used by the

readers in order to understand the content of the information source they are assigned to read;

2. those skills are taught as the students read (or in this case listen to) the information source and

3. the information source is assigned in order to teach the content it contains rather than teaching the reading skill per se (Herber, 1975, p. 26)

While the usual approach to teaching in the content areas relies heavily on questioning students, Herber suggests questioning only after we have taught students what it is that we would like them to master. Questioning is "assumptive." Whether at the literal, interpretive or applied level, questioning assumes that students have the skills in comprehending that are necessary to answer the questions. However this is seldom the case when teachers daily ask their students to read and listen to new and unfamiliar information in their subject areas. Herber recommends "simulation," in place of traditional questioning. Simulation, as defined by Herber and Nelson (1975), is "an artificial representation of real experience; a contrived series of activities which when taken together approximate the experience or procedure that is ultimately to be applied independently."

Using this "functional teaching" framework as a guide, taped instructional messages can be written and/or adapted from text materials for use with identified students first of all because the message contains the content relevant to the instructional objectives. Once created, the taped message is then examined to see what skills are necessary for the message to be comprehended. For example the organizational patterns of messages might differ depending on subject matter content. Messages might be organized so as to require that students understand sequential steps in a process such as photosynthesis, or so that they understand comparisons and contrasts or in some instances so that organization is more of a simple factual listening. The skills taught will depend upon the content and organizational structure of the message. In the case of instructional tapes these skills can be incorporated within the taped instructional message.

For purposes of illustrating this approach, a lesson that was written and taped for identified students in a fifth grade science class follows. Prior to this tape, students were introduced to the idea that a zoologist is a scientist who studies animals, and that he does so by classifying or grouping animals. All students were also provided with an activity that demonstrated the difficulties that the zoologist can experience in classifying animals. Students were given a worksheet of strange animals and asked to examine them for common features that could be used in order to decide upon a classification system. Different solutions were possible and encouraged. The need for the scientist to know the answers to many questions before classifying an animal was demonstrated.

Assigned tape or text, depending upon the individual students, next introduced students to the two large groups of animals, vertebrates and invertebrates. The narration that follows is that of a third tape. The organizing idea of the tape is that fish, the simplest vertebrates, live in water, have fins, and breathe through gills. The instructional options that students were guided to listen for were literal and interpretive levels of comprehension and the organizational pattern of the message which was a simple factual listing. It should be noted that none of these options are directly stated to the student but rather simulated by the materials in the guides. Students have a study guide that accompanies the tape. The guides were created in two formats. Some of the guides listed only illustrations and the letters corresponding to the sentences, and others contained the illustrations and the letters plus the sentences. An example of a taped instructional message follows:

Tape Two — Animals With Backbones

Tape two in the series called *Animals With Backbones* is about fish. Before you listen to tape two, you will hear two sentences. Listen to the sentences and then listen for these ideas in the taped reading. Sometimes exactly the same words will be used. Other times the taped reading will use different words to express the same ideas. Listen to these sentences.

Sentence A. Fish are the simplest invertebrates.
Sentence A. Fish are the simplest invertebrates.

Sentence B. Fish live in water and breathe through gills.
Sentence B. Fish live in water and breathe through gills.

Sentence C. The limbs of the fish are its' fins.
Sentence C. The limbs of the fish are its' fins.

Now listen for this information in the taped reading:

Out of the five groups of vertebrates that we will study, fish, amphibians and reptiles are cold blooded animals. We say that an animal is cold blooded if its body changes temperature as it moves between hot and cold places. Fish are the first group of vertebrates you will hear about. Fish are the simplest examples of the animals we call vertebrates. They are cold blooded because their body temperature changes as the temperature of the water around them changes. Although fish live in water, they do need oxygen in order to stay alive. How do they get this oxygen? In order to breathe, fish take water into their mouths and force it out past their gills. These gills are located on the sides of the fish. The arrow in picture one in your study guide points to the flap which covers a gill of the fish. When water which the fish has taken into its mouth, moves past the gills, oxygen in the water passes into the bloodstream of the fish. The groups of cells or tissues which make up the gills are very delicate. If a fish is out of the water and in air too long, the gills dry quickly and are damaged. The fish will die if it is kept out of the water very long.

All fish have limbs called fins. The arrow in picture number two of your study guide points to the fins. Most fish have scales which cover their body, but some fish are scaleless. The streamlined shape of the fish helps it to move swiftly through the water. Most fish lay eggs. The eggs of the fish have soft shells. New baby fish hatch from these eggs.

The seahorse and the eel, shown in pictures three and four in your study guide, are fish that have unusual shapes. Notice how different they look from the fish in pictures one and two.

Now look at picture five, which shows a whale, and at picture six, which shows you a porpoise. Whales and porpoises look like fish — they have bodies that are shaped like fish. But since both whales and porpoises breathe through lungs instead of gills they are not fish.

Now listen once again to Sentences A, B, and C. If a sentence states an idea that you have just heard in the tape section about fish, circle the letter of the sentence in your study guide. Make sure that you could replay the tape and find the information that shows why you did or did not circle the letter of a sentence. Make sure that you can explain your choices.

Sentence A. Fish are the simplest invertebrates.
Sentence A. Fish are the simplest invertebrates.

If you heard this idea in the tape, circle the letter A in your study guide.

It should be pointed out to the reader that this literal level listening is not identical to a true or false activity. Conceivably Sentence C may not have been mentioned in the reading. Yet if Sentence C were in the guide, it would still be true, though the student would not be justified in circling C in such an instance. Sentences B and C would also be repeated again. The student would be told, "If you need to listen to the tape again push the rewind button and then replay the tape. Otherwise continue to listen."

> Get ready to listen for three new sentences. These sentences may or may not relate to or combine the ideas which you will hear in the tape. After listening to the tape you will be asked to circle the letter of a sentence if you believe that the tape contained information which would support the sentence. Listen now to sentences D, E, and F.
>
> Sentence D. Fish are cold blooded only when they are in cold water.
> Sentence D. Fish are cold blooded only when they are in cold water.
>
> Sentence E. The shape of an animal can help to determine what an animal can or cannot do.
> Sentence E. The shape of an animal can help to determine what an animal can or cannot do.
>
> Sentence F. Knowing the shape of an animal is not enough information to place the animal in its correct group.
> Sentence F. Knowing the shape of an animal is not enough information to place it in its correct group.

The identical fish tape would then be read once again for the student. After the taped narration has been read again, the sentences and directions for this level of comprehension would be repeated. The approach could be simplified by having students listen for only one sentence at a time during the reading. The approach could be made more difficult by altering the level of sophistication of the sentences.

The fact that this taped narrative was organized by means of only simple factual listing makes this second activity appropriate. The activity would be taped and also appear in the students' study guide.

In this activity you will hear some phrases about fish. Your job is to place a check next to those phrases that correctly describe fish. Fish do the following things:

1. breathe through gills
2. breathe through lungs
3. always have scales
4. sometimes have scales
5. are warm blooded
6. are cold blooded
7. live in only salt water
8. live in both fresh and salt water
9. are invertebrates
10. are vertebrates

11. are born alive
12. are hatched from eggs
13. have gills that are delicate
14. have strong tough gills
15. have limbs called flippers
16. have limbs called fins

Other tapes in this series would use similar activities depending upon the content and the organizational pattern of the narration. In addition vocabulary instruction is a strong emphasis in this approach. (Hammond and Messineo, 1979) The taped lesson illustrated above is just one approach that can be and has been successfully used for designing and building a nontextbook instructional sequence. In addition to systematically producing materials, it should be pointed out that commercially prepared materials could be carefully selected and purchased. Activities in either the listening or reading modality that incorporate Herber's methodology could be created as pre- and post-listening and viewing guides for these materials.

Storage and Retrieval

In the past, collections of instructional materials have seldom been systematically developed at the local level and/or carefully selected from the vast array of commercially available materials so that they relate directly to both learner characteristics and instructional objectives. As school systems come to realize the central versus the supplemental importance of nontextbook instructional delivery systems, their approaches for storing and retrieving these materials will need to interface with both learner characteristics and the hierarchy of curriculum objectives. This classification system might take the form of indicating grade level, subject area, specific content topic, specific instructional objectives addressed, the content level of the material and modality used. A systematic approach for developing materials means that objective materials in alternative instructional modes and emphasizing various instructional tasks will need to be readily available for each.

Evaluation

The evaluation component of an instructional model such as the one outlined should provide data on the effectiveness of the instructional packages. Pre- and post-tests were developed to assess these packages. These tests provide information on the validity of the instructional packages as well as evaluate the performances of individual students. The testing at this level must, of course, match the modality of the instructional package.

The second level of evaluation involves measurement of the degree to which curriculum objectives have been attained. This is accomplished through locally developed criterion-referenced tests. These tests are used to measure mastery of specific objectives and are administered at designated times throughout the course of instruction. As in all testing, the content level is constant for most all students but the code vehicle used to transmit the test is varied. In certain cases tests might be individually administered.

The third level of evaluation uses standardized achievement tests and is more general in nature than the other forms of evaluation. Modification of these tests coupled with mastery test information can provide information on individual students. But since these achievement tests are norm-referenced tests, they also provide an external measure of the effectiveness of the instructional system on a local and nationwide level.

Conclusion

The nontextbook instructional model outlined in this chapter is in no way offered as a simple solution to learner problems. Rather the major objective of the approach is to provide the student with instruction at their highest level of cognitive functioning in each subject area. While new information evolving from research in cognitive psychology could certainly be used to improve upon our testing, task analysis, monitoring of individual performance on task components (Glaser, 1980; Resnick and Glaser, 1981), given the staffing constraints in most public school systems, the model outlined in this chapter provides a framework within which we can begin to systematically deliver instruction to specified target populations. The approach bypasses the student's weak modality and capitalizes on his or her strongest modality to provide instruction in areas such as science and social studies. However, it is important to note that instruction to correct or remediate code vehicle deficits in reading and listening must remain the most important area of instruction. Continual monitoring of the remediation process must constantly occur in order to determine at what point it becomes more beneficial to alter our instructional decisions regarding the content and modality of the message a student receives. This dual approach should provide a greater number of students the opportunity to achieve their academic potential.

REFERENCES

Anderberg, J.R. *Cluster Analysis for Applications.* New York: Academic Press, 1973.

Anderson, J.R. and G.H. Bower. *Human Associative Memory.* New York: Winston, 1973.

Berko, J.J. Psychological and linguistic implications of brain damage in children. In M.J. Meacham (ed.), *Communication Training In Childhood Brain Damage.* Springfield, Illinois: Charles C Thomas, Publisher, 1966.

Brown, C.T. Studies on listening comprehension. *Speech Monographs,* 1965, 32 129-138. Dumbie, J. In S. Duker (ed.), *Listening Bibliography.* Metuchen, New Jersey: Scarecrow Press, 1976. S>

Gagne, R.M. Curriculum research and the promotion of learning. In R. Tyler, R. Gagne and M. Scriven (eds.), *AERA Monograph Series on Curriculum Evaluation.* Chicago: Rand McNally, 1967.

Glaser, R. Instructional Psychology: Past Present and Future. Paper presented at the University of Leuven in Leuven, Belgium, in May, 1980.

Hammond, Kathleen L. and Louis Messineo. The design of instructional packages. *International Journal of Instructional Media,* 1979, 18, 271-290.

Herber, H.L. *Teaching Reading in Content Areas.* Englewood Cliffs, New Jersey: Prentice-Hall, 1978.

Herber, H.L. and J. Nelson. Questioning is not the answer. *Journal of Developmental Reading, 18,*512-517, 1975.

Messineo, L.V. Messineo, J.F. and R. Loiacono. *Degree of intellectual utilization in learning disabled children in relation to mode of instruction.* Unpublished manuscript, Syracuse University, 1975.

Messineo, L.V. *Matching Instruction to the Students Information Processing Ability.* Paper presented at the Special Education Conference at BOCES 2, Spencerport, New York, 1973.

Messineo, L.V. and R. Loiacono. A Non-Textbook Instructional Model. *International Journal of Instructional Technology, 18,* 1979.

Oaken, R., Wiener, M., and W. Cromer. Identification, organization and reading comprehension for good and poor readers. *Journal of Educational Psychology, 62,* 71-78, 1971.

Osgood, C.E. Motivational dynamics of language behavior. In M. Jones (ed.), *Nebraska Symposium on Motivation.* Lincoln, Nebraska: University of Nebraska Press, 1957.

Osgood, C.E. In P.L. Newcomer and D.D. Hammil. *Psycholinguistics in the Schools.* Columbus, Ohio: C. Merrill, 1976.

Perfetti, C.A. and Lesgold, A.M. Coding and comprehension in skilled reading. In L.B. Resnick and P. Weaver (eds.), *Theory and Practice of Early Reading.* Hillsdale, New Jersey: Erlbaum, 1979.

Sticht, Thomas G. Applications of the audread model to reading evaluation and instruction. In L.B. Resnick and P. Weaver (eds.), *Theory and Practice of Early Reading.* Hillsdale, New Jersey: Erlbaum, 1979.

Vineyard, E.E. and Bailey, R.B. Interrelationships of reading ability, listening skill, intelligence and scholastic achievement. *Journal of Developmental Reading, 3,* 174-178, 1960.

Vygotsky, L.S. *Mind In Society: The Development of Higher Level Psychological Processes.* Cambridge, Mass: Harvard University Press, 1978.

Wepman, J. Neurological approaches to mental retardation. In R.L. Copeland and J.O. Smith (eds.), *Language and Mental Retardation.* New York: Holt, Rinehart & Winston Inc., 1967.

CHAPTER 17

IMPLEMENTATION OF QUESTIONING STRATEGIES TO ADDRESS LEARNER ERRORS

Jo Mary Hendrickson

THE universality (Belch, 1975) and high frequency, e.g. Floyd, 1969 and Moyer, 1966, with which teachers employ questions in one-to-one interactions, small-group discussions and large-group presentations is astounding. Teachers are literally asking students hundreds of questions each day. Whether in a classroom of developmentally normal (Belch, 1975) or exceptional learners with a wide range of learning characteristics, e.g. Gallagher, Aschner & Jenne, 1967; Hendrickson & Stowitschek, 1980; Zetlin & Gallimore, 1980, teachers are questioning students at a high rate. Their purpose is to assess mastery and progress, promote thinking and listening skills, test memory and awareness, provide stimulation, and initiate or maintain teacher-student interaction. Information gained from questioning can be general, e.g. assess the level of a student's attention or very specific, e.g. pinpoint the exact difficulty in a verbal reasoning problem (Armstrong, 1977). Questioning strategies can be employed to lead students to mastery of new knowledge and skills (French & MacLure, 1977) and provide useful models for resolving problems pupils encounter when the teacher is not present (Marksberry, 1979). Questions used as direct teaching tactics may promote acquisition, mastery and generalization of academic skills (Armstrong, 1977), expressive language repertoires (Hendrickson & Stowitschek, 1980) and social skills (Hendrickson & Freedman, 1980; Hester & Hendrickson, 1977).

Questioning strategies may range from simple to fairly complex. Questions may be one component of an instructional tactic, e.g. Rogers-Warren & Warren, 1980, or the instructional tactic, e.g. Armstrong, 1977. They can be used as general setting events or as specific antecedents to student responding. Questions may be

153

employed as general or corrective feedback following student errors. With relative ease questioning strategies used with individual students can be modified to teach multiple objectives or be applied in group instructional situations (Stowitschek, Day, Stowitschek, & Hendrickson, in press). Unfortunately, many of the questions used in classrooms today appear to be random and with little instructional worth. On the other hand, it is likely that minor modifications in the current questioning approaches of teachers will enhance the instructional merit of their questions greatly.

To date a major hindrance to widespread utilization of effective questioning strategies has been the lack of systematic empirical research to precisely document the relationship between teacher behavior, i.e. questioning, and student performance (Gall, Ward, Berliner, Cahen, Winne, Elashoff, & Stanton, 1978; Hendrickson & Stowitschek, 1980; Shores, Roberts, & Nelson, 1976). There also has been a negligence on the part of teacher educators to thoroughly instruct preservice teachers on the uses of questions and to measure their competence employing questioning strategies in practicum or student teaching internships. While numerous educators have written about or investigated the importance of questioning, e.g. Aschner, 1961; Gall, 1971; Loughlin, 1961; Rice, 1977; Zahorick, 1971, few have reported in a straight-forward, easily understandable manner the ways questions can be used more effectively by classroom teachers.

The purpose of this chapter is to provide guidelines and detailed examples for teachers and other practitioners to use when selecting and designing questioning strategies. Two primary functions that questions may serve, to prevent and remediate or correct errors, will be discussed. Illustrations of questioning strategies that have been applied in different curricular areas are provided.

Guidelines for Questioning Students

During any given instructional day teachers may question students as a means of systematically preventing errors, pinpointing deficiencies and providing corrective feedback. In addition teachers will be spontaneously using questions to prompt, cue, probe and redirect students. Whether the teacher is implementing prespecified series of questions or using questions spontaneously, there are several guidelines which, if followed, will improve the instructional value of teacher questions:

1. Ask one question at a time. Whether teaching in a one-to-one or small group format, do not fire the same question or different questions at your students. Wait for a response. Give the students enough time to formulate their answers. This is especially important if you are asking higher level questions, i.e. questions that require abstract or creative thinking. When asking your students questions that include such terms as predict, compare, justify and evaluate, allow ample time for them to ponder and fully answer the question.

2. Correct student errors consistently and immediately.

3. Give the same high level of praise and positive feedback you would when employing any other teaching strategy.

4. Evaluate your questions. Are they properly worded? Are they stated as clearly and concisely and possible?

5. Avoid casual rewording or restating of questions. Restate questions only in response to a student error or misinterpretation.

6. Avoid random questioning.

7. Do not rely too heavily on Yes-No questions or lower order questions, i.e. questions that require only simple memory or factual recall. Consider other types of questions available, e.g. multiple choice, open-ended, and select questions most suited to your instructional objective.

8. Use age-appropriate language when questioning adolescents and young adults. Simplify your questions and strive for extra clarity with language deficient students.

9. Ask questions that are specific, relevant and directly related to the curriculum and instructional materials being used. The objective of your question(s) should be apparent to the student(s).

10. Be enthusiastic and alert to the nuances of student responding. Your enthusiasm will generate attention and your attention will help you refine your questioning strategies.

Defining the Instructional Objective

As Gall (1970) advocated, question types, e.g. simple memory or recall questions versus abstract reasoning questions, should not be the primary consideration of the teacher selecting a questioning strategy. Instead, the educational objective should guide the formulation of the questioning strategy. Only after the objective is written and student behavior defined in observable terms is the teacher ready to choose the questioning tactic and design a simple data collection system.

The questioning strategies presented here are primarily for use in one-to-one and small-group instruction. Some sequences are specific to a particular content area, e.g. the oral reading corrective feedback hierarchy, others appear to have applicability across skill areas, e.g. the diagnostic questioning sequence. Both are discussed later.

The Basic Question-Answer Sequence

The simplest and most commonly used question-answer sequence consists of a teacher-child-teacher interaction. Typically the question-answer sequence begins with a teacher question. The ideal interaction is followed by a correct student response and is consummated with positive teacher behavior. Over 70 percent of all question-answer sequences used in classrooms begin with a wh-question (Belch, 1975). Wh-questions, often the focal point of many instructional objectives, function differently in the classroom from outside the classroom. For instance, a teacher asking, "What day is it?", is probably not curious about the day of the week and date of the month. Rather, the teacher is asking a question directly related to an educational objective such as, "The student will state orally the name of the day and date of the month nine out of ten times when so asked by the teacher for five consecutive days."

Addressing Learner Errors

Questioning strategies may be used to assist students learning to respond to specific questions or problems in any academic or nonacademic skill area. Cues and support to a student may be provided either before or after the key question is asked. Questioning strategies which precede the teacher's key question may be called *lead* questions. Questioning sequences that follow the teacher's key question may be called *response-dependent* questions. Lead questions and response-dependent questions may be part of the same instructional sequence or used separately and independently.

Implementing Lead Questions (LQs) to Prevent Errors

Lead questions are utterances which generally, but not always, take the form of a question. A lead question precedes the teacher's key question, e.g. "What day is it?", and focuses the student's attention. Lead questions are employed primarily for these reasons: (1) to focus the child's attention on the topic or experience about which a key question is to be asked when that topic or experience is physically present, (2) to bring to mind a topic or experience that is not physically present and (3) to introduce and teach new knowledge and concepts. The functions of lead questions are similar to those described by French and MacLure (1977) for performulators.

Sample Lead Questions (Three Types)

Type 1 Experience Questioned is Physically Present

General Objective: To tell the day and date

T: LQ:	Do you see this calendar? See all the days crossed off? (Teacher displays a calendar with days marked off with an X.)
C: Attending:	Yes.
T: Wh-question:	What day and date is it?
C: Correct Answer:	Wednesday, April 3rd.
T: Consequence:	Yes, it is Wednesday, April 3rd!

Type 2 Experience Shared Between Teacher and Child is Not Present

General Objective: To tell one thing each of ten zoo animals was doing yesterday

T: LQ:	Do you remember the mother lion and her baby?
C: Attending:	Yes.
T: Wh-question:	What was mother lion doing?

C: Correct Answer: Mother lion was cleaning the baby.
T: Consequence: Good! You remembered what the lions were
                     doing.

Type 3 New Knowledge or Concept

General Objective: To sort colors into light and dark shades

T: LQ: See? These boxes are painted light blue,
                     light green and light brown.
C: Attending: Nods head.
T: LQ: See? These boxes are painted dark blue,
                     dark green and dark brown.
C: Attending: Nods head.
T: Wh-question: Where does this box go?
C: Correct Answer: Goes there. (Places the new light purple box
                     with others.)
T: Consequence: That's right! That is a *light* purple box. It
                     goes with the light colored boxes.

Each educational objective should be defined with consideration given to the number and kinds of LQs necessary for the student to respond correctly. A shifting criterion design (see Eaton, 1978, for explanation of static versus dynamic aims) may be very useful for establishing high mastery standards in a step-by-step manner. (In shifting criterion designs the teacher aims for increasingly higher standards for the student based on his or her past performance.) In addition to considering the frequency and kinds of LQs, teachers need to specify whether student response will be verbal, nonverbal or a combination of both.

Implementing Response-Dependent Questions (RQs) to Remediate/Correct Errors

If the child does not answer the key wh-question correctly despite careful use of lead questions, the teacher may ask another question to cue the child or restrict his/her response alternatives. Response-dependent questions are asked *after* an incorrect response. In selecting questions to cue and redirect the student, teachers should assess each question according to the amount of support it provides. In addition to answering key questions correctly, the goal of instruction is to provide fewer and less restrictive response-dependent questions.

Sample Response-Dependent Questions

T: LQ:	Can you find the robin? (Shows picture of a robin eating a worm.)	Orienting question
C: Attending:	Yes.	
T: Wh-question:	What is the robin *doing*?	Key question
C: No Response:		
T: RQ:	What is the robin *eating*?	More specific question

In this sequence, the RQ, "What is the robin eating?", is a more specific question and provides information regarding the type of answer that is expected. Eating is a subset of doing. If this first response-dependent question does not gain an answer, the key question may be repeated or a second RQ presented.

T: RQ 1:	What is the robin eating?	More specific question
C: No Response:		
T: RQ 2:	Is the robin carrying something?	Same semantic category

In RQ 2 the child must assess the semantic correctness of a category of action, e.g. carrying. RQ 2 still affords the child an opportunity to answer the question correctly with fairly minimal direct support, e.g., the child might say, "No, the robin's eating something."

RQ 3 might be a question requiring a positive response, e.g. "Is the robin eating something?" A fourth response-dependent question might restrict the response alternatives even further, e.g. "Is the robin carrying or eating?" The fifth and most supportive question might merely require an affirmation, e.g. "The robin's eating a worm, isn't it?"

When establishing a response-dependent questioning sequence to remediate errors the teacher will begin usually by ordering the questions from least to most restrictive. That is, questions that provide more and more support are added consecutively to the questioning strategy.

CURRICULAR APPLICATIONS

Mathematics

Armstrong (1977) reported a response-dependent questioning sequence she called diagnostic questioning to teach reasoning skills. The strategy provided evaluative information that could be used as feedback on pupil performance and strategy effectiveness. This strategy also enabled teachers to pinpoint and remediate student errors. The strategy may be used on a one-to-one basis or in a roving tutorial format, i.e. when students work independently and the teacher moves around the room monitoring their efforts.

Teachers employing diagnostic questioning to teach verbal reasoning or other problem-solving skills will find that in the early stages of learning more prompting or restrictive questions are required to gain correct responses. Later, less restrictive and more open-ended questions will lead to correct responding.

A diagnostic questioning sequence used effectively with elementary-aged learning disabled children (Armstrong, 1977) is described here. In this sequence as in other response-dependent questioning sequences a series of question types were designed with the intention of gaining certain responses from the students. Next the questions were ordered from those questions that required a complete answer to those that requested only a partial solution. The Armstrong (1977) strategy includes five questions and begins with the least supportive questions and ends with a question that greatly restricts student response alternatives.

Question 1:   Opening Question (OQ). This question immediately follows the reading of a problem by the subject or by the teacher, e.g. "What is the equation?" The student then writes and solves the entire equation before proceeding to the next problem.

Question 2:   Constructed Response (CR). This question is intended to elicit a single response or phrase from the pupil, e.g. "Which words tell us what we need to find out?" It is more restricted than the opening question, but still requires the student to construct a response. This is the *first* question in the *remediation* series.

Question 3:   Multiple Choice (MC). The student is given a choice of two responses, one of which is the correct response, e.g. "Do we multiply or divide?" The MC question follows an error on the CR question.

Question 4:   Restricted Alternative (RA). This question eliminates the incorrect alternative provided in the MC question, but does not provide a model, e.g. "We don't multiply, so what do we do?" This question follows an error on the RA.

Question 5:   Complete Model (CM). The complete model is given if the student errors on the RA. The teacher then proceeds to the next problem.

Armstrong (1977) used her questioning sequence to address the four basic components of solving a word problem in mathematics. The student was required to complete four steps: (1) to restate the problem, (2) to state the operation, (3) to identify the first and second numerals of the operation, and (4) to solve the equation. During instruction, the student is given a number of word problems and an answer sheet with spaces for filling in each component of the equation to be solved, e.g. ____ $\Box$ ____ = ____. The teacher used the questioning sequence to help the student complete any or all of the four components necessary for answering the word problem. In the example below and in all verbal reasoning problems the opening question was asked only one time. If the student erred on the opening question, the series of response-dependent questions was initiated.

Sample Problem

If there are *20* apples in a basket, and *5* boys want to share the apples equally, how many apples will each boy get?

In each sample diagnostic questioning sequence it is assumed that the student does not answer correctly until the last question in the sequence.

Sample Diagnostic Questioning Sequence for Verbal Reasoning

First Step: To restate the problem
   CR 1 - Which words tell us what we need to find out?

MC 2 - Do we find out how many apples each boy will get or how many boys want to share apples?

R A 3 - We already know how many boys want to share apples, so what do we need to find out?

C M 4 - Say, we need to find out how many apples each boy will get.

After any correct response, the teacher should underline the words in the problem that tell what is to be found out and proceed to determining the operation.

Second Step: To state the operation

C R 1 - What is the operation to use in this problem?

M C 2 - Do you multiply or divide?

R A 3 - Not multiply, so what do we do?

C M 4 - Say, we divide.

After any correct response or at the end of the sequence the child puts the appropriate sign in the box and proceeds to writing the equation.

Third Step: To state the equation (the first numeral)

C R 1 - What is the equation?

M C 2 - Is the number that tells us how many objects are to be divided 20 or 5?

R A 3 - Not 5, so what is it?

C M 4 - Say, 20 objects are to be divided.

After any correct response *but the first*, the child writes the number in the first blank. Teacher proceeds to the second numeral of the equation.

Fourth Step: To state the equation (the second numeral)

C R 1 - What is the equation?

M C 2 - Does the number 5 tell us how many groups we have or how many objects are to be divided?

R A 3 - It's not how many objects are to be divided, so what is it?

C M 4 - Say, 5 tells us how many groups we have.

After a correct response or at the end of the sequence, the child writes the appropriate number in the second blank and the teacher proceeds to solving the problem.

Fifth Step: To solve the problem

CR 1 - What is the answer to the equation?

MC 2 - Is it $20 \div 5 = 3$ (Teacher reads incorrect equation.) or is it $20 \div 5 = 4$ (Teacher reads the correct equation.)?

RA 3 - $20 \div 5$ does not equal 3 (incorrect), so $20 \div 5 = $ what?

CM 4 - Say, $20 \div 5 = 4$.

(Armstrong, 1977, pp. 87-89)

After the correct response the child writes the answer in the third blank and the teacher proceeds to the next problem.

Diagnostic questioning used in this manner is very effective for teaching verbal reasoning skills in mathematics, an area that usually presents difficulty for special learners (Armstrong, 1977).

Word problems taught using diagnostic questioning sequences are likely to be more manageable if they are grouped by process — addition, subtraction, multiplication and division, or according to type of applied mathematics skills, e.g. time, money. Once the teacher and student are familiar with the questioning strategy, mixed problem types can be presented. Acquisition of other complex skills, e.g. reading comprehension, may also be amendable to this type of questioning strategy. Initially, reading comprehension might be divided into distinct categories also, e.g. fact information, vocabulary information and inference information. Adaptations of the questioning sequence used to remediate any skill should reflect the age, skill level and special learning characteristics of each pupil.

Language

Response-dependent questioning approaches have been investigated to evaluate their potential for teaching young handicapped children expressive language (Hendrickson & Stowitschek, 1980). These investigators assessed the relative effectiveness of two strategies, the Full Model-Open Question sequence and the Open Question-Full Model sequence. While the actual response topographies targeted varied from child to child, each strategy was shown to be useful in developing verbal repertoires in young language and developmentally delayed children.

During the Open Question-Full Model (OQ-FM) sequence progressively more restricted question types were used. The Full Model-Open Question sequence consisted of the procedure applied in reverse order. The questioning sequence is similar to the strategy employed by Armstrong (1977).

1 - Open Question (OQ).	This type of question (or statement) is intended to gain a single word, short phrase or complete sentence response, e.g. "Tell me about this."
2 - Multiple Choice (MC).	This type of question presents alternative responses that include the correct response, e.g. "Is it a *cat* or is it a *cow*?" (More alternatives may be added.)
3 - Restricted Alternative (RA).	This type of question eliminates the alternative incorrect response without presenting a complete model of the correct response, e.g. "It's not a cow. What is it?"
4 - Full Model (FM).	This may be a question or a statement followed by a direct model intended to gain a correct imitative response. The teacher requests the student to imitate the answer, e.g. "Say, It's a cat." The teacher follows a correct child response with praise, and then repeats the original Open Question, i.e. "Tell me about this."

If the student did not successfully imitate the full model, a partial model (PM), i.e. a limited number of the words in the target response, was provided. For instance, the teacher may have directed, "Say, It's a __." After the child repeated, "It's a __," the entire model was given again.

Young handicapped children and students with severe deficits appear to learn better with the Full Model-Open Question sequence. Positive responses are more likely to occur earlier and more frequently in the training session when models and restrictive question types introduce the questioning sequence. Unfortunately, exposure to different question types is less frequent with early modeling. Therefore, the teacher must consider the objective of the learning session carefully when selecting a questioning sequence. A teacher that has multiple objectives, e.g. for the student to answer in complete sentences *and* to reply to a variety of question types, would choose the Open Question-Full Model sequence, which would most readily allow these objectives to be met. On the other hand, the current behavioral repertoire of the student must also be considered. Students with very limited repertoires need supportive, structured learning environments, other more capable students may benefit more from being presented with wider response alternatives. For instance, for students who have spontaneously exhibited the desired behavior on previous occasions or who are being prepared to make a transition to a less restrictive, less supportive environment, e.g. mainstreamed students, the Open Question-Full Model strategy with its early provision for greater options by the student might be more appropriate. Indeed, regular education and many special education teachers prefer not to provide models or other support until late in their instructional sequence (Stowitschek, Day, Stowitschek & Hendrickson, in press).

Spelling

Questioning sequences may be applied effectively to teach spelling. For instance, in a typical response-dependent questioning sequence, the error made by the child can be brought to his or her attention through a question which in itself may lead to a self-correction.

Sample Response-Dependent Questioning Tactic for Teaching Spelling

GENERAL OBJECTIVE: To spell *calendar* correctly aloud

T: How do you spell calendar?	1 - Key Question
C: c-a-l-l-e-n-d-a-r	
T: c-a-l-l-e-n-d-a-r?	2 - Repetition of Error Question

C: error
T: Do you spell calendar c-a-l-e-n-d-a-r   2 - Multiple   Choice
   or c-a-l-l-e-n-d-a-r?   Question
T: error
T: You spell calendar, c-a-l-e-n-d-a-r.   4 - Full Model
C: c-a-l-e-n-d-a-r

Oral Reading

Response-dependent questioning strategies may be sequenced in a number of ways to improve the oral reading skills of students. One format for employing an increasingly restrictive questioning sequence is to apply questions to the corrective feedback hierarchy described by Hansen and Eaton (1978). After the child makes an error in reading a passage orally, the teacher presents a series of questions corresponding to the hierarchy and aimed at cuing the student until he or she responds correctly.

Corrective Feedback Hierarchy

Seven Step Hierarchy

1 - Purpose of question: Cue the student that has read a word incorrectly.

2 - Purpose of question: Have student finish sentence and and guess the word.

3 - Purpose of question: Have the student break the word into parts and pronounce each one.

4 - Purpose of question: Provide student with aided visual cue to decrease the stimuli.

5 - Purpose of question: Provide the student with a phonic cue to indicate location of his finger.

Possible Teacher Questions

1 - What is the word after "famous" or how do you pronounce the last word in the sentence?

2 - Can you reread the sentence correctly?

3 - Do you see any smaller words in that word? What does "b-a-t-t-l-e" spell?

4 - What word do you see if you cover a part of the word, e.g. "b-a-t-t-l-e," with your finger?

5 - If you cover all the letters two or three at a time, e.g. "b-a,"what sound(s) do you have?

6 - Purpose of question: Provide the student with a choice of the correct word and incorrect word.	6 - Is the word "cattleship" or "battleship?"
7 - Purpose of question: Provide the student with the correct word.	7 - The word is "battleship." Read the word and the complete sentence.

(Hansen & Eaton, 1978, p. 73)

In addition to using this strategy as a tactic for directly intervening upon student errors, teachers could train students to learn the strategy as a self-correction procedure when reading alone. For instance, once a student recognizes he or she has made an error, the student could apply steps 2, 3, 4, and 5 substituting the word "I" for "you." In this way, students might correct a number of their errors spontaneously.

QUESTIONS AS COMPONENTS OF OTHER DIRECT TEACHING STRATEGIES

Mand-Model Strategy

The mand-model strategy for promoting language development was designed to be employed as a primary direct teaching tactic or a secondary tactic to facilitate generalization (Rogers-Warren & Warren, 1980).

The mand-model strategy capitalizes on the interest and attention of the child at the time and generally is employed in relatively unstructured, naturalistic settings. It is used primarily to increase the rate of child utterances and overall reliance on verbalization. The mand-model strategy is implemented in a seemingly spontaneous fashion whenever the teacher observes (or creates) a credible teacher-child interaction. A simple mand-model sequence follows:

GENERAL GOAL: Increase rate of verbalization

Teacher	*Basic Definition*	*WH-Question*
1 - Question	An inquiry that does not require a yes or no answer	What do you want?
2 - Mand	Request for verbal reply.	*Tell* me what you want.

| 3 - Model | Demonstration of verbal response | Say, train. |
| 4 - Praise for Verbaliz- ing. | Show of approval for talking | Great talking! Here's the train. |

The function of the question is to *initiate* an interaction sequence which in turn will lead to the child verbalizing. Particularly important to reiterate is the fact that the child's answer is very functional *for the child*, e.g. it leads to acquisition of desired object.

Communicative-Interactive Model

In the communicative interaction model the teacher says or does whatever is probable of evoking a child response which in turn will lead to a child initiation which in turn helps to maintain dialogue. The teacher functions as a facilitator for establishing and maintaining dialogue by doing or saying things to evoke communicative behavior (Allen, 1980). For example:

GENERAL GOAL: To maintain dialogue

Child	*Teacher*
1 - Points	2 - You want the train? Say, train.
3 - Nods, makes sound like "tr-r-ā."	4 - Gives child the train.
1 - Tommy!	2 - Look, Tommy's getting wet.
3 - Hair is wet.	4 - Yes, and his face, and hands, and _____.
5 - Shirt, too.	6 - Oh, oh. His shirt, too!
1 - What are you doing?	2 - Watch, what am I going to do?
3 - Build blocks? Me play?	4 - Okay. What do you want to build?

At times the questions and utterances will vary from topic to topic as the child's attention shifts. Regardless of topical shifts the teacher continues to question and comment in a nonthreatening though directive manner. The instructional objective, for instance, might be to increase the duration of teacher-child interactions and/or the number of child initiations.

Generative Questions-Answering Strategies

Clark and Sherman (1975) taught new linguistic structures and generative responding with simple question-modeling strategies. Initially the teacher models every answer the child will be expected to give. After the answers are under the stimulus control of specific questions that have been paired with the modeled answers, the child is likely to emit new examples of the trained linguistic forms spontaneously. A sample of Clark and Sherman's (1975) teaching sequence is provided.

GENERAL GOAL: Answer wh-questions with correct inflectional endings

Teacher: He is a *baker*.	(Statement including stimulus form)
Teacher: What did he do yesterday?	(Question — past tense)
Child: Yesterday he *baked*.	(Answer — stimulus item with /t/ inflection)
Teacher: He is a *baker*.	(Statement including stimulus form)
Teacher: What will he do tomorrow?	(Question — future tense)
Child: Tomorrow he will *bake*.	(Answer — stimulus item with no specific inflection)
Teacher: He is a *baker*.	(Statement including stimulus item)
Teacher: What is his job?	(Question)
Child: His job is *baking*.	(Answer — stimulus item with /ing/ inflection)
	(Clark & Sherman, 1975, p. 323)

OTHER APPLICATIONS

Questions may be used as the total teaching tactic or a component of a teaching procedure. The variety of educational objectives that may be addressed via questions therefore seems endless. Of worth mentioning, however, is the instructional merit questions may have in the following situations:

1. Kaczmarek and Dell (1981) pointed out the educational

value of teaching to multiple objectives rather than the traditional one objective-one activity teaching. Upon reflection it would appear that questions and questioning sequences may be of particular utility when teaching to multiple objectives. For instance, the goal of increasing a child's rate of verbalizing may be both a language and a social behavior objective. Questions can be used effectively to evoke increased amounts of verbalization and are by definition interactive in nature.

2. Questions are useful for teaching small groups of students separate objectives while they are engaged in similar tasks. A teacher, for example, can ask different students questions about shape, size, function and quantity while each pupil works on his/her own puzzle, construction or drawing.

3. Questions are frequently used with large groups of students, i.e. the entire class. In such instances each question and follow-up procedure (error correction tactic) should be well-planned in advance. Unfortunately, this is the time that many instructional agents employ questions least effectively. Whenever possible the teacher should attempt to increase the number of students asked to respond as well as the time that *all* students are actively responding. Large group teaching activities should include drill and practice sessions in particular. The length of such sessions should be kept short, however such activities can be distributed across the day. One technique teachers can use to introduce drill and practice to large groups is to have students respond with flash answer cards rather than orally. In that way the teacher literally is able to "see" each student's response and note errors without risking embarrassing anyone. Following a reading exercise, for instance, comprehension questions can be asked so that TRUE-FALSE or YES-NO answers are needed. Students simply flash their answer to the teacher.

4. In every classroom there are students who can contribute to the development of other students and participate more actively in the instructional process as a means of enhancing their own skills. Peers are an often overlooked resource available to almost all teachers. Peers can be taught to use

questions to initiate interactions with other children. They can be taught appropriate ways to respond to the initiations of others. Peers will be of tremendous importance in the maintenance of linguistic, social and general cognitive behavior of their classmates, particularly as they progress through school. It is to the teacher's advantage to use peers in meaningful instructional activities, teaching them appropriate question-asking/answering and giving them an opportunity to refine their skills.

Conclusion

Teacher use of questions may be one of the most powerful instructional tactics available to educators or a frustrating and fruitless teaching activity depending on how questions are selected and how they are applied in the classroom. While the direct effect of questioning strategies on student performance is just beginning to be investigated, the promise of questions as preventive and remedial/corrective teaching strategies is already apparent. For teachers wishing to improve the instructional worth of their questioning tactics the following summary seems most appropriate: (1) select and/or design questioning strategies in direct relation to pre-established educational objectives, (2) be systematic in the implementation and evaluation of these strategies, and (3) view your steadfast experimentation with questioning strategies as potentially leading to the development of one or some of the most productive teaching strategies ever used.

REFERENCES

Armstrong, J. The use of a diagnostic strategy to teach educationally handicapped children to solve verbal reasoning problems (Education specialist thesis, George Peabody College for Teachers, 1977.) Nashville: Peabody College, 1977.

Floyd, W. An analysis of the oral questioning activity in selected Colorado primary classrooms (Doctoral dissertation, Colorado State College). Ann Arbor: University Microfilms, No. 60. 2653, 1960.

Gallagher, J., M. Aschner, and W. Jenne. Productive thinking of gifted children in classroom interaction. Research Monograph No. B-5. Washington, D.C.: The Council for Exceptional Children, 1967.

Hendrickson, J. and J. Freedman. Peer tutoring of conversational skills: A mini-facilitator in the preschool classroom. Nashville: Peabody College (ERIC

Document No. Ed 209 917), 1980.

Hillman, S. The effect of question type and position on four types of learning among mentally handicapped children (Doctoral dissertation, Indiana University). Ann Arbor: University Microfilms, No. 73-2714, 1960.

Moyer, J. An exploratory study of questioning in the instructional process in selecting elementary schools (Doctoral Dissertation, Columbia University, 1966). *Dissertation Abstracts,* XXVII-A, July: 147, 1966.

Schreiber, J. Teachers' question-asking techniques in social studies (Doctoral Dissertation, University of Iowa, 1967). *Dissertation Abstracts,* XXVIII-A, 0523, July, 1967.

REFERENCES

Aschner, M.: Asking questions to trigger thinking. *National Education Association Journal, 50*:44-46, 1961.

Belch, P.: The question of teachers' questions. *Teaching Exceptional Children, 7*: 46-50, 1975.

Clark, H., and J. Sherman: Teaching generative use of sentence answers to three forms of questions. *Journal of Applied Behavior Analysis, 8*:321-330, 1975.

Eaton, M.: Data decisions and evaluation. In N. Haring; T. Lovitt; M. Eaton, and C. Hansen (Eds.), *The Fourth R: Research in the Classroom.* Columbus, Merrill, 167-190, 1978.

Fine, M., C. Allen and A. Medvene: Verbal interaction patterns in regular and special classrooms. *Psychology in the Schools, 5*: 265-271, 1968.

French, P., and M. MacLure: Getting the right answer and getting the right answer. *Research in Education,* November: 1-23, 1979.

Gall, M.: The use of questions in teaching. *Review of Educational Research, 40*:707-721, 1970.

Gall, M.; B. Ward; D. Berliner; L. Cahen; P. Winne; J. Elashoff, and G. Stanton: Effects of questioning techniques and recitation on student learning. *American Educational Research Journal, 15*:175-199, 1978.

Hansen, C., and M. Eaton: Reading. In N. Haring; T. Lovitt; M. Eaton; and C. Hansen (Eds.), *The Fourth R: Research in the Classroom,* Columbus: Merrill, 41-92, 1978.

Hendrickson, J., and C. Stowitschek: Teacher of diagnostic questioning and modeling in language development, *Journal of Special Education Technology, 4*: 17-27, 1980.

Hester, P. and J. Hendrickson: Teaching functional expressive language: the acquisition and generalization of five-element syntactic responses. *Journal of Applied Behavior Analysis, 10*: 312, 1977.

Kaczmarek, L., and A. Dell: Designing instructional activities for young handicapped children. *Journal of the Division for Early Childhood, 2*: 74-83, 1981.

Loughlin, R.: On questioning. *The Educational Forum, 25*: 481-482, 1961.

Marksberry, M.: Student questioning: An instructional strategy, *Educational Horizons,* Summer: 190-195, 1979.

Rice, D.: The effect of question-asking instruction on preservice elementary science teachers. *Journal of Research Science Teaching, 14*: 353-359, 1977.

Rogers-Warren, A., and S. Warren: Mands for verbalization: Facilitating the display of newly trained language in children. *Behavior Modification, 4*: 361-382, 1980.

Shores, R.; M., Roberts, and C. Nelson: An empirical model for the development of competencies of children with behavior disorders. *Behavior Disorders, 1*: 123-132, 1976.

Stevens, R.: The question as a measure of efficiency in instruction: A critical study of classroom practice. Teachers College Contribution to Education. New York: Teachers College, Columbia University, No. 48, 1912.

Stowitschek, J.; R. Day; C. Stowitschek and J. Hendrickson: *Direct Teaching and Supervision Tactics for Exceptional Children.* Rockville, Maryland: Aspen Systems Corporation, in press.

Zahorick, J.: Questioning in the classroom. *Education, 4*: 358-363, 1974.

Zetlin, A., and R. Gallimore: A cognitive skills training program for moderately retarded learners, *Education and Training of the Mentally Retarded, 15*: 121-131, 1980.

CHAPTER 18

IMPLEMENTATION OF INSTRUCTION IN SPECIAL EDUCATION THROUGH THE C.R.E.A.T.E. SYSTEMS APPROACH

VYKUNTAPATHI THOTA

THE changing social and economic structure of the United States during the late 1950s and early 1960s threw the special needs of certain groups of people into sharp focus. The Vocational Education Act of 1963 recognized that some youth and adults may require specialized instruction to become functioning members of society and to earn a living. As a result of 1963 and 1968 vocational legislation, two categories of special needs students were recognized: disadvantaged, and handicapped. The handicaps included in the 1976 legislation can be summarized as: mental handicaps, physical handicaps, emotional handicaps, and specific learning disabilities. Modern treatment and instructional methods enable many people to prepare for a productive life who would formerly have been consigned to long-term custodial care.

MENTAL HANDICAPS. Mentally handicapped persons are generally considered to be those who have an IQ below 75, although this is subject to state and local interpretation. These persons are usually classified as educable or trainable.

PHYSICAL HANDICAPS. Physical handicaps may result from birth defects, injury, or illness. These handicaps range from perceptual difficulties, such as blindness or limited vision and deafness or impaired hearing, to loss of a limb or a crippling condition.

EMOTIONAL HANDICAPS. The behavior of emotionally disturbed students is sometimes disruptive in the classroom. They may be unstable or hyperactive and often overreact to situations. Socially maladjusted students cause trouble at home and school, and they may be truants, predelinquents, delinquents, or incorrigibles (Young).

SPECIFIC LEARNING DISABILITIES. It is estimated that one of every fifteen school children has a specific learning disability (SLD). Even though SLD students usually have average or above-average intelligence, their handicaps inhibit learning. The SLD student is usually male and often has well-educated parents (Cline & Ishee).

Although specialized programs may have been necessary because of the extreme shortage of teachers trained to work with handicapped persons, federal legislation now mandates that these students be mainstreamed whenever possible. Mainstreaming handicapped students reduces their isolation and prepares them for a more normal life.

Adaptions in material, methods, and content may be necessary for handicapped learners. Many of these adaptions can be used for mainstreamed learners as well as for those in special education classes. In teaching individuals with special education problems, a teacher should keep in mind and use certain guidelines as a basis for implementation of instruction. A sincere interest in these individuals can overcome many problems. A teacher must get acquainted with the students and become aware of each one's abilities and interests. In addition to personal acceptance, the teacher should encourage the other students to be understanding and accepting. The handicapped learner needs acceptance, encouragement, and positive reinforcement, just like other people.

Today many teachers have special needs, or exceptional students in their classes. Some of these teachers work in schools or classrooms exclusively for special needs students. Many schools integrate handicapped students into regular classrooms with other students. Whiteford indicates that most teachers have received little or no specialized training to teach exceptional students.

Innovation, like charity, begins at home. In the days of tight money, unique solutions should be developed for obtaining innovations desired, and creative use of resources placed at our disposal is imperative. Special programs may be needed to help students of special education. A system is needed to help students progress to the point that they can succeed in the regular program.

Individualized instruction has long been a goal of our American education concern for the individual child and meeting his/her needs dates back to the one-room school. Educators who have recognized the need for individualizing of instruction have hesitated to undertake the task because of the lack of an effective system for implementation. A system now exists. It has proven its effectiveness and is readily available through the C.R.E.A.T.E. Systems approach. The primary function of the C.R.E.A.T.E. Systems approach is to guide the student through a highly structured program of multimedia packages. The multimedia package is not a panacea for all our money, class size and time problem, but it does provide us with a vehicle that makes the implementation of instruction feasible.

It is not enough to decide what students are to learn. There must also be a definite plan to help them attain objectives. The C.R.E.A.T.E. Systems approach developed by the author is designed to help handicaps learn what is desired. The model includes a variety of activities because different students learn in different ways.

Sometimes multimedia packages must be developed when nothing is available that can be adapted for handicaps. Teachers often find that they must develop multimedia packages, and many enjoy the creative aspects of such an activity. Chisholm and Ely list the following advantages of inexpensive and locally made packages:

1. The package most closely matches the particular need of the teacher, students and setting.
2. Parts of the materials can usually be readily adapted to meet changing needs.
3. Production requires understanding of the subject content and often serves as motivation.
4. Students can participate in production activities, which often serve as motivation.
5. Production often encourages students and teachers to work cooperatively.
6. Local production is often less costly, so more students and teachers can be served.
7. Production can often be done by less able students and so help to develop self-confidence. Locally produced packages can be more up-to-date, be more specifically oriented geographically, and capture local flavor.

The C.R.E.A.T.E. System approach is intended to serve as a means for implementation of instruction in special education. Not only will multimedia packages give the teacher a new status and role in the classrooms, but they will bring a new excitement into teaching and learning, making it a truly creative experience for teachers and students of special education.

C.R.E.A.T.E SYSTEMS APPROACH

We are a visual culture, living in an environment impacted by commercial print and nonprint media. One of the most important responsibilities of today's special education teacher is to develop creative thinking among his/her students. Students learn from a wide variety of experiences. To stimulate students to reach their full potential, the innovative teacher motivates by using a wide variety of instructional materials. It is therefore vitally important that every effort be made to use existing materials and equipment to their fullest extent in the learning and teaching process.

The teacher who thinks creatively finds that the C.R.E.A.T.E. systems approach provides unlimited possibilities for implementation of instruction for handicaps. The C.R.E.A.T.E. systems approach is composed of six stages: 1. Collecting, 2. Recognizing, 3. Employing, 4. Arranging, 5. Transmitting, and 6. Evaluating.

In conclusion, the teacher requires systematic attention to a number of questions in implementation of instruction through the C.R.E.A.T.E. systems approach:

1. Is there an important need for the communication module?
2. What behavioral changes are to be sought through using the

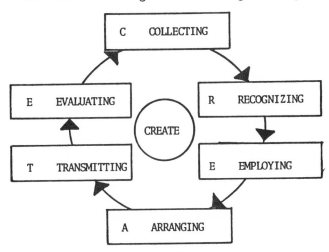

Figure 18-1.

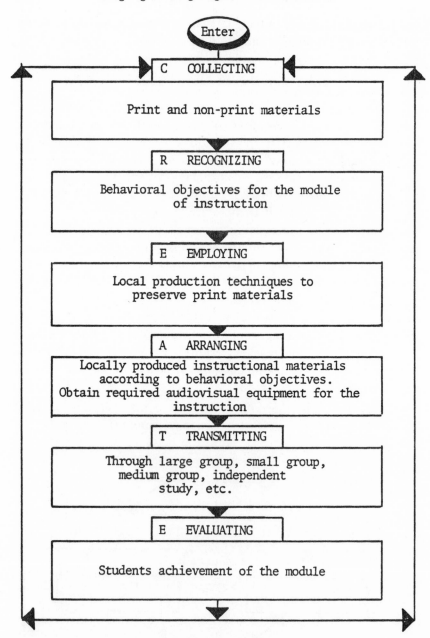

Figure 18-2. Functional Flow Chart.

module?

3. What production costs will be involved?
4. What should be the module's message content?
5. What procedures should be initiated to monitor up-to-dateness and revision as necessary?

REFERENCES

Chisholm, M.E. and D.P. Ely. *Media Personnel in Education.* Englewood Cliffs, N.J.: Prentice-Hall, 1976.

Cline, B.S., and B. Ishee. "Specific Learning Disabilities" *Today's Education.* 61(1), 18-22, January 1972.

Federal Register. *Vocational Education, State Programs and Commissioner's Discretionary Programs.* Washington, D.C.: U.S. Government Printing Office. 1977.

Polloway, E.A., and J.E. Smith. *Teaching Language Skills to Exceptional Learners.* Denver: Love Publishing Co., 1982.

Thota, V., *C.R.E.A.T.E.: An Instructional Development Model.* Petersburg: Virginia State University. 1981.

Younie, W.J. *Instructional Approaches to Slow Learning.* New York: Teachers College Press, 1967.

Young, E.B. (Ed). *Vocational Education For Handicapped Persons: Handbook For Program Implementation.* National Conference on Vocational Education for Handicapped Persons, Washington, D.C., 1969.

CHAPTER 19

IMPLEMENTATION OF PERCEPTUAL FACTORS IN READING PROGRAMS

RICHARD H. BLOOMER

P ERHAPS nowhere in the field of education has the study of perception had such an impact as in the area of teaching reading. Reading is usually defined as the achievement of meaning from the written word. This process has three components. The first, sensation, is the impact of the stimulus on the optic nerve. This process which involves stimulation of the total visual field produces such a vast amount of information as to be meaningless. An intermediary step between visual sensation and the third component, meaning, involves attention, selection and focusing on aspects of the complex visual field. In order to achieve the third component of meaning, these intermediary processes, the substance of the hypothetical construct perception, are necessary. Perception is then a number of interactive processes between the reader and the stimuli which serve to organize the stimuli field into components for meaningful processing. Disorders in reading may be attributed to poor visual sensation, poor perceptual processes, or failure to achieve meaning. Since disorders of visual sensation are relatively rare and reading materials are generally selected with the child's ability to understand in mind, many reading disorders are attributed to this intermediary processing termed perception. This chapter will be divided into three sections, the first section dealing with approaches to the interaction of perception and meaning, the second dealing with perceptual principles applied to the construction of reading programs, and the third discusses the results of some applications of these principles in reading programs.

APPROACHES TO PERCEPTION AND READING

There are primarily two ways of looking at the problem of poor reading in relation to perception. The first model, the perceptual deficit model, attributes poor reading to faulty perceptual processes on the part of the child; the second attributes poor reading to the organization of teaching stimulus materials used in the teaching of reading.

It is clear that the first approach is the more popular one at the present time. There are a myriad of tests available to determine the quality of a child's perceptual abilities, ranging from such instruments as the Wepman Auditory Discrimination Test (1973) designed to determine the strengths and weaknesses in terms of mode of processing, the Developmental Test of Visual Perception (Frostig et al., 1964), and the Purdue Perceptual Motor Survey (Roach and Kephart, 1966) designed to determine sensory motor integration, to a number of experiments done on hemispheric laterality (Wellman, 1980) designed to determine whether or not the child perceives and processes material with the appropriate side of the brain.

In general, the perceptual deficit argument is that if a child is introduced into a reading program where some children succeed and others fail, the child who fails must have some flaw in his perceptual processing abilities that will not allow him to succeed where others do. There is considerable face validity to this position and the various approaches to remediating perceptual processing have given rise to numbers of curricula which purport to change and enhance the manner in which the child deals with the visual material or converts visual material into auditory or motor material. For the most part, these programs have been somewhat successful in changing the scores on various tests to which they are aligned. It does appear, therefore, that insofar as tests of perceptual ability are constructed, appropriate training can increase the scores on these tests of perceptual ability. There is, however, as Coles (1978) points out, a serious flaw in this argument. The ultimate goal is changes in reading ability as a function of perceptual training. Here the success of perceptual training has not been satisfactory at all. Children who go through perceptual training programs and do in fact increase in the ability to perform perceptual tasks on tests are not found to be better readers. The net effect of research in this area seems to indicate that perceptual training itself does not relate to reading ability. One might ask the question whether perception, in spite of its face validity, relates to reading at all?

The answer to this question lies in the alternative approach, the perceptual teaching model. The basic stance of this approach is somewhat different than the perceptual deficit approach. People in the audiovisual area are somewhat more comfortable with the perceptual teaching model in that it involves the selection and manipulation of stimuli for effective teaching purposes.

In its simplest form, the argument states that perceptual problems do not exist if the stimulus is simple enough and is presented alone. Take for example the famous "b-d" confusion which is presumed by the child deficit group to be indicative of perceptual difficulties or mirror vision. If "d" did not exist, "b" would not be a problem. It is basically the interaction between these two stimuli that generates a difficulty in telling one from the other. Without the pair of similar stimuli, there is no reason to suspect that the letter "b" in and of itself would cause any more reading difficulties than the letter "l" or the letter "o", or any other single letter of the alphabet. Therefore, perceptual problems as seen from this approach can, at least in part, be related to the stimuli themselves rather than to the child. It follows that if the stimuli could be organized into a teaching curriculum in such a way as to minimize these perceptual difficulties, a considerably greater number of children might accomplish adequate reading skills and avoid the stigma of various perceptual handicaps. It is fundamentally this approach that we will concern ourselves with in the present chapter.

SOME RULES FOR ORGANIZATION OF STIMULI

1. Teach only one thing at a time. Application of this rule avoids a variety of problems stemming from the limited short-term memory of children as well as any potential confusions that might arise early in the teaching process. Simple and clear as this rule may seem, most reading methods do not follow it. They tend, for example, to present all of the beginning sounds at one time or all of the ending sounds at one time or a number of sight-words in a group.

2. Teach the stimulus in its absolutely simplest form. It is well known that complex stimuli are more likely to produce difficulties than the simple ones. In reading, some of the early perception studies indicate that more letters could be perceived at one exposure if they were combined into words; then hence, in the field of reading, words are commonly the teaching unit (Cattell, 1886). However, we have long known the learning efficiency is negatively related to the

complexity and size of the unit to be learned (Krulee, Podell and Romeo, 1954), as well as numerous other researchers. These data suggest for instance that the use of the complex stimuli in analytic phonics as opposed to the single letter sound combination of synthetic phonics increases the complexity and therefore the difficulty of learning (Chall, 1965).

3. Stimulus consistency. A stimulus that is presented in a consistent form is easier to learn than one that is presented in varied forms. In teaching in schools, the letter stimuli occur in several different forms, i.e. in cursive caps and small, in manuscript caps and small, in serif and sans serif type. Thus, each stimulus occurs in a number of forms and the child must learn to respond to the multiple varieties of stimuli.

The English language spelling presents a second problem in that the same letter may require different responses depending upon whether it is long or short. Irregular uses of letter sound correspondence in English spelling increase the difficulty of learning English. Good practice therefore is to limit letters to single form and the words to single letter sound correspondences, thus avoiding difficulties with having to learn multiple responses to the same stimuli.

4. Stimulus discriminability. With a beginning learner, two stimuli which are very similar tend to be confusing. If, on the other hand, these two stimuli are learned well separately, the confusion is mitigated and the potential for perceptual difficulty disappears (Gibson, 1953). "B" and "d" are again a case in point. Being similar in both sound and shape, they are much more likely to be confused than most of the other letters. "F" and "v" for example have an equal similarity in sound but are not often confused because the shapes differ. "B" and "h" are quite similar in shape but are not often confused because of the difference in sound. Good organizational practice for curriculum, then, involves separating any two very similar items in the curriculum sequence and teaching one of them very well before the other one is introduced. Further, for example, if we chose to teach in capital letters rather than small letters, "b" and "d" are no longer a problem since visually they are highly discriminable.

5. The more ways a child responds, the better his learning. Thus a child who responds with a verbal response to a visual stimulus will not learn as well as a child who responds verbally to a visual

stimulus and with written response to an auditory stimulus. Children who produce their own materials will do better than children who are given materials to read.

These simple rules can be combined into a reading/teaching technique called progressive part. Progressive part was developed as a resolution to the whole-part controversy in learning. Essentially the procedure is as follows:

1. Learning Unit A is taught.
2. Learning Unit B is taught.
3. Learning Units A and B are combined into a larger "whole."
4. Learning Unit C is taught.
5. Units, A, B, and C are combined into a larger "whole."

An illustration of the organization of progressive part into a reading program to minimize perceptual problems is given in Figure 19-1. The system proceeds through all the letter sound combinations. Rules are adhered to in that a single letter sound is taught in capital

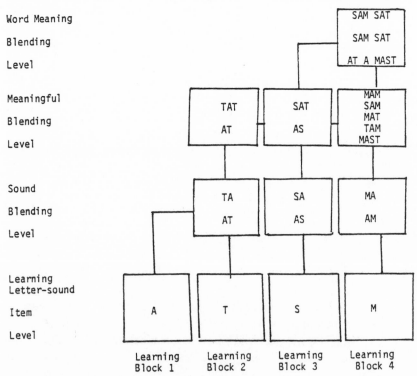

Figure 19-1. Conceptual lattice for progressive part reading teaching.

form for each learning block. Children both say and write the material composed of only previously learned letters and sounds. The words presented are phonetically consistent and the sequence separates letters that are confusing in either sound or shape. Thus, the program design seeks to avoid difficult or complex perceptual problems while achieving the basic goal of teaching reading.

The net effect of using the progressive part design in the teaching of reading in the regular class was done in two forms. The first, a form using writing as a medium and the second used the typewriter as a medium. The results of both of these experiments are presented in the third section of this chapter.

EXPERIMENTAL RESULTS

The first experimental program was tried in a suburban middle-class first grade with the control group coming from the same school who used a basal reading system. The progressive part program used print script capital letters as a medium and the children wrote regularly as a part of the program. Children were assigned on a haphazard basis to the classes by the principal. The Gates Primary Reading Test was given in June of the first grade. The following are the results broken down by year of achievement.

TABLE 19-I

PERCENTAGES OF CHILDREN WHO ACHIEVED AT VARIOUS
GRADE LEVELS ON THE FINAL GATES PRIMARY READING TESTS

Achieved Grade Level	Group	N	Word Recognition	Sentence Reading	Paragraph Reading	Average Reading
1.0-1.99	Exp	32	0	6	12	0
	Cont	30	17	33	17	17
2.0-2.99	Exp	32	53	63	50	63
	Cont	30	53	46	60	56
3.0-3.99	Exp	32	47	31	38	38
	Cont	30	30	23	23	27

Note that important differences occur in the number of children who are achieving below grade level and that the differences are somewhat diminished as the complexity of the stimuli increases from words to paragraphs. Analyses of variance indicated that all differences significantly favored the experimental group: word recognition F w/w 1/60 df = 2.71 > .01, sentence reading F w/w 1/60 df = 2.13 > .05 and paragraph reading F w/w 1/60 df = 1.90 > .05.

The second experimental program used the typewriter as a medium of teaching. This experimental program has been in existence since 1966 in a small New England milltown with a primarily lower socioeconomic group. Children were randomly assigned to treatment. Children were in the reading/typing program in grades 1 and 2, and then joined the control group in basal readers for grades 3 to 8.

There are certain advantages to using the typewriter as a medium for teaching reading. The first of which is a reduction in the confusion of letter order in words or reversal, as is common in other programs, since the typewriter only goes in one direction. And, since the children are writing every word that they read, this reversal tendency is remarkably decreased.

Since the typewriter takes the burden of letter formation from the child and puts it on the typewriter, and since the child habitually writes, the written verbal fluency is considerably increased. This verbal fluency was tested at the end of second grade; the average number of words per story by a reading/typing child was 156, basal reader children produced eighty-eight words. The number of words produced by children who had typing, in a test of handwritten compositions, was 113, almost twenty-five words greater than the basal reader pupils. The number of complex sentences, an indicator of verbal fluency, was almost twice as great and sentence length was increased from 6.8 for controls to 9.7 for reading/typing children F w/w 1/45 df = 8.20 p = .01.

The results of the first two-year study have been previously reported by Bloomer and Bernazza (1967) and Bloomer, Bernazza and Cline (1968). In general, pupils in the Reading/Typing Program were superior to pupils in the Scott-Foresman Program in vocabulary and in spelling and at the end of the grade were slightly superior, but not significantly superior, in reading comprehension.

Typewriters in the experimental program lasted twelve years on the average. Concurrent with a second grant of typewriters from the Smith Corona Corporation, it was determined to follow up the reading/typing children through seventh grade. Comprehensive Test of Basic Skills data was available at the third, fifth, and seventh grade levels and for children through the present grade 8. Thus, third grade data was available for all children presently in grades 5 through 9, and seventh grade data was available for present 7th and 8th graders. The seventh and eighth grade data was collected from the local junior high school. To reduce other influences, only pupils who had gone to the experimental school at the elementary level were included in the study. Overall, 439 test results from 150 reading/typing and 289 basal reader children were found.

The reading/typing children were superior to Basal Reading Programs in vocabulary, F w/w 1/437 df = 9.62, p = .002; reading comprehension, F w/w 1/437 df = 12.92, = .0005. Signficant differences occurred at each grade level. Figures 2-4 show accelerated growth of the reading/typing pupils through grade 7. Similar results were found for language skills, (for language mechanics, F w/w 1/437 df = 7.56, p = .006 language expression, F w/w 1/437 df = 15.07, p = .0001 and spelling, F w/w 1/437 df = 12.85, p = .004) as with the reading skills. Pupils in the reading/typing program accelerated in growth over the basal reading pupils from the same school.

The net effect of structuring reading teaching according to perceptual rules is most clearly seen in remedial instruction. In our follow-up study the number of pupils who were engaged in remedial programs, Title I, emotionally disturbed or learning disabled, were recorded. For control group basal reader children, 32.4 percent were engaged in some form of remedial instruction. For children who had had the reading/typing program, 11.8 percent received remedial instruction in any form, a difference of over 20 percent.

Since economics is important to education at the present time, some economic comparisons are in order. The reading/typing program, including typewriter costs and repairs, costs the same amount as a basal program on a ten-year basis. Taking costs from our experimental program, the per class, per year savings in remedial education costs is over $5,500, considerably more than the cost of the typewriters.

Most tests of perceptual ability for academic purposes include letter recognition and the standard clue for learning disabilities is the presence of a "b" -"d" confusion. Using the Reading Skills Diagnostic

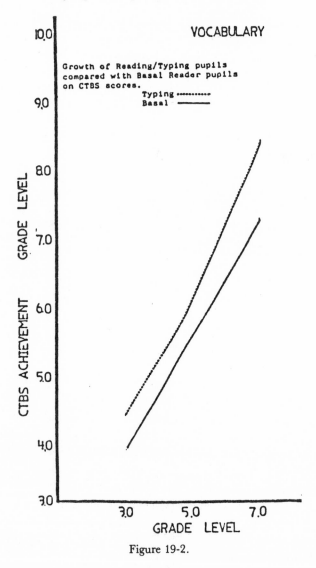

Figure 19-2.

Test, RSDT III, Level 2: Letter Recognition (Bloomer, 1967), a criterion-referenced tool, 65.2 percent of the reading/typing first graders reached the criterion of 100 percent of the letters correct, whereas only 45.6 percent of the control groups achieved this result. At the end of the second grade, 65.5 percent of the controls and 86.4 percent of the reading/typing children had reached criterion. By the letter recognition measure of perceptual ability, organization of

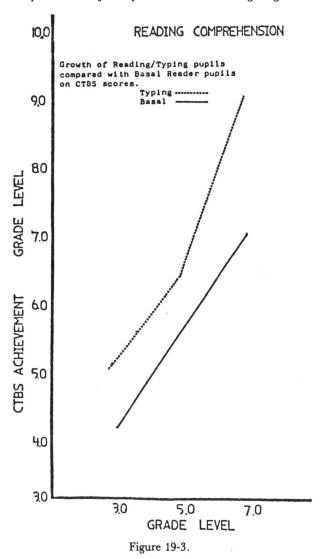

Figure 19-3.

stimuli to minimize perceptual problems produces significantly fewer errors.

Summary

Our research into the area of perception has shown that the application of the perceptual deficit model has been successful in rais-

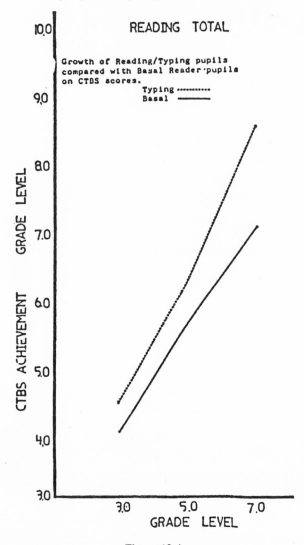

Figure 19-4.

ing scores on various perceptual deficit tests but has been generally unsuccessful in changing reading abilities.

The alternative view takes the position that perceptual difficulties are a function of the interaction between the stimuli and the organization of the curriculum along simple perceptual principles as rules can prevent many of the perceptual problems deemed to cause reading failure. The rules or principles are as follows:

1. Teach only one thing at a time.
2. Use the simplest stimulus possible.
3. Teach only one constant stimulus.
4. Separate and teach separately stimuli that are similar.
5. Have the child respond in as many ways as possible.

Using these perceptual principles to organize materials for reading teaching was demonstrated experimentally in two studies to significantly increase reading vocabulary, language arts and spelling abilities, to increase verbal writing fluency, and to reduce the number of students requiring special education services. The application of perceptual principles to the design of teaching materials has a long-standing effect as indicated by an increased rate of learning in children whose initial training followed these principles over standard school reading programs.

REFERENCES

Bloomer, R.H., and A.M. Bernazza. An experimental reading/typing program with rural disadvantaged children. *Teaching Exceptional Children, 1*:112-116, 1969.

Bloomer, R.H.; A.M. Bernazza, and H. Cline. An experimental reading/typing program. Proceedings National Reading Conference, 1970.

Bloomer, R.H., and A.J. Bernazza. *The Reading/Typing Program.* Brador Publications, 1983 (in press).

Cattell, J. Mc. The inertia of the eye and brain. *Brain 8*:295-312, 188b.

Chall, J. *Learning to Read: The Great Debate.* New York, McGraw-Hill, 1967.

Coles, G. The learning disabilities test battery: empirical and social issues. *Harvard Education Review, 48(3)*, 313-340, 1978.

Frostig, M.; W. Lefeuer, and J.R. Whittlesey. *The Marianne Frostig Developmental Test of Visual Perception.* Palo Alto: Consulting Psychologists Press, 1964.

Gibson, E. Improvement in perceptual judgements as a function of controlled practice or training. *Psychological Bulletin, 46*:603-340.

Krulee, G.K.; J.E. Podell, and P.G. Romeo. Effect of number of alternatives involved in a particular visual discrimination and the ease of making such a discrimination. *Journal of Experimental Psychology, 45*:75-80, 1954.

Roach, E.F., and N.C. Kephart. *Purdue Perceptual Motor Survey.* Columbus, OH, 1966.

Wellman, M. Hemispheric laterality and reading. Doctoral dissertation, The University of Connecticut, Storrs, CT, 1981.

Wepman, J.M. *Auditory Discrimination Test.* Chicago: Language Research Associates, 1973.

CHAPTER 20

IMPLEMENTATION OF A READING PROGRAM FOR THOSE STUDENTS, GRADES 3-12, WHO HAVE NOT LEARNED TO READ FROM STANDARD CURRICULA

RUTH WORDEN FRANK

GENERALLY classified as learning disabilities, students who have not learned to read in the early grades are often referred to as perceptually handicapped, neurologically impaired, or dyslexics. Whatever the nomenclature, these are the students with near average, average, or above average intelligence, for whom standard reading instruction in basal, phonetic, and linguistic curricula does not result in their learning to read. Discrepancies between their attained grade levels on standardized reading achievement tests and the grade levels one would expect from students with their mental ages can range from one to nine years.

Early reporting of teachers' clinical observations of these children's reading difficulties is extremely important. Depressed scores on standardized reading achievement tests will support the clinical evidence, but will not identify the specific reading problem. Fine screening must follow so that the students can be correctly diagnosed and provided with an appropriate educational prescription. An oral reading diagnostic test (Gates-McKillop or *Phonetic Reading Chain*) should be administered first. Subnormal scores indicate a decoding disability. The primary problem lies in the learning-to-read area. Average or above-average scores on such a test signify a comprehension disability, a reading-to-learn problem which should be investigated further.

Neither the decoding-disabled nor the comprehension-disabled are functioning properly. For the former, the problem is at the automatic level of organization. For the latter, it is at the representational level of learning. Since different brain functions are involved at each of these levels, it is crucial that the diagnosis be correct. Some are doubly disabled in both comprehension and decoding. Diagnosticians should be aware that, when there is a wide discrepancy between a decoding-disabled student's actual reading level and expected reading level, learning-to-read is a prerequisite of reading-to-learn.

This chapter deals with the decoding-disabled who have varying degrees of disability in the areas of visual memory, auditory memory, directionality, symbol use, and who are markedly deficient at the automatic level of organization. Of these deficits, the most damaging is their inability to properly organize and process information at the automatic level. A properly functioning automatic level of organization (sometimes called the integration or perceptual organizational level) is needed in attaining automaticity and generalization of all word recognition skills. Children who experience no difficulty in learning to read automatically integrate phonetic information (learned or deduced) and apply it to unknown words. The decoding-disabled are unable to do this. Something occurs (or fails to occur) to, in, or from their brains as stimuli are presented and processed, resulting in distorted perception and inadequate processing. Consequently, internalized misrepresentations and misstated responses feed back into the child's system, further confusing the situation. At the automatic level of learning, the brain records garbled information just as readily as it records correct information. If the decoding-disabled are to learn to read, they must be provided with a reading program which circumvents their lack of a well-functioning automatic level of organization by doing for them what they cannot do for themselves. Instructional techniques and reading materials must overcome each of their deficits within the shortest possible time, *but for the long term*! Everlasting benefits for the decoding-disabled cannot be accomplished by adapting standard basals, or standard phonetic and linguistic programs. Such curricula are written for students with no perceptual, organizational, directional, or memory problems.

Instead, a highly structured system must be designed that will not only organize the automatic level of learning for these students but will also overcome learning deficiencies relating to perception, symbol use, direction, and memory. Such a program for the decoding-disabled should include: (1) use of all sensory modalities (visual, auditory, kinesthetic, tactile) so as to ensure that decoding information is properly integrated in spite of perceptual difficulties. Standard reading instruction is predominantly a visual exercise; (2) use of Robert Gagné's chaining concept, so that there is always a continuous, on-going reinforcement of all previously learned decoding information as new material is introduced; (3) varied use of repetition because the decoding-disabled need much more repetition in order to permanently stabilize the letter-sound associations. They must overlearn; (4) elimination of confusion for teachers and students by means of a sensible, highly-structured organizational plan; (5) controlled oral reading practice material which will provide an opportunity to read without guessing. Words should be comprised of *learned* letter-sound associations only. The text should not be illustrated so that meaning is derived from words, not pictures; (6) multisyllabic words from beginning to end so that, upon completion of the program, students will be able to read everything. The decoding-disabled cannot automatically bridge the gap between monosyllabic and polysyllabic words; (7) a set-up in which the students are totally involved; (8) behavioral objectives with the easily reached goal of 90 percent to 100 percent accuracy; and, (9) systematically administered *cumulative* tests.

This author has designed a reading series which circumvents the learning to read problems of the decoding-disabled. *The Phonetic Reading Chain Series* is guaranteed to teach groups of students in grades three through twelve (and adults) to read all monosyllabic and polysyllabic words in a minimum of two years, provided that (1) all exercises of the daily format are used from the first day to the last, (2) the approximately one thousand pages of oral reading material are read and monitored as indicated, and (3) the program's cumulative tests are administered at the end of each unit so as to determine whether each student is achieving mastery. The time frame is based on daily classes of forty-five minutes' to one hour's duration.

The Phonetic Reading Chain Series is a system which processes the stimuli successfully in spite of the students' difficulties. This is accomplished by means of a highly structured organizational design, controlled oral reading content, a multisensory approach, and the maximum use of Robert Gagné's chaining concept. It consists of thirty-eight units that include all letter-sound associations. Inclusion of every conceivable combination is essential because provisions must be made for these student's inability to generalize — their inability to make inferences at the automatic level of learning.

To eliminate confusion and to ensure everlasting stabilization, each short vowel is introduced separately in the first five units and is reinforced throughout the first twenty-six units. Long vowels are introduced in Units 27A and 27B, after the students have successfully read about seven hundred pages of material, which include 5,280 short vowel multisyllabic words. This separation makes sense because only 15 percent to 20 percent of English words contain long vowels, and about 82 percent of those are not of the one syllable "vowel-consonant-e" variety (tame, while). By separating the introduction of the short and long vowels by 21 to 26 units, the students need to deal only with the one most-used sound for each vowel as they are experiencing success in learning to read. When the long vowels are introduced, also one at a time, the students make the transition from reading multisyllabic short vowel words to reading multisyllabic long vowel words with facility.

Hard c and g are separated from soft c and g by twenty-two units. Hard *c* and *g* must be completely stabilized before students are exposed to the large number of soft *c* and *g* words whose correct pronunciation depends on knowing that, generally, soft *c* and *g* precede *e* and *i*.

The ambiguities of the language are covered in Units 28 through 38. Because of their successful experiences in reading about 825 pages of controlled reading material which includes approximately 6,160 nonambiguous multisyllabic words, students are able to deal effectively with the ambiguities.

The oral reading material and the exercises of the daily format are designed to enable the students to easily attain the behavioral objectives. Cumulative tests evaluate the objectives after each unit is completed.

Behavioral Objectives

1. Students will be able to rapidly read the names and vocalize the sounds of all letter-sound associations in Unit 1 through Unit__ (last unit taught) with 100 percent accuracy.
2. Students will be able to respond with the letter names of all letter-sound associations in Unit 1 through Unit__ with 100

percent accuracy when their sounds are uttered in rapid-fire fashion.

3. Students will be able to write in cursive writing "pure" (no schwa) phonetic words that combine all letter-sound associations in Unit 1 through Unit__ with 90 percent to 100 percent accuracy.

4. In context, and from a one-hundred word list, students will be able to read orally the polysyllabic words selected from Unit 1 through Unit__ with 90 percent to 100 percent accuracy.

5. Students will be able to read orally the sight words in Unit 1 through Unit__ with 100 percent accuracy.

6. Students will be able to write in cursive writing the sight words in Unit 1 through Unit__ with 90 percent to 100 percent accuracy.

Daily Format

Each exercise of the daily format reinforces the previous ones: flash card drill, VAKT, sight word reading and spelling, word attack training, and oral reading practice. Students are totally involved in each exercise. Parts of the first two exercises are adaptations of techniques suggested by Gillingham and Stillman (1940).

Flash Card Drill: This is a fast-paced, rhythmical, two-part exercise that uses the visual, auditory, and kinesthetic (speech) modalities. In Part I, the students and the teacher say the letter's name and sound; in Part 2, the teacher gives the sound and the students, as a group, respond with the letter name. Daily card drill enables the students to meet Objectives 1 and 2. Observation of their daily performance is the evaluation.

VAKT: This is a visual-auditory-kinesthetic-tactile exercise that (1) further reinforces the letter-sound associations; (2) teaches the students the cursive equivalent of the letters; (3) teaches the students to properly combine the learned letter-sound associations in spelling dictated words; (4) teaches the students to automatically write letter-sound associations alone and in combination, a necessary prerequisite to expressive written language; (5) uses the kinesthetic modality twice as the cursive letters are written and articulated; (6) provides some of the skills needed in reading multisyllabic words; (7)

improves penmanship, and (8) totally involves the students. There is minimum use of the tactile modality because students use pens or pencils. Writing with their index fingers on sandpaper would make excellent use of the tactile modality. In VAKT, the students write a letter (or a combination of letters) several times *as* they say its name and sound. The teacher then dictates words in which the particular letter-sound association is used. Objective 3's goals are easily reached through the inclusion of the VAKT exercise in the daily format. Cumulative phonetic written tests evaluate their competency.

SIGHT WORD READING AND SPELLING: The students are taught to read and spell sight words in a combined teaching procedure. Because *The Phonetic Reading Chain Series*, in dealing so thoroughly with the phonetic aspects of our language, trains the students in attending to word parts, sight word mastery is facilitated. Nearly all sight words have some phonetic elements. Since these are known by the students, their attention can be focused on the nonphonetic irregularities through the use of special techniques involving all learning modalities. These techniques are a modification of Grace Fernald's (1943): (1) The teacher writes the sight word on the board in cursive writing, pronounces it, and establishes its meaning; (2) Phonetic letters are noted; (3) The irregularity is noted; (4) As the students look at the word on the board, they pronounce it. Then, in the manner of VAKT, they write the individual letters (orally emphasizing the irregularity), as they continue to look at the word on the board; (5) The same procedure is followed without the visual model; (6) The same procedure is followed, using a pencil and paper. Students must not copy the words because copying tends to be a motor exercise, with minimal visual and auditory stimulation. Daily attention to sight-word reading and spelling enables the students to meet Objectives 5 and 6. Cumulative sight-word spelling tests evaluate their competency.

WORD ATTACK TRAINING AND ORAL READING PRACTICE: Elimination of confusion is readily apparent in the composition of the oral reading content. At the beginning of the first twenty-five units are repetitive oral-reading exercises that provide not only repetition of a particular unit's newly taught letter-sound, but also reinforcement of letter-sound associations taught in all of the preceding units.

These practice exercises are comprised of nonwords so that z's, q's, and other less commonly used letters can be included, and so that b's, d's and p's can be emphasized. In the first eleven units, vowel discrimination is a major element of the repetitive exercises: for example, *stan, stin, ston, stun, sten*. Generally, the format of the practice exercises includes vertical rows of clumps, five nonwords to a clump. To effectively provide the opportunity for processing a vast amount of repetition rapidly, the students must deal with only one phonetic change from word to word to clump to clump. In the above example, the vowel changed. In the following samples, the first or last letter changes: *fin, pin, din, zin, quin; fab, fap, fat, faz, fan.*

Following the practice exercises is a highly structured continuum of real word exercises, each of which builds on the preceding one. All of these include monosyllabic and polysyllabic words comprised of only the letter-sound associations taught from Unit 1 through the unit being read: for instance, *orthodontist* and *historian* are a part of the *or* unit. *Absorbency, aorta,* and *notorious* are not. They are used in Units 26 (soft c), 27A (long a), and 36 (ious ending) respectively. Chaining the words in this fashion is extremely beneficial to the decoding-disabled because they no longer have to deal with unknown letter-sound associations by guessing. All words are readable.

In each unit, there is a deliberate uniformity in the design and hierarchical progression of the various oral reading exercises that follow the repetitive practice pages. Generally, a list of words is followed by sentences, paragraphs, or a story in which the words in the list are used. But it is the unique organization of these lists which provides for the unique needs of the decoding-disabled. Remember that after each of the following lists, its words are used in interesting oral reading material: (1) one syllable words; (2) two syllable words, with accented first syllable; (3) two syllable words, with accented second syllable; (4) three syllable words, with accented first syllable; (5) three syllable words, with accented second syllable; (6) three syllable words, with accented third syllable. This type of patterning continues through words of four, five, six and seven syllables. For further simplification, the words within a section are subdivided into similar or identical phonetic groupings: for example, in Unit 26, *convalesce, acquiesce,* and *reminisce;* in Unit 15, *inscription, subscription, conscription, description,* and *prescription.*

The author's focus on sounds and syllables is important because their correct pronunciation is crucial to comprehension. Sounds and syllables have meaning. For example, the vowel in these words determines the meaning: lust, list, last; suction, section. In these, the consonants do it: pedal, medal; internal, infernal. And in these, it is the syllable which determines the meaning: *at*tic, *rus*tic, *op*tic, *sep*tic; *in*stitute, *des*titute, *pros*titute.

To decrease confusion further, accented syllables are underlined in the word lists, but not in context, and not one standard syllabication rule is taught. The underlining of accented syllables is a concrete learning aid which highlights word parts for word attack training purposes. As the students learn and apply the accented syllable and unaccented syllable rules throughout the series, they inductively learn all they need to know about syllabication. The only two reading rules taught in this series are:

Accented syllables:	Higher voice, Louder voice.
	The vowel has a sound of its own.
Unaccented syllables:	Lower voice. Softer voice.
	The vowel has no sound of its own.

These rules apply to all multisyllabic words.

Because so many decoding-disabled students have been instructed with the whole word approach (look-say), they think they must read a multisyllabic word as if it were one long syllable. Therefore, they must be taught how to sequence sound clusters from left to right within words, and how to stress the accented syllable. Every language has a rhythm and cadence, a predictability. In *The Phonetic Reading Chain Series*, the decoding-disabled effectively learn these rhythmical patterns (and correct pronunciations) because of the phenomenal amount of controlled practice material devoted to word attack training. In addition to the repetitive oral reading exercises already discussed, another type that deals with accenting practice is included in the first eight units in a vertical layout: for example, *ban*na, *dan*na, *han*na, *lan*na, *ran*na; or, la*min*, la*man*, la*mon*, la*men*, la*mun*; or, da*muz*zal, da*mez*zal, da*moz*zal, da*miz*zal, da*maz*zal. Finally, word building exercises are used throughout the series, also in a vertical layout: *ap*, *ap*pa, appa*rat*, appa*rat*us; *del*, *del*ic, *del*ica, *del*ica*tes*, *del*ica*tes*sen.

Since the objective is to raise their reading vocabularies to the level of their speaking and listening vocabularies, the inclusion of multisyllabic words, from Unit 1 on, is crucial in teaching the decoding-disabled to read. Merely learning the letter-sound associations and their application in reading one syllable words will not automatically enable these students to read multisyllabic words. Practice, and more practice, in sequencing syllables in "safe" real words and nonwords will ultimately result in the decoding-disabled being able to recognize multisyllabic words as automatically as the normal reader. In this series, repetition in many guises allows for the necessary review and reinforcement of decoding skills so that the goal of automaticity is achieved. Reading orally is a must for the decoding-disabled because every possible learning "pathway" must be used simultaneously for long-lasting results.

To give the students maximum opportunity for reading practice, they are taught to subvocalize while the others are reading aloud in turns. Subvocalization provides for the use of the visual, auditory, and kinesthetic (speech) modalities, just as oral reading does. Subvocalization is a whispered "mouthing" of the words. The words are articulated exactly as if they were being read aloud.

Language lessons are correlated with the oral reading units so as to provide silent reading experience, vocabulary growth, and practice in getting meaning from context. Their content is also controlled so that all words contain only learned letter-sound associations.

By following the daily format and reading the oral reading books as indicated, the students will easily attain Objective 4. Cumulative oral reading tests determine their competency.

Students retain what they are taught in *The Phonetic Reading Chain Series* because of its unique design. When the course is completed, the skills they have learned will automatically be reinforced as they read material pertinent to their education or their earning a living.

While this series is technically a learning-to-read (decoding) program, students who have completed it have consistently demonstrated impressive growth on standardized reading achievement tests, which measure comprehension skills. The decoding-disabled, whose strengths at the representational (meaningful) level are sound, only need to learn to read.

Consult the Teacher's Manual of *The Phonetic Reading Chain Series* for additional detailed information regarding this proven series. Its components are: nine oral reading books, a language workbook, a teacher's manual, flash cards, and two cumulative test books.

REFERENCES

Crosby, R. *The Waysiders*. New York: Delacorte Press, 1968.

Fernald, G. *Remedial Technique in Basic School Subjects*. New York: McGraw-Hill, 1943.

Frank, R.W. *The Phonetic Reading Chain Series*. Johnstown, Pennsylvania: Mafex Associates, Inc., 1977.

Gagné, R. *The Conditions of Learning*. New York: Holt, Rinehart & Winston, 1965.

Gillingham, A., B. Stillman. *Remedial Training For Children With Specific Disability in Reading, Spelling, and Penmanship*. New York: Sackett and Wilhelms, 1940.

Johnson, D., H. Myklebust. *Learning Disabilities*. New York and London: Grune & Stratton, 1967.

Messineo, L. *Comparison Between Poor And Good Readers In Relation To Skill Development At The Automatic Level Of Organization*. Doctoral dissertation, University of Syracuse, 1971.

Money, J. *Reading Disability: Progress and Research Needs In Dyslexia*. Baltimore: Johns Hopkins Press, 1962.

Osgood, C.D. *A Behavioristic Analysis of Perception And Language As Cognitive Phenomena. Contemporary Approaches To Cognition*. Cambridge: Howard University Press, 1957.

Whiting, D., M. Schnell, and C. Drake. *Automatization In Dyslexic And Normal Children*. Minneapolis, 1966.

CHAPTER 21

IMPLEMENTATION OF MATHEMATICS PROGRAMS

Robert A. Shaw

INTRODUCTION

IMPLEMENTATION is one of the steps in the total curriculum development process. To make a new or revised program functional this step becomes essential. In terms of mathematics programs for learners with special needs the curriculum development steps and decisions must be placed within the proper framework. For the purposes of this chapter of this book the curriculum development steps will include: (1) needs assessment — an examination of the current state of affairs, (2) criteria for program development, (3) a program model, (4) suggested implementation procedures, and (5) evaluation procedures. Decisions on *what* and *how* to teach become a part of the program model.

NEEDS ASSESSMENT

The rationale for a needs assessment often begins when something is not functioning properly or because of some external pressure. To exemplify and to develop an awareness of this situation a portion of a curriculum evaluation report of a K-9 mathematics program in which the author participated is presented.

The Evolution of a Mathematics Program

In thinking about designing learning programs in mathematics for students with special learning needs it is necessary to explore the current status of mathematics programs from a functional approach.

It appears that programs in mathematics evolve in a direct relationship to the interests and abilities of those individuals in charge of such programs, often without specific guidelines for even an element like time. For example, in a particular K-6 elementary school the mathematics program has evolved as independent segments across *and* within grades with each teacher determining the amount of time allocated for instruction in mathematics. This time range within this school was from thirty-five minutes to five hours *per week*. Observations of mathematics-related activities gave evidence that the actual instructional time was even less since three to five different instructional groups existed within the classes.

In efforts to individualize, these interclass groupings are made and, again, time devoted to instruction is reduced proportionally by the number of groups. An economy-of-time principle emerges with: (1) each group being introduced to new material and given an assignment, (2) selected core (basic concepts and skills) areas receiving emphasis, and (3) levels of output behavior by the learners being reduced to factual information in a recall mode.

Regardless of whether a written or an "understood" curriculum guide exists, a textbook (or workbook) is selected to help implement the program in mathematics. This textbook serves to guide an instructor in presenting mathematics concepts to the learners. Often decisions are made to work through the textbook in somewhat of a random manner, depending on external pressures for including or excluding selected topics. In the school system of the evaluation report 90 percent of the learners in grade 5 had never been exposed to fractions on *any* developmental level. Geometry and measurement topics were not regularly presented. These topics were only included if extra time remained at the end of the school year.

In many situations such procedures are established and refined. With this refinement comes efficiency and success at this defined level. A given instructor now has two options: to broaden the scope and thus, introduce more decision making into this phase of the mathematics program or to continue on the established narrow path. The latter option appears to be the most dominant choice; thus, attitudes and belief systems become solidified and there is a resistance to change. If allowed to continue in this manner a mathematics program results that resembles swiss cheese — a program with many instructional and, in turn, conceptual gaps.

Some programs in some schools (as in this report) have arrived at this point and deficiencies are beginning to show in assessment and evaluation data. The results are cumulative. Criticism begins to occur and attention is drawn to the total program situation. Time appears to be an appropriate variable again, because the longer a given program is in existence with a given staff the more difficult it is to change. This situation and similar ones certainly indicate that curriculum revision is necessary.

Trends

Other contributing factors that serve to initiate a needs assessment come from society in general, education theorists and practitioners, content and method specialists, and federal and state regulations. The focus of this section will be on content and method as they relate to the learners with special needs.

For a period of time the emphasis in special education was on *what to teach*. The words of Inskeep (1938), Ingram (1968), and Meyer (1972) reflect this trend from the thirties through the sixties. Curriculum guides became very popular, even at the state level. After the content revolution in mathematics in the 1960s and early 1970s, the trend changed from the *what* to the *how* and methods books became abundant. In the 1970s and 1980s systems of instruction that link the *how* and the *what* were explored, for example, *Project MATH* (1976).

From research work in education and psychology a *new* trend developed. This current trend concerns developmental and diagnostic teaching of school mathematics which (hopefully) will lead to better problem solvers in the future. In less than ten years diagnostic work has progressed from error analysis to learning style or mode analysis with at least two books in this area: Reisman (1978) and Underhill et al. (1980).

In the 1980s the emergence of the microcomputers presents another influence and source that must be explored in terms of potential for presenting content in a different modality.

Under these conditions a needs assessment may indicate that a particular program in mathematics is out-of-date and not meeting the needs of the learners. Whatever the circumstances the current trends and needs provide us with a new opportunity to design and develop a mathematics program for all learners.

CRITERIA FOR PROGRAM DEVELOPMENT

An integrated (one that involves both the *what* and the *how*) approach to the selection and/or development of content in mathematics to meet the special learning needs of students implies that alterations to the present program or alternative programs are necessary. A comprehensive approach is implied. Cawley (1977) established minimum criteria by saying that comprehensive programming will have to include: (1) contrasting approaches based upon different curriculum models such as subject-matter *vs* broadfield *vs* child-centered, (2) varying approaches to the selection, development and presentation of content such as those within the broad areas of social studies and science, and (3) different approaches to basic skills such as those in language arts and mathematics.

Some of the reasons for alternative approaches for learners with special needs are: (1) this is what general education has offered to its participants, (2) no single school of thought has proven its superiority in meeting the needs of these learners, and (3) the needs of some learners may be better met via one approach than by another. The ingredients for every approach should be: (1) procedures for individual assessment in both individual and group situations, (2) assignment to and selection of instructional practices that are linked to assessment, (3) procedures for continuous assessment, (4) long-term patterns of organization of the scope and sequence of content, (5) appropriate sets of instructional materials and provisions for in-service training, and (6) some modest pre-implementation evaluation (Cawley, 1977).

The essence of such a program is a combination of curriculum (content) and instruction (method) which will represent: (1) a balanced representation of mathematics without an undue reliance upon arithmetical computation, (2) a reasonably well-defined relationship between assessment and program, (3) the capability to parcel out the effects of a problem in one area, e.g. reading problems, upon performance in another area, e.g. verbal problems, and (4) experiences that will tend to enhance the developmental status of the student in areas other than mathematics, e.g. logical thinking, concept development, Cawley et al. (1978).

Implications

If individuals who are responsible for the mathematics programs see the same needs as outlined in these sections and accept the given criteria, what implications are suggested? First, the concepts and skills of mathematics must be organized vertically [across the grade (age) levels] and horizontally (within grades) according to the developmental characteristics of the learners. The developmental characteristics must not be limited to just the cognitive ones. We must include attitudes and emotional development, social development, and physical growth and development. Considering these characteristics, it is obvious that each individual's development is unique and, by definition, handicapped learners are individuals whose developmental characteristics are not intact. For some, it is developmental delay and overall slower rates of development; for others it may be sensory impairments; for others it may be identifiable or nonidentifiable specific learning disabilities; and for others the source may be emotional. In regard to these learners curriculum development becomes more than the selection of content and the organizing of this content into a scope and sequence chart. Cawley (1977) stated that curriculum development for the learners with special needs must stand the rigors of the requirement which suggests that any learning deficiencies be: (1) prevented, (2) ameliorated, or (3) compensated for.

A second implication is that mathematics must be taught developmentally from verbal development to experience with real objects to representations that create visual images to the use of symbols. Heddens (1980) identifies these stages of concept development to be concrete, semiconcrete, semiabstract, and abstract.

Developmental teaching is an instructional process that involves selecting and using strategies and methods that take into account the developing characteristics of learners. In developmental teaching of mathematics the added dimension of a logical sequence of content is included in the decision-making process. The instructional procedures include the *input* behaviors of the teacher and the *output* behaviors of the learners in various interactive combinations. For example, the most common interactive is for an instructor to select or develop a worksheet and present this to the learners as a group and the learners respond by developing written responses to the questions or exercises in the worksheet. The input information is symbolic (in written form) as is the output information. Delimiting the instructional procedures only to this interactive reduces the chance of communicating with all of the learners.

The third implication is that if developmental teaching of mathematical concepts and skills was never attempted or the development was incomplete, then diagnostic-prescriptive teaching is necessary. This is especially true of grades five through nine. With these implications there is now the need to establish a program model that will give ample consideration to the needs and characteristics of the learners and assure a reasonable representation of mathematics.

A MATHEMATICS PROGRAM

Under strict conditions a mathematics program may be defined as that subset of mathematical concepts and skills that the majority, e.g. 75 to 80 percent, of the learners acquire and maintain for a period of time (as evidenced by test results). These concepts and skills are acquired from direct and indirect teaching-learning activities and will be a portion of all of the information presented or implied (thus, the subset designation). The presented information may also represent a subset of the total mathematics curriculum for a given level of learners. With this expansion to the total curriculum a framework has been established, which ranges from some form of a curriculum guide to what is presented in the classroom to what is learned and maintained. Defining a program in this manner serves to identify levels for decision making and provides a starting point for curriculum revision. Focusing on what the learners have acquired and what the teacher does from this point produces a program model.

A Program Model

General steps in program development begin with a content definition. First, define the program elements by identifying strand of content (S), content area (A), concepts and/or skills (C or K), e.g. S: whole numbers, A: Operations, C: Addition.

The lowest level (concepts and skills) represents the content of the criterion behaviors (desired learner performance level). In terms of a content taxonomy the next step is to determine where the particular concept or skill belongs, e.g. using Wilson's (from Glennon and

Wilson (1972) content taxonomy whole numbers would appear in D-1-. . .). In addition, find the placement of this element within a given curriculum guide and/or textbook series. Third, determine the general behaviors that will be expected of the learners, e.g. in whole number addition, rounding addends, estimating the sum, speculating on whether the estimated answer will be larger or smaller than the actual answer, and computing the answer are such behaviors. Fourth, determine the specific behaviors required, e.g. knowledge and skills for each step in an algorithm. Fifth, hypothesize if the placement and behaviors "fit" the "normal" growth patterns of learners in terms of affective, social, physical, cognitive, and psychomotor development. Are the learners ready for instruction in the area? If the answer is *no*, adjustments are necessary. If the answer is *yes*, then a base exists from which to determine any deficiencies. Sixth, select the simplest element within the given concept and determine the placement as was completed with the criterion behavior. A scope is now defined for selected topics and a task analysis, as outlined in Underhill et al.'s (1980) book, will present a sequence. The right section of the model in Figure 21-1 depicts the development thus far. To complete this section we need to determine the necessary prerequisite concepts and skills to begin a given topic (step seven) and to determine the developmental steps for each particular element of the sequence (step eight). For example, the prerequisite information for development of addition of whole numbers includes: sorting, classifying, counting, labeling and matching activities; the development involves objects, movement of the objects, naming and labeling "how many," drawing pictures, and writing number symbols. The sliding scale in the top left section of the model in Figure 21-1 represents this concern.

As mentioned previously, mathematics programming for the special needs learner involves more than determining scope and sequence; therefore, if the model in Figure 21-1 is reduced and scaled to represent a scope and sequence within a given grade or age level, other elements can be included (see Figure 21-2).

An essential element in program planning is screening and placement by using survey and analytical testing (Underhill et al., 1980) devices to determine where each learner is in concept and skill attainment — to determine his or her present level of functioning. As the screening element of the model in Figure 21-2 indicates, we

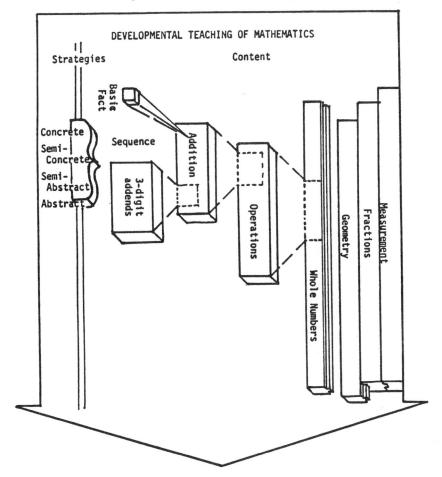

Figure 21-1. Program Model, Part 1.

should be able to identify levels of achievement within the content strands and place the learner accordingly. Information obtained from the initial screening situation can serve one of two functions: (1) to refer the learner for more detailed diagnostic analysis and remediation or (2) to place the learner within the instructional program. Clinical interviews and observations may be necessary to determine exactly what interactive (what combination of teacher input information *and* learner output behavior) works best for various learners.

If the criteria previously mentioned are to be adhered to, the conditions indicate that a continuous-progress program must be

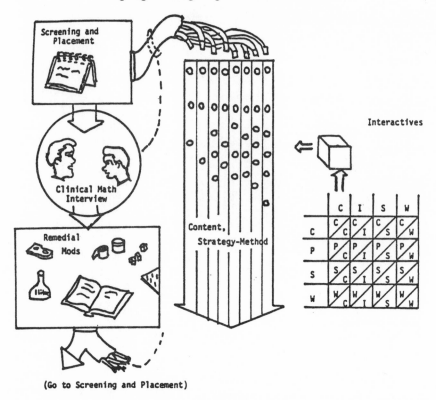

Figure 21-2. Program Model, Part 2.

established in mathematics in which each learner can function according to his or her abilities. An individualized program where only the rate differs *is not* being outlined because several research studies have indicated that this is not enough. Learners *need* large group instruction and interrelations; small group instruction so that they can gain a broader view of the concepts being presented while obtaining answers to individual questions; and individual work that includes personal attention and a time to think. Another element that is not present in many programs is a multiple-option curriculum defined in terms of the interactives (previously discussed). Such an interactive unit is described in detail in an article by Cawley et al. (1978). The matrix of the unit is included in Figure 21-2. The entire model has a research base in *Project MATH* (1976).

SUGGESTED IMPLEMENTATION PROCEDURES

What has been developed in this chapter is a mathematics programming concept that has a good chance of meeting the special mathematical learning needs of students at different levels. Implementation involves selling a concept rather than a particular program. Data from national and regional assessments suggest that we need to approach the teaching of mathematics in different ways and establish a continuous progress mathematics program where one acquired concept or skill builds a base for other concepts and skills. The first phase of an implementation procedure is to develop an awareness of what needs to be done and what is possible. We need to answer such questions concerning the teaching of mathematics as: (1) what do we say we are doing? (2) do we do what we say we are doing? (3) how well are we doing it? Articulation within and across grade levels is a necessity as we need to communicate. To develop and refine a new program concept such procedural models as The Concerns-Based Adoption Model (CBAM) from the Research and Development Center for Teacher Education of the University of Texas at Austin could be used. This model involves a change facilitator and such activities as probing, determining levels of use, and intervention if necessary.

In terms of a mathematics program we can start in the regular classroom by assessing current status, grouping for instruction, giving individual attention, identifying appropriate workmates, giving differentiated assignments and tests, and letting the learners use alternatives in learning and evaluation, e.g. tapes or slides. Cooperative arrangements with other individuals is the next phase if the classroom teacher needs diagnostic assistance. Monitoring of progress leads to the evaluation phase.

EVALUATION

In terms of the learners with special needs formative evaluation is essential. There is a need to know if a learner is progressing toward the selected criterion behaviors and if he or she is responding to the prescriptive mode(s) of instruction that has been identified. It should be noted that if the learners are involved in different modes of functioning, then these particular modes should also appear in the evaluation phase, whether it involves written responses, oral responses, or a demonstration.

A CONCLUDING STATEMENT

In this chapter the heart of the mathematics curriculum has been examined — the teaching-learning process as it relates to learners with special needs. It has been demonstrated that there are many needs in this area. Evidence indicates that we are teaching along a narrow path and content and method options must be expanded. A suggested model for such an expansion has been developed in this chapter. With a model such as this we have a base. The research needs are apparent and, with the renewed interest in the area, we have the opportunities to develop and implement a personalized teaching-learning mathematics program.

REFERENCES

Cawley, John F. Curriculum: One Perspective for Special Education. *Changing Perspectives in Special Education.* Columbus: Charles E. Merrill Publishing Co., 1977.

Cawley, John F.; Anne M. Fitzmaurice, Robert A. Shaw, Harris Kahn, and Herman Bates III. Mathematics and Learning Disabled Youth: The Upper Grade Levels. *Learning Disability Quarterly, 1*:37, 1978.

Glennon, Vincent J. and Wilson, John W. Diagnostic-Prescriptive Teaching. *The Slow Learner in Mathematics.* Washington, D.C., National Council of Teachers of Mathematics, 1972.

Heddens, James W. *Today's Mathematics.* Chicago: Science Research Associates, Inc., 1980.

Ingram, C. *Education of the Slow-Learning Child.* New York: Ronald Press, 1968.

Inskeep, A. *Teaching Dull and Retarded Children.* New York: The Macmillan Co., 1938.

Meyer, E. *Developing Units of Instruction: For the Mentally Retarded and Other Children with Learning Problems.* Dubuque: W.C. Brown Co., 1972.

Project MATH. Tulsa, Educational Progress Corporation, 1976.

Reisman, Fredricka K. *A Guide to the Diagnostic Teaching of Arithmetic.* Columbus: Charles E. Merrill Publishing Co., 1978.

Underhill, Robert G., A. Edward Uprichard, and James W. Heddens. *Diagnosing Mathematical Difficulties.* Columbus: Charles E. Merrill Publishing Co., 1980.

CHAPTER 22

IMPLEMENTATION OF CAREER EDUCATION PROGRAMS

Alfred J. Mannebach

INTRODUCTION

IN 1971, former Commissioner of Education Dr. Sidney P. Marland, Jr. (1971) delivered an important address entitled, "Career Education Now" to the Convention of the National Association of Secondary School Principals in Houston, Texas. Since that time the educational, business, and industrial community has been exposed to many thoughts, theories, conceptualizations and possibilities of career education. Pilot programs have been initiated, the public has been informed, personnel from business, industry and the community have been involved, a multitude of speeches have been presented, and millions of dollars have been spent. A massive effort has been made to develop the career education concept and to infuse it into school curricula. As Hoyt, et al. (1972) stated, "Few concepts introduced into the policy circles of American education have ever been met with such instant acclaim as career education."

Marland's address synthesized the isolated thoughts and positive concepts of many educators regarding the development of an educational system that would be better able to meet the emerging needs of all students. This is not surprising, for Herr (1972) pointed out that the concepts of career education are rooted deeply in our contemporary society historically, philosophically, sociologically, and legislatively. Goldhammer and Taylor (1972) stated that "Career Education is an idea whose time has come." Support for this statement was evidenced by the endorsements that the U.S. Office of Education and many organizations and associations provided nationally and by the interest and leadership provided at the state and local levels over the past twelve years.

The public has had little trouble identifying with and agreeing to the basic tenets of career education. Many school administrators, counselors, and teachers also endorse career education concepts.

However, when it comes to implementation, many have seen career education as massive educational reform, as something beyond the scope of which they were capable. They became uneasy when confronted with reorienting the entire curriculum or restructuring the total educational system around the career development concept. Yet, as Herr (1969) has written, such restructuring is possible and necessary. Bruner (1973) concurs that more positive ways are needed to provide continuity of learning for our youth when he writes, ". . . the first order of business in the transformation of our mode of educating is to revolutionize and revivify the idea of vocation or occupation." He goes on to state, "We are living . . . in a time of deep revolutionary change. Tinkering with the details of school organization without making room for a means of absorbing the wider revolution into our ways of educating is surely unworthy of us as a species."

School administrators, to a large extent, realize the problem. They may see the many possibilities of career education for individuals with special needs, but many lack concrete ideas regarding how to install or implement career education in their local school systems. They need help in initiating and implementing career education concepts, in analyzing career education components present, and in identifying essential elements needed to teach special needs learners effectively. For the most part, they are eager to implement career education, because if properly implemented, career education has many positive implications for special needs learners. However, as Hoyt et al. (1972) point out, "No matter how attractive as a concept, career education can emerge only from concrete efforts at implementation which must occur at two levels: (1) the policy level at which legislators, school boards, and administrators, perhaps influenced by public opinion, opt for a career education emphasis and (2) the classroom level at which teachers and counselors must develop or revise specific materials outlining and facilitating career education and apply them in their instructional activities. The danger for career education is that too many may endorse its concept while waiting for someone else to push for its implementation."

While career education was designed to meet the needs of all students, the Education For All Handicapped Children Act (P.L. 94-142), passed in 1975, mandated actions that would insure educational benefits and rights for handicapped children and their families. Shortly thereafter, Public Law 94-482, "The Educational Amendments of 1976," was passed. It included a complete revision of the Vocational Education Act of 1963. This act reflected a major change in the nation's social and economic awareness by focusing on the preparation of all students for employment. Legislation enacted during this period of time offered greater educational opportunities to handicapped and disadvantaged students who in many cases had been excluded from educational programs in the past.

The first time the Congress authorized the use of federal funds for career education was in 1974 when it enacted, as part of the Elementary and Secondary Education Act Ammendments of 1974, Section 406 — "Career Education" (Hoyt, 1981). Section 406 provided funds for the purpose of demonstrating the effectiveness of career education. In 1978, Public Law 95-207 — "Career Education Incentive Act" was passed by Congress to provide assistance to those who on their own decided to embrace the career education concept. Under this act, funds could be used to implement career education. However, the intent of Congress was that the implementation of K-12 career education be a state and local responsibility, not a federal responsibility. In 1983, the last year of P.L. 95-207, funds for the implementation of career education will no longer be available from the federal government. Clearly, with the role of the federal government in career education diminishing, the implementation of career education at the state and local level takes on special significance.

IMPLEMENTING CAREER EDUCATION AT THE STATE LEVEL

The onus for providing leadership in implementing career education during the 1980s is at the state level. Many states have moved forward successfully in implementing career education programs. States that have been successful in the implementation of career education have adhered to some basic principles of implementation. The following are basic principles that have been most significant in states' implementation programs.

1. Obtain a State Board of Education Policy Statement. To be

effective, career education must be included as a priority at the highest levels. A policy statement provides the framework for the development of programs and procedures.

2. Develop and publish a Philosophy of Career Education. Many definitions, theories, thoughts, and conceptualizations exist regarding career education. A broad definition of career education and a written philosophy that includes key beliefs provides the foundation upon which the local programs can be built.

3. Develop Goals and Objectives of Career Education. A clear specification of the intents and expected outcomes of career education programs, including attainable objectives for learners with special needs, furnishes program planners with the framework needed to develop viable programs.

4. Involve all Relevant Agencies and Organizations. When representatives from education, agriculture, business, industry, labor and the general public are informed about and involved in career education, the stage is set for cooperative and collaborative efforts to develop.

5. Agree on Methods of Financing Career Education. Because career education is generic in nature, much can be done by shifting or reallocating existing resources. However, state monies that provide the incentive for local school systems to get involved in career education are essential.

6. Provide Technical Assistance in Program Design. Local school personnel need help in designing programs for their system. Technical assistance from the state level helps local educators plan and initiate viable programs more quickly than without such assistance.

7. Establish Program Approval and Evaluation Procedures. Viable programs must adhere to predetermined standards and be accountable. State guidelines for the approval and evaluation of local programs stimulate quality program planning and implementation.

8. Plan and Develop Pre-Service and In-Service Educational Programs. Pre-service teacher education programs should include components that prepare prospective teachers to help special needs learners formulate realistic career development plans. Planned in-service educational programs help present teachers infuse career education concepts, information and activities into ongoing programs.

9. Establish Curriculum Development and Dissemination Centers. Persons involved with career education need access to information regarding career education. Such centers provide the information, resources and materials needed by local educators and the public to implement a viable career education program.

10. Develop Guidelines for Implementing Career Education in Local Schools. Local educational personnel need assistance in planning, organizing, implementing and evaluating career education programs. Guidelines regarding procedures to be followed in initiating career education are beneficial to local educational personnel.

While many other principles are involved in conducting quality career education programs, the above principles are most significant at the state level.

IMPLEMENTATION AT THE LOCAL LEVEL

The purpose of this section is to (1) identify strategies that can be used to enhance the implementation of career education, and (2) provide local school personnel and the public with an overview of their roles and responsibilities regarding the implementation of career education. As the chief change agents in the school system, school administrators are the key personnel in implementing career education. The superintendent at the district level and the principals at the building levels must provide the primary leadership. Administrative commitment and leadership are essential to the successful implementation of career education.

Mannebach (1973) and Mannebach and Stilwell (1974) developed a systems approach to installing career education. Key concepts identified in those publications will be reiterated here with specific reference to meeting the needs of special needs learners. The key components of implementing the program at the local level follow.

INVOLVE AND ORIENT KEY GROUPS. To be successful in designing programs for students with special needs, the involvement of many groups and individuals is necessary. Career education coordinators and special education teachers and coordinators must be involved in designing or planning the program. If various agencies within the community are to be involved, representative members must be included in the planning from the start. Those responsible for, involved with and affected by the program must be involved in the planning, implementing, and evaluating of the program.

One of the first actions needed is to obtain administrative commitment and board of education policy. School administrators, as the chief change agents, must be familiar with the concepts of career education and must be committed to implementing them in the school system. Unless the school administration realizes the potential of career education and opens the school system to the public for its input, support and understanding, career education will have little chance of reaching its full potential as a pervasive influence in the lives of students with special needs.

The Board of Education should write a policy statement specifying that implementation of career education is a priority educational goal. Goals that state the desired outcome of career education should be specified. Policies regarding community involvement should be reviewed and adequate resources should be allocated to attain the goals specified. Administrative commitment and Board of Education policy are crucial first steps in career education implementation.

The involvement of parents, employers, workers, educators, students and representatives from other organized groups and agencies in the community is also important. An advisory committee composed of interested and committed persons can be organized. Advisory committee members should show interest in career education, should be representative of the community, and should have time to serve. The primary function of the advisory committee will be to open doors to positive school-community involvement. Advisory committee members can serve as the liaison between the school, business and industry, and various community agencies and organizations. They will compose the core group to serve as change agents in the community.

School personnel and members of the advisory committee should explore career education programs presently in operation. Schools having career education programs can be visited and observed. Discussion and interaction regarding the positive and negative aspects of such programs can serve as the basis for assessing the career education concepts. Particular attention can be given assessing provisions made for students with special needs. Through assessment and evaluation, preliminary plans can be made to synthesize essential components and design an optimum career education program for the local community.

ANALYZE EDUCATION SYSTEM. After involving and orienting the community to the concept of career education, an analysis of the local education system can be made. Data can be collected regarding how well the system is meeting the needs of the school population and the community. Parents, employers, workers, former students and present students can be surveyed to determine the extent to which the curriculum is meeting their needs. An analysis of employment needs, including the knowledge, skills and attitudes needed for successful employment can be made. The educational needs of students with special needs should be identified. Evidence regarding the special needs of students can be collected and analyzed in regard to the implications for career education.

The next step is to evaluate the present curriculum. Questions regarding how well it prepares students to attain their educational and occupational objectives should be asked. The degree to which the curriculum helps students of all levels and needs become aware, explore and prepare for educational and occupational decisions should be analyzed. The present components of career education evident in the curriculum can be identified and those found lacking should be specified. An inventory of the students' knowledge and awareness of self, the world of work, and the social pressures that bear upon their educational and occupational decisions can be conducted. The evaluation of the curriculum should make evident the strengths and weaknesses of the educational system in regard to its implications for career development.

It is then necessary to identify and inventory the resources available to implement career education. An inventory can be made of the funds available to conduct career education activities, the provision for released teacher time, funds for curriculum development and review, staff time to observe successful career education programs, and changes needed in school plant, facilities, and equipment. A survey of untapped community resources should be made. Cooperative and collaborative arrangements as identified by Hoyt (1981) that utilize the community as the classroom should be considered. The inventory of resources can also include an evaluation of the attitudes of the community, students and faculty toward change, career education, and programs needed to assist special needs learners.

DEFINE GOALS. Following analysis of the educational system, the goals of the career education program should be defined. The goals can be specified for two major categories. Goals regarding the number of schools and students served, the time and scope of implementation, the completion of inservice education, and the integration of career education units and concepts constitute process goals. They are needed to provide a benchmark regarding progress made in implementing career education.

Goals regarding the desired career development outcomes of students within the educational system are also needed. These goals are stated as product goals. The overall product goals of the career education program should be specified. In addition, sub-goals for various grade levels should be defined. Sub-goals can be developed for grades K-3, 4-6, 7-8, 9-10, and 11-12 as well as for the individualized educational plans of learners with special needs. In addition, product goals for adult and continuing education can be specified. All sub-goals and objectives later developed should contribute to the overall product goals of the career education program.

SELECT/CREATE CAREER PROGRAM. After the process and product goals are specified, the optimum career education program for the school system can be selected and/or created. The program developed should be designed to attain the goals specified. In making decisions regarding the optimum program of career education to be implemented, several options can be considered. Certain aspects of the career education program can be adopted. Components identified while exploring career education pilot programs that will contribute to the attainment of the goals specified are especially suited for adoption. If changes in pilot programs observed are identified, the career education program will need to be adapted to the needs of the local educational system. It may be necessary to create certain components to compose a comprehensive career education program. Ultimately, a decision regarding program concept and structure must be made. The decision made should incorporate the most desirable elements of programs observed or conceptualized, should meet the needs of the community served by the school system, and should be designed to attain the goals and objectives specified.

PREPARE FOR PROGRAM INSTALLATION. After a decision has been made regarding the program concept and structure, a broader range of key personnel should be identified to prepare for program installation. Key personnel in the school system include the administrative, supervisory and guidance staffs and a core group of representative teachers. The core teachers should be instrumental in preparing the concept/content guidelines and in providing continuous in-service education to other teachers. Therefore, they should have the respect of their peers and should be able to work well with fellow teachers. Selection of key personnel is crucial to the implementation of career education in the school system.

The next step is to conduct in-service education for the key personnel. Various amounts of time may be needed, depending on the purposes and desired outcomes of the inservice education program. Consultants who are knowledgeable about the concept and structure being proposed should be used. A close working relationship between the consultants and those involved in the in-service education program should be developed. The consultant should help key personnel to become oriented to the philosophy and goals of career education, to gain an understanding of the concept/structure being proposed, to plan career education activities that will help attain the product goals specified, and to articulate and implement the career education program. Adequate time must be allocated for the key personnel to define their respective roles and to prepare concept/content guidelines. The guidelines developed should be compatible with the program concept/structure that has been selected to attain the product goals specified. Provision should be made for continuous involvement of advisory committee members and community personnel. The community should be informed of efforts being made to prepare for initiation of career education in the school system.

IMPLEMENT CAREER EDUCATION PROGRAM. The implementation of the career education program will involve the cooperation of many persons in the school and community. The key personnel in the school system should encourage and promote the implementation of career education. Key teachers who have participated in the in-service educational program should serve as the core group to implement career education in the school system. They can involve many persons in the community to assist in initiating and implementing career education activities appropriate to their level of teaching. Successful experience in implementing career education activities can help them attain the self-assurance and confidence they need to provide continuing in-service education for other teachers in the school system.

Key teachers who have participated in the in-service educational program and have attained success in integrating career education concepts in their teaching are the best resource persons to use in continuing in-service education. They can relate to the problems and concerns of their fellow teachers and are well prepared to help them initiate, integrate and implement career education concepts and activities.

Administrators, supervisors, counselors, and other school personnel can also participate in continuous in-service education. They can promote the implementation of career education, open the doors of the school to the public and facilitate school-community collaborative relationships. They can also publicize successful career education activities and caution against the use of practices that have proven to be unsuccessful.

The implementation of career education concepts and units will follow closely the continuing in-service education. As the teachers in the school system are provided continuing in-service education, they will begin to initiate and implement career education concepts in their teaching. Successful experience with career education activities will provide the impetus for further initiation, integration and implementation of career education concepts. After a period of time, each teacher will have developed certain generic skills that will facilitate the integration of career education concepts into their teaching on a continuing basis.

EVALUATE CAREER EDUCATON PROGRAM. The career education program must be evaluated to determine the extent to which needs are being fulfilled, process and product goals are attained, and decisions regarding program content/structure are realized.

Evaluations conducted can be continuous and periodic. The conduction of external evaluation constitutes periodic evaluation. Persons outside the local educational system who are involved in career education in other settings can be utilized periodically to review the career education programs being implemented. Personnel involved in external evaluation should be used as resource personnel and should not be regarded as evaluators. They should be familiar with the needs, goals and program content/structure being implemented. Periodic use of an outside evaluator can increase staff morale, question concepts being implemented, and provide new ideas.

The primary type of evaluation conducted should be continuous self-evaluation. Local people must be involved in program evaluation because they are the ones affected by the program and they are the ones responsible for implementing program changes. Through self-evaluation, program modifications can be made continuously and/or periodically. The school staff, in cooperation with the community and through interaction with parents, employers, workers, and members of the advisory committee, should adjust the career education program continuously and make process changes that will lead to program improvement. Periodically, specific data should be collected by the school staff to determine progress made toward process and product goals.

Analysis and reporting of findings should be carried on continuously as well as periodically. Communication is important to the success of the program. The evaluation made should be analyzed and reported to those involved with, responsible for and affected by the program. Continuous interaction among all those involved in the installation and implementation of career education should be encouraged. Sharing of experiences and ideas is essential. Periodic newsletters can be published and distributed to relate staff activities, community involvement, and successful techniques and concepts used and developed. Feedback is essential regarding the degree to which the career education program is meeting the needs identified and the process and product goals specified. The evaluation findings should have implications for modifying the program concept/structure selected and for improving the concept/content guidelines specified. Through evaluation and feedback, the system can be modified and improved until career education is an integral part of the total school system.

IMPLEMENTATION AT THE CLASSROOM LEVEL

Many successful ways have been demonstrated to implement career education in the classroom and in the community. A school may arrive at a particular approach depending on its philosophy, pupil needs, staff orientation, community readiness and other factors. According to Phipps (1974) three career education approaches commonly used to help students attain career development goals are the isolated activities approach, the unit approach, and the integrated curriculum approach.

THE ISOLATED ACTIVITIES APPROACH. This approach consists of conducting career education activities periodically throughout the year within the classroom, on field trips, or during school assembly programs. The activities are usually not correlated with the curriculum nor are they part of a systematic school-wide plan. The isolated activities approach is probably the easiest, although not the most effective way of implementing career education in a school. Individual teachers may conduct such activities successfully, however, a major disadvantage is that students may be unable to relate the isolated activities to their total school experience.

THE UNIT APPROACH. The unit approach involves spending a designated amount of time, usually from one to six weeks, on a particular theme or topic such as "Community Helpers" or "The Grocery Store." During the unit, most classroom activities focus on the unit theme. The unit approach is popular at the elementary level. It can be an effective means of imparting career information and providing hands-on experience for students. To be used system-wide, however, close coordination is required. The program must be articulated from grade level to grade level to ensure that duplication of units does not occur and that key concepts and activities are not omitted. The program should also be logically organized, psychologically sound and developmental in nature.

THE INTEGRATED CURRICULUM APPROACH. The integrated curriculum approach, or infusion as it is sometimes called, is endorsed by many authorities as the most effective approach to career education. It involves the integration or infusion of career education activities and concepts into the total curriculum. When this approach is used, all school subjects and activities relate to the career development needs of the student and become more relevant and interesting. The career implications of all subject matter taught are emphasized. While many individual teachers have mastered the infusion approach, few school systems have been totally successful in implementing the integrated curriculum approach. Schools have been successful in infusing career education concepts into the educational program when they have followed a planned process similar to the one described in the last section.

While the three approaches described tend to be most widely used, other approaches are possible. Mannebach and Stilwell (1974, 1978) advocate a Career Activity Team (CAT) to initiate career education learning activities. Whatever their composition, within the school a CAT may:

1. visit schools that have viable career education programs
2. attend career education conferences and workshops
3. provide in-service education for other teachers
4. share ideas and successful career education experiences
5. help teachers utilize the career education resources of the guidance department
6. inform the school administration of needs
7. team teach certain career education concepts
8. serve as resource persons
9. plan displays to depict careers
10. construct bulletin boards on career opportunities
11. plan and assist in conducting a career fair
12. develop a placement service for students
13. compile a list of career-related materials
14. review career education materials and resources
15. identify career education concepts to be taught
16. articulate career education content and objectives
17. identify resources needed
18. disseminate successful career education ideas and materials
19. compile a list of people who are willing to serve as resource persons in the classroom
20. present career education concepts at PTA meetings

Within the community, a CAT may:

1. identify potential field trip sites
2. identify part-time employment opportunities for students
3. involve lay citizens in an advisory capacity
4. identify community resources available for career education
5. survey how senior citizens can become involved
6. visit business and industrial firms to become aware of employment opportunities
7. interview early school leavers to determine why they left school
8. inform people in the community of the role they can play in career education
9. survey the community regarding the need for adult education

10. identify new formats for learning

The above are only a few of the direct activities in which a CAT may become involved. In addition, a CAT may plan many activities in which the students can get involved. Through two-way communication between teachers and students, relevant activities can be identified and undertaken. Student involvement is essential in a successful career education program. Students will have the opportunity to become involved only after teachers become aware of their career awareness, and plan meaningful career-related student activities. The initiation and establishment of CAT's within the school setting serves as a viable way to accomplish the task.

Summary

As career education becomes a more dominant aspect of school curricula, the special needs of all students must be addressed. The trend for the 1980s seems to be that the initiative for developing career education programs for learners with special needs must come increasingly from the state and local levels. In this chapter, suggestions have been presented that can chart the direction for the further development of career education programs, which will assist students in the career development process and help them to make mature career decisions.

REFERENCES

Bruner, Jerome. Continuity of Learning, *Saturday Review of Education, 1*:21-24, March, 1973.

Goldhammer, Keith and Robert E. Taylor. *Career Education. Prospective and Promise.* Columbus, Ohio: Charles E. Merrill Pub. Co., 1972.

Herr, Edwin L. *Review and Synthesis of Foundations for Career Education, Series 61.* The Center for Vocational and Technical Education, Columbus, Ohio: The Ohio State University, 1972, 82 pp.

Herr, E.L. "Unifying an Entire System of Education Around a Career Development Theme." Paper presented at the National Conference on Exemplary Programs and Projects, Atlanta, Georgia, March, 1969.

Hoyt, Kenneth B. *Career Education: Retrospect and Prospect.* Washington, D.C.: U.S. Government Printing Office, 1981.

Hoyt, Kenneth B., et al. *Career Education — What It Is and How To Do It.* Salt Lake City, Utah: The Olympus Publishing Co., 1972.

Mannebach, Alfred J. "A System for Installing Career Education at the Local Level." Paper presented at the annual meeting of the American Educational Research Association, New Orleans, Louisiana, March, 1973.

Mannebach, Alfred J. and William E. Stilwell. "Career Activities Team System." Paper presented at the annual meeting of the American Educational Research Association, Chicago, Illinois, April, 1974.

Mannebach, Alfred J. and William E. Stilwell. Developing Career Education Programs: A Team Approach. *The Vocational Guidance Quarterly, 26*:308-317, June, 1978.

Mannebach, Alfred J. and William E. Stilwell. Installing Career Education: A Systems Approach. *The Vocational Guidance Quarterly, 22*:180-188, March, 1974.

Marland, Sidney P., Jr., "Career Education Now." Speech delivered at the convention of the National Association of Secondary School Principals. Houston, Texas, January 23, 1971.

Phipps, Curtis, *Developmental Career Guidance Guide.* Division of Guidance Services, Kentucky State Department of Education, Frankfort, Kentucky, 1974.

CHAPTER 23

IMPLEMENTATION OF VOCATIONAL EDUCATION PROGRAMS

RICHARD W. WHINFIELD

W HILE all education may be considered as important, even necessary for today's job market, vocational education is specifically designed to prepare persons for occupations. Vocational education is frequently referred to as "the bridge between school and work."

The historical development of that specific education called Vocational has resulted in a general agreement that it is of less than baccalaureate degree level. In fact it is so defined in federal legislation. By contrast, occupational training at the baccalaureate level and above is, by quiet consent, "professional" education. This is a somewhat elitest distinction, but it is generally accepted, and so applied here.

Special needs as applied in this chapter cover a wide range of students. Each category probably has different vocational educational needs and students within categories also have different needs. Fortunately, one of the characteristics of employment is that there is a wide range of special skills and knowledge needed in a wide range of occupations. Some occupations may require a great variety of skills and special depths of knowledge in one or more subject areas, while other occupations may require minimal skills and knowledge. The variety is great enough to permit each student to prepare for several, even many jobs.

The trick is to be able to match student skills and knowledge with job skills and knowledge.

The role of vocational education in this interface process is to first understand the nature of the labor market, its needs and expectations, to translate those into educational programs, and finally to help students select programs that are appropriate, based on the student's experiences, interests and aptitudes.

It is an equation trying to be balanced in the most efficient way possible.

LABOR SUPPLY — LABOR NEEDS

The more stable, intractable side of that equation is the labor needs side. It is controlled by economics, technology, available resources and consumer demand. There is some flexibility in how job roles are defined, but for the most part, there are limitations on how many carpenters, nurses or typists will be required to perform the nation's work.

While the labor need requirements are more stable than labor supply, it is nonetheless constantly changing. Jobs in our society are tending to require ever increasing expectations. Increasingly high level skills are required, and an increasingly thorough knowledge base is anticipated; higher level decision making is also becoming more commonplace. Technology has further created a wide range of new occupations with a variety of restrictions and expectations for each.

Since humans are capable of a wide variety of skills, the supply side of the equation is expected to respond to labor need. Vocational Education must therefore build programs that reflect labor need and make these compatable with human potential.

On the labor supply side (the worker) of the equation vocational education is challenged to prepare persons with higher level skills and more sound knowledge bases for those entering the labor market, as well as those already in the labor market.

The problem of doing this is compounded by the fact that society is demanding that certain groups who were previously excluded from or restricted in the labor market now must be included universally. These include the physically and mentally handicapped, minorities, various ethnic groups and both sexes.

The simple equation of labor supply and labor demand is really not simple at all! Both sides of the equation are in constant flux and this places a very difficult burden on vocational education.

In simpler times, vocational education addressed the problem quite clearly, a student selected a job, took shop or learned to trade, and then went to work. But times are no longer simple. Educational solutions are not easy to come by.

VOCATIONAL EDUCATION STRATEGIES

There are two basic instructional modes used to provide vocational education in-school, and a combination of in-school/on-the-job education.

Additionally there are strategies to help individual students select appropriate occupations and occupational programs. The broadest strategy is one of career education. Starting at the elementary school, students are helped to develop career awareness, self-awareness, career expectations and career preparation.

This simple notion is not easily implemented however, and is discussed elsewhere in this book.

Another device used is vocational counseling. With the use of group and individual counseling, the process is aimed at helping each student understand his/her abilities, aptitudes and interests on the one hand, and to provide occupational information on the other. The hopeful, though not controlled outcome is occupational choice. Thus, youths and adults will be able to make occupational selections that will permit them to make maximum use of their skills and knowledge.

A further device used to help people prepare for jobs is the use of Individual Educational Plans (IEP's) developed by Pupil Planning Teams (PPTs). These have been mandated by law for certain youth. They are monitored, evaluated and modified on a regular basis. In high schools, these plans usually include some vocational education.

School/Work Instruction

One of the more promising devices for successfully creating the bridge between school and work are programs that provide real life experiences on real jobs. This requires that employers provide some instruction. Attention is given to individual learning that cannot be incorporated into school settings. It has the benefit of preparing students with the expectations of the work force. Those simple but elusive bits of knowledge such as regular attendance, promptness, proper attire, human relations, and productivity are made quite visible when a student is confronted with pay schedules.

Several variations of this process are currently being used.

Work Experience Programs

This is not generally a controlled learning experience, but it is intended to be a supervised experience in a work place. The object is to learn a particular set of skills, learn how to behave in a work place and learn how to become a productive employee.

A student is released from school for a portion of the day into an approved and monitored work place. If he is a productive worker, he may receive high school credit. What he/she learns is not necessarily related to the work performed in school.

This has a particular advantage for students who need to earn money to support themselves or their families and still be permitted to remain in school. However, though learning usually takes place, it is uncontrolled.

Diversified Occupational Education (DO), or Cooperative Work Experience (CWE)

This is similar to the work experience program but different students are placed into different occupational settings, based upon a student's occupational goals. A contract is developed for the school, the employing agency and the student, detailing the tasks to be learned in a specified time period.

Each student spends a portion of each day in school taking regular subjects as well as a course directly related to employment. In addition, each student is supervised on the job periodically by a CWE or DO coordinator, and in cooperation with the supervisor in the work place, evaluates the student's progress.

This has some real advantages for learning jobs of a semiskilled level. Since it is highly individualized, persons with handicaps can also participate.

Special Cooperative Work Experience

Groups of students in business education (typing, accounting, etc.) distributive education (merchandising, advertising, display, etc.) trades and industry (machinists, carpenters, etc.), agriculture (farming, farm equipment repair, etc.) and health occupations (nurse's aides, hospital workers) are placed part of the day in the work place. These are similar to CWE, but the on-the-job aspect is the culminating activity of skilled training in high school, or post-high school. After one or two years of learning special skills, students are placed in work places where they can apply those skills to real work situations. A course in school provides seminar-like activities so students may compare experiences and gain job-related information. This is a model similar to that of the medical intern.

Apprenticeship

This training program is usually for persons who have completed high school. Under a contract developed between an employer and a group representing the employee (a state government agency, an apprenticeship advisory committee, a labor union), a clearly defined training program that includes skills to be learned on-the-job and knowledge to be gained by attending school usually once a week is agreed upon. It is a long-term program of three to five years. A part of the contract includes a differential pay scale. As the apprentice becomes more proficient, the pay scale rises.

Once, apprenticeship was an exemplary program. But for achieving modern day learning efficiency and occupational specialization, it has tended to become obsolete, except for a few very traditional trades. It is also being used by some industries for leadership training. Midmanagement personnel come from those who have completed an apprenticeship program.

On-the-Job Training (OJT)

This is a modification of the apprenticeship program. Under a contract, trainees are placed in the work place, paid on a differential scale and are supervised periodically by the representative of some agency. Agencies such as CETA use the technique extensively. There is usually no classroom work associated with the program.

These five programs are, in theory, designed to provide a high level of individualized instruction.

Problems of School-Work Learning

In general, the less school-related the program, the lower level is the job. A concomitant of this is, the lower the level of pay, the lower the level of intellectual ability required.

There are inherent problems with all of these on-the-job programs:

THE PRODUCTION PROBLEM. The quality of the learning depends upon the interest of the employer in having the student learn. However, the employer must be production oriented, because his business success is based on that premise. Education of a trainee who may or may not continue in his employ is not likely to be a high priority for many employers.

SUPERVISION QUALITY. Even with the best industry, the skill of the on-the-job teacher will be highly diverse. Who the teacher is, is uncontrolled by the schools. Since they are generally unprepared to teach, the quality of teaching is likely to be low.

THE AVAILABILITY OF TRAINING SITES. This is subject to the whims of the economy. Such sites are more available in prosperous times than in recession times, quite the reverse of the need.

JOB MODIFICATION. The variety of training sites is a matter of chance. Employers must maintain continuity, and are unlikely to interrupt that continuity with periodic temporary employees, particularly trainees.

UNSTABLE EMPLOYMENT. Employers are not bound to follow contracts. They can and do terminate employees with little or no notice, creating administrative and scheduling problems for schools, as well as seriously interrupting a student's learning.

A variety of incentives and practices have been devised to help alleviate some of these problems. Tax breaks, special relief from minimum pay laws and special provisions in government contracts have opened up more job sites. A concerted effort to bring about cooperation is underway with local, state, and national vocational advisory committees and manpower committees. These are all efforts to try to alleviate some of the problems.

SCHOOL INSTRUCTION

The other major process being used by vocational education to prepare persons for employment is the institutional training practice, which is the traditional in-school program. This provides important learning opportunities to a wide range of students.

In-school means just what it sounds like. Vocational skills, knowledge and attitudes are taught within the school. It is, in most cases, the most time-efficient way to prepare persons for employment. The curriculum can be highly organized, controlled and properly evaluated. It can be individualized to a substantial degree. It can create, to a large extent, the atmosphere of a business or industry. But in most schools, the in-school vocational education is limited in its potential effectiveness by having to conform to schedules that severely cut into learning. Where a student in one of the on-the-job programs has a half day at work, he/she can become quite involved. But when there is a limit of two, or even one school period (and a period can be as short as 45 minutes in high school), not much practice or learning can occur in a shop or office practice room, where setup and cleanup are a part of the activities.

In addition, in-school programs have the problem of inflexibility. Equipment becomes dated in ever-shortening time and replacement is increasingly more expensive. Curriculum tends to become stagnant, because teachers, as well as equipment and facilities have trouble keeping up-dated. The teacher problem becomes more significant by the fact that teachers' salaries are falling even further behind business and industrial incomes and many vocational teachers are attracted away from education.

In-school vocational instruction appears to be becoming increasingly difficult to maintain. The increasing diversity of students has still further created a problem, for vocational teachers are generally ill-prepared to deal with the diversity.

Efforts have been and are being made to modify these in-school programs. The modifications are directed at providing a maximum of individualized learning.

Competency-based vocational education is one of the bases of such instruction. Job skills and knowledge are carefully analyzed, and goals stated with measurable behavioral achievement identified. Modules of instruction can be assembled in different ways for different students and for different occupational goals.

Various administrative structures have been designed to bring together enough students to meet the enrollment requirements for employing teachers and for the development of facilities. Several small school systems share facilities, or a special agency such as New York's Board of Cooperative Education, or Connecticut's Educational Service Center may be developed. And finally, special vocational schools may be developed for students with similar learning abilities.

Problems of In-School Vocational Instruction

There are three problems associated with in-school vocational education.

COST. The cost of institutionalized vocational instruction is generally higher than for general education. The greater the number of students, the higher the cost. That is not always the case with academic programs where the principle cost is the teacher.

TIME. The time a student is actually learning a job in the school setting is quite limited, particularly in Comprehensive High Schools with schedules controlled by the academic side of the program. A large portion of a period is taken up with setting up and cleaning up.

ARTIFICIALITY. A school shop cannot provide effective shop situations that relate to actually working on the job. The environment is primarily for learning, not for productivity. Shop or lab behavior is not influenced by older workers, or pay incentives.

Conclusions

It is common for educators, primarily academic educators to believe that students who have academic problems might be better off in "shop."

"Can't work with his head — let him work with his hands," is perhaps a blatant statement but one many educators believe in. It is of course, not necessarily true. But there are two factors that are educationally important in the action of placing non-academically skilled youth into vocational programs.

1. Preparation of employment is, by nature or at least by definition, an attempt to match a person's skills and knowledge to job needs. If a match can be made (and since there is variety not only in the kinds of jobs but in levels of skills required) these students in vocational education should not fail. The competitive edge is minimized and it is generally agreed that students will learn if they succeed. And if they succeed, they will stay in school.

2. Students who are not skilled in dealing with academic subjects are frequently unmotivated to learn those subjects because they are "dull." In the related instructions of vocational education, math, science and even English can be made very meaningful and students can succeed.

Bright students can profit from vocational education, too. Having job skills and knowledge can provide alternative career paths or serve as a basis for further higher level skills and knowledge. Vocational education can be for all persons.

Summary

Vocational education is designed to prepare students for work (1) because of the diversity of jobs in the labor market and (2) because most students will spend a large portion of their lives in some kind of occupational pursuit. Vocational education is an important component of education, not just for youth, but for all ages of the work life and even after.

To meet the diverse needs of the many kinds of students who need vocational preparation or upgrading, vocational education is trying to provide individualized guidance and instruction. A variety of strategies are being used, both within the school and within the labor force. Of all phases of education, vocational education is one of the most pragmatic aspects of education. Instruction is for both social productivity and for individual survival. It is potentially important to all groups of special needs students.

REFERENCES

Finch, Curtis R., and John R. Crunkilton. *Curriculum Development in Vocational and Technical Education.* Boston, MA: Allyn & Bacon.

Mitchell, E.F. *Cooperative Vocational Education: Principles, Methods, and Problems.* Boston, MA: Allyn & Bacon, 1975.

Phelps, L. Allen; and Ronald J. Lutz. *Career Exploration and Preparation for the Special Need Learner.* Boston, MA: Allyn & Bacon, 1979.

Wenrich, Ralph C. and J. William Wenrich. *Leadership in Administration of Vocational and Technical Education.* Columbus, OH: Charles E. Merrill Pub. Co., 1974.

Wentling, Tim L. *Evaluating Occupational Education and Training Programs.* Boston, MA: Allyn & Bacon, 1980.

Section IV

Research and Evaluation

CHAPTER 24

INCORPORATING PROGRAM EVALUATION INTO SPECIAL EDUCATION SERVICES: A SYSTEMS APPROACH TO SPECIAL EDUCATION PROGRAM EVALUATION

CHARLES A. MAHER, MARY KATHERINE HAWRYLUK, AND DAVID W. WINIKUR

INCREASINGLY, special education program evaluation, commonly defined as a process of gathering information and making judgments about special education program effectiveness, quality, or worth, has been recognized as an essential part of a special education service delivery system (Cronbach & Associates, 1980; Salvia & Ysseldyke, 1981; Maher & Bennett, in press). However, whether the special education system is embedded in a school or school district, or exists as part of an intermediate unit or state agency, a common concern seems to unite practitioners involved in special education program evaluation: how to incorporate program evaluation into the system so that trustworthy information can be obtained and so that meaningful evaluation can occur. More specifically, when attempting to establish special education program evaluation into normal operating routines, several questions seem prominent to those involved in the task:

1. What is special education program evaluation?
2. How can a school or school district organize for special education program evaluation?
3. How can special education services be viewed so that important questions, issues, and concerns can be addressed?
4. What kinds of programs are most amenable to evaluation, and how can other programs be placed in a form ready for evaluation?
5. What kinds of evaluation methods and procedures are most appropriate?

The task of incorporating program evaluation into a special education service delivery system is essentially a complex endeavor: It requires the involvement of people and processes in various parts of the larger school system; it requires a comprehensive view on evaluation and where it meshes with other system components. The purpose of this paper is to describe the major procedures of a systems approach to special education program evaluation, an approach that has been applied by the authors in numerous school settings and, most recently, in a New Jersey statewide planned change effort, entitled "Project to Study the Effectiveness of Alternative Special Education Service Delivery Systems."

The systems approach consists of a set of procedures that are usefully seen in terms of seven phases:

1. Developing a Program Evaluation Team;
2. Describing the Current Special Education System;
3. Planning Special Education Program Evaluations;
4. Implementing the Special Education Program Evaluation;
5. Reviewing and Disseminating Evaluation Information;
6. Describing Special Education System Changes;
7. Evaluating Special Education Program Evaluation Services.

These seven phases and their related procedures are appropriately considered a systems approach to special education program evaluation for three primary reasons. First, within the context of the seven phases of the approach, program evaluation is seen as one part of a special education system, being affected by and affecting the nature of that system. Second, within the same context, program evaluation also is considered a "system" that includes different parts that must mesh in some efficient and effective fashion. Third, through application of the procedures during each phase of the approach, the complexities of a special education system became apparent, particularly the various stages of development of the various special education programs that currently do exist as well as the inter-relatedness between and among the different programs. Due to space limitation, it is not possible in this paper to detail all aspects of the systems approach, including particular organizational assessment and other evaluation materials discussed. Where appropriate, relevant references for additional information have been cited. Each phase of the approach is now described below.

Developing a Program Evaluation Team

In school systems, a range of program decision makers is involved in the planning and provision of special education services, including school administrators, special and regular education teachers, and pupil personnel services staff. Each of these groups possesses a somewhat different perspective on what constitutes quality special education and on the types of information needed in the special education service planning process. The utility of special education program evaluation is determined in large part by the extent to which evaluation activities and results address the needs of these different groups (Maher & Illback, in press). Thus, it is recommended that the task of evaluating special education services be carried out by a team of school personnel who represent relevant special education decision-making groups. Typically, a school district's Special Education Program Evaluation Team (hereafter referred to as Team) is comprised of five to eight members:

1. the Director of Special Services who typically serves as Team chairperson;
2. a special education teacher;
3. a regular education teacher;
4. a pupil personnel service staff person, e.g. a school psychologist;
5. a school administrator, e.g. a building principal, and, in some cases,
6. a parent of a special education student.

In addition, a professional program evaluator (either a member of the district's research and evaluation unit, or an external consultant) often serves in an advisory capacity to the Team, providing technical assistance with evaluation activities, as well as training in program evaluation principles and group decision-making methods. (For information about training of Teams, the reader should contact the first author.)

The Team has three major functions: To plan and develop the special education program evaluation conducted each year; to oversee the implementation of special education program evaluation activities; and to evaluate the worth of the special education program evaluation services provided each year. The Team exercises these functions through a series of evaluation activities conducted over the course of the school year which occur within the context of the remaining six phases of the systems approach.

Describing the Current Special Education System

The first task of the Team, usually carried out at the beginning of a school year (or every two or three years depending on the stability of the system), is to describe the current status and characteristics of the district's special service delivery system, from an organizational perspective. This description, referred to as an Organizational Assessment (O.A.), provides answers to three evaluation questions. The first question is, "What special education services are currently being provided in the five areas of special education service and in terms of constituent service programs?" There are service areas and examples of constituent programs in each area:

1. *Assessment Services*, consisting of programs such as a kindergarten screening program, preplacement evaluation, IEP annual review, and formative instruction evaluation.
2. *Instructional Services*, consisting of programs such as, reading programs, mathematics programs, resource rooms, special classrooms, physical education programs.
3. *Related Services*, such as counseling programs, physical and occupational therapy, and transportation.
4. *Administrative Services*, such as case management, cost analysis, and information management.

The second question is, "What are the characteristics of the various programs through which these services are provided?" The third question is, "How are these programs perceived?" The information obtained through this O.A. serves as "baseline" data in the measurement of organizational change in special services delivery over time, i.e. over the school year.

During this first phase, the Team engages in three sets of activities: selection and/or development of O.A. procedures; management of the implementation of the O.A.; and review and synthesis of the O.A. results. In terms of O.A. procedures, two general types of data are collected in order to describe the special education system. First, program design data about all special education service programs provided in the district are obtained. These data serve to delineate program goals and procedures, as well as the number and characteristics of program clients and personnel. Second, perceptual data are obtained about the special education services that have been provided. These data are obtained from service providers and program consumers, e.g. pupils, parents, focusing on their understanding of the purpose and methods of different programs, as well as their satisfaction with program outcomes. The above kinds of program data are generally obtained by means of Program Profile Questionnaires completed by an administrator or staff member or every program. Perceptual data typically are collected by means of surveys administered to randomly selected members of different groups of special education service providers (teachers, administrators and pupil personnel staff) and consumers (parents, students). (A complete set of Organizational Assessment materials can be obtained upon request from the first author).

Management of the implementation of the O.A. requires that the Team educate program administrators and staff as to the purpose of this evaluation activity; monitor the appropriateness and adequacy of the administration of O.A procedures to program personnel; and address procedural problems, e.g. confusion of school personnel on the meaning of certain survey questions, as well as "political" issues, e.g. administrator resistance to the O.A. because of time demands, which arise in relation to O.A. activities.

The Team's final task during this Phase is to review and summarize the information collected through the O.A. This involves compilation of the Program Profiles for each program, and analysis of the consumer and service provider perceptual data. Typically, salient points of information emerging from the O.A. are dissminated to school administrators, and in some cases, to all personnel, through a brief written report and/or an oral presentation at a faculty meeting.

Planning Special Education Program Evaluations

During this second phase, which occurs at the beginning of the school year, the Team prepares for the special education program evaluations to be conducted over the course of the year. This phase requires that the Team accomplish three tasks:

1. selection of the special education programs to be evaluated during the year,
2. development of an Evaluation Program Design for each program selected, and
3. development of a written Special Education Evaluation Plan.

The task of selecting the programs to be evaluated requires that the Team survey the district's special education program decision makers, by means of interview or written questionnaires, to identify their evaluation information needs. Then the Team determines whether, and how, these information needs might be met during the coming year, and makes a final selection of programs to be evaluated. Four questions serve to guide the Team's selection of programs to be evaluated:

1. For which special education programs is evaluation information needed, and for what purposes, e.g. for decision making about program continuation?
2. What factors seem to have influenced program decision makers' desire for evaluation information on each program, e.g. anticipated funding cuts?
3. What resources are needed to evaluate each program, and what resources are available?
4. What are the anticipated benefits and possible negative consequences of evaluating each program at this time?

Following program selection, the Team develops an Evaluation Program Design (EPD) for each program. The EPD is a written statement of the evaluation to be conducted for each selected program. The EPD describes the following:

1. the general purposes of the evaluation;
2. the evaluation questions posed by program decision makers, describing their information needs;
3. procedures to be used for data collection;
4. procedures for ensuring that client and staff rights are protected, e.g. confidentiality measures;
5. data analytic procedures;
6. expected informational outcomes of the evaluation;
7. resources to be allocated for evaluation activities, i.e. personnel to be involved and their specific responsibilities, amount of funding requested, and technological resources to be used; and
8. the timeline for evaluation activities.

Development of the EPD for each program requires close collaboration between the Team and program administrators and staff, in order to match available resources with the needs of the program personnel. In addition, technical assistance from a professional program evaluator may be needed in order to ensure that evaluation procedures are selected which are appropriate to the type of program being evaluated, the evaluation questions being asked, and the desired informational outcomes. Table 25-I outlines sample evaluation questions, procedures and outcomes for programs belonging to each of the five special education service areas.

Once the EPD for each selected program has been completed, the Team develops a written Special Education Program Evaluation Plan for the year. The Evaluation Plan provides an overview of all of the program evaluation services to be provided over the course of the year and has the following components:

1. Statement of the general purpose and goals of the evaluation services.
2. Listing of the programs to be evaluated, with a brief rationale for their selection.
3. Written EPD for each program.
4. "Timeline — and Resource Allocation Chart" for all of the evaluation services to be provided during the year.
5. Description of administrative policies and procedures to be followed by the Team in managing program evaluation activities, i.e. the roles and responsibilities of each Team member and of key program decision makers in each program, lines and methods of communication between the Team and program personnel, procedures to be used for conflict resolution within the Team and between the Team and other school personnel.

Once the Evaluation Plan has been written, it is disseminated to relevant school administrators and other program decision makers for review. The final Plan then becomes a "public" document, available to all interested school personnel.

Implementing Special Education Program Evaluations

After the program evaluation services to be provided during the year have been delineated in a written Evaluation Plan, the activities of the Team center on ensuring that the evaluation services are carried out as intended. During this phase, the Team has two tasks: preparation of school personnel for involvement in evaluation ac-

TABLE 24-I

SAMPLE EVALUATION QUESTIONS, PROCEDURES AND OUTCOMES

Program Type	Typical Evaluation Question	Evaluation Model and Procedures	Evaluation Outcome
1. Assessment Preplacement Evaluation Program	Are the district's procedures for determining special education eligibility technically adequate and fair?	Accreditation model procedures, using APA standards for the use of tests	Delineation of the extent to which evaluation procedures adhere to APA standards
2. Instruction Reading Instruction Program for learning disabled students at the high school level	To what extent are students in this program progressing toward designated skill goals?	Goal-based Model, using goal attainment scaling	Pre- and Post-goal Attainment Scores Goal Attainment Change Scores
3. Related Services Group Counseling Program for emotionally disturbed students in the middle school	To what extent is disruptive behavior on the part of those students decreasing?	Goal-based Model, measuring attainment of behavioral objectives	Delineation of the degree of counseling goal attainment
4. Personnel Development Teacher Consultation by School Psychologists	To what extent do teachers find consultative services helpful in working with handicapped students?	Consumer satisfaction surveys	Delineation of level of teacher satisfaction with different aspects of consultation
5. Administrative Multidisciplinary Evaluation Team	To what extent are Team decision-making practices effective and efficient?	Transactional Model, using interviews with Team members	Description of Team members' perceptions of the Team decision-making process

tivities; and monitoring the implementation of each program evaluation.

The Team's personnel preparation efforts include "technical training" of program personnel responsible for carrying out various evaluation activities, as well as more general education of all program personnel as to the nature, purpose, and implications of the evaluation being conducted. Technical training of program staff is provided by means of evaluation workshops, written instructional material, as well as ongoing consultation from Team members over the course of the evaluation. Brief presentations at staff meetings and written memos are the methods typically used for informing other program personnel about evaluation activities.

The Team's monitoring efforts during this phase are guided by three questions about the implementation of each evaluation:

1. Are evaluation procedures (data collection, data analysis) being carried out according to the EPD?
2. Are there any unintended positive or negative side effects that appear to be related to the evaluation, e.g. teacher concern about job security?
3. What measures should the Team take to address difficulties that have arisen in the course of evaluation activities, e.g. additional meetings with program personnel in order to correct misunderstandings about the evaluation, revision of planned evaluation procedures.

In carrying out its monitoring tasks, the Team uses a variety of formal and informal methods to assess implementation of the evaluations including interviews with program staff, review of documents and records emanating from evaluation activities, e.g. data sheets, and on-site observation of evaluation activities.

Reviewing and Disseminating Evaluation Information

As each program evaluation in the Special Education Evaluation Plan is completed, the Team reviews the evaluation results and disseminates them to relevant program decision makers. The Team's principal goal during this phase is to make the evaluation information as useful as possible for program planning and development purposes. In this regard, five questions guide the Team's review of the results of each evaluation:

1. What were the original evaluation questions and how do these results relate to these questions?
2. Which results appear to be most relevant to the program decision makers current informational needs?
3. What factors related to the implementation of the evaluation must be taken into account in interpreting and using these results, e.g. difficulties with data collection?
4. What factors "external" to the actual program evaluation must be considered in relation to these results, e.g. modifications in the structure of the program being evaluated?
5. In what form should these results be disseminated to the program decision makers?

Usually, the Team arrives at the answers to these questions through discussion among its members with program personnel. However, in some cases, especially when the evaluation design is complex or when extensive, sophisticated statistical analyses of the data should have been performed, it is important to obtain assistance from a professional program evaluation consultant.

In its dissemination of evaluation results, the Team attends both to the *content* of the information given to program decision makers and to the *mode* of presentation of this information. In terms of content, the most salient results, directly relevant to the decision makers' program planning concerns, should be emphasized (Maher & Bennett, in press). In addition, the results should generally be accompanied by specific suggestions as to how they can be used in program decision making (Maher, 1981). The selection of the mode(s) of presentation should be guided by expressed preferences of the program decision makers. In general, however, it is useful to provide evaluation results in both oral and written form. Furthermore, evaluation reports (both oral and written) should be succinct, use clear language, and be appropriate to the level of sophistication of the program decision makers' understanding about the evaluation. Furthermore, it is essential that evaluation results be disseminated to program decision makers in a timely manner — i.e. well before the planning decisions requiring the evaluation information are to be made (Cox, 1977).

Describing Changes in the Special Education System

During this phase, which occurs toward the end of the school year, the Team conducts a follow-up Organization Assessment (O.A.), using the same data collection procedures used for the baseline organization assessment (Phase 2). Once the follow-up O.A. has been implemented, the Team has two tasks: to review the follow-up data to determine what organizational changes have occurred in special education service delivery over the course of the year, and to describe these changes in the form of summary reports disseminated to special education program decision makers.

The Team's review of the results of the follow-up O.A. is a two-step precedure. The first step is comparison of the program profile and perceptual data collected during this phase with those from the baseline O.A., in order to identify changes in the special education system. In this regard, the Team examines both quantitative changes, e.g. on increase in the number of clients served by a particular program, a decrease in funds allocated for certain services and qualitative changes, e.g. modification of program goal, adoption of new instructional methods. Procedures used for this comparative analysis generally include narrative description, and procedures such as descriptive statistics and some inferential statistical methods.

The second step of the review process involves formulation of hypotheses about "internal" and "external" factors that may be related to the identified changes in special service delivery. Three questions serve to guide this hyposthesis generation process:

1. What changes in the nature, availability or allocation of resources within the school system or special education department might be related to the observed organizational changes, e.g. reassignment of program personnel?
2. What environmental influences may be associated with observed changes in the district's special education system, e.g. state or federal funding decreases, new special education legislation, community support for a particular program?
3. How many quantitative or qualitative changes in one special education program can be related to changes in another pro-

gram, e.g. an increase in the number of students served in one program might result in a decrease in the students served by a related program?

Methods used in formulating hypotheses about the O.A. results include Team discussion, as well as interviews with relevant program personnel, with assistance, as needed, from the evaluation consultant. Throughout this process, however, the tentativeness of the hypotheses generated is emphasized. It is recognized that O.A. results are not those of a controlled experimental study, and that the number of internal and external influences impinging on special service delivery in a given year preclude definitive statements about "causes" of observed changes.

After the results of the follow-up O.A have been reviewed, the Team reaches consensus on the findings that are most relevant to special education service planning and disseminates the findings to relevant program decision makers. Typically, the O.A. results are disseminated by means of written summary reports given to program administrators, being supplemented by oral presentations to all special education personnel at faculty meetings.

Evaluating Special Education Program Evaluation Services

In order to ensure the utility and quality of special education program evaluation itself, the Team undertakes an evaluation of the evaluation services that have been provided. This evaluation phase, which generally occurs in June of the school year, involves two interrelated activities: (1) Assessment of Team functioning and effectiveness; and (2) Examination of the adequacy and appropriateness of the evaluation services provided during the year.

Three questions serve to focus the Team's evaluation of its own functioning: (1) To what extent were Team members able to involve school personnel in various evaluation activities, e.g. responding to O.A. surveys, carrying out data collection procedures? (2) To what extent was Team decision making efficient? (3) To what extent was the Team perceived as helpful and effective in its training, consultation, monitoring and information dissemination activities? These evaluation questions are addressed through team discussion, as well as interviews or surveys of program personnel who were involved with the Team over the year.

In the Team's evaluation of evaluation services five criteria for quality program evaluation are examined:

1. *Usefulness* of evaluation information for program decision making.
2. *Practicality* of evaluation activities, i.e. the extent to which they could be incorporated into ongoing special education service delivery.
3. *Perceived Worth* of the program evaluations conducted, in relation to their cost, i.e. financial and human effort cost.
4. The extent to which evaluation activities adhered to *Legal* and *Ethical* standards.
5. *Technical Adequacy* of data collection, data analytic and dissemination methods.

Methods used in assessing evaluation services according to these criteria include Team discussion, structured interviews with program decision makers, an Evaluation Satisfaction Questionnaire administered to all special education personnel, and independent judgments from the program evaluation consultant. Input from a professional evaluation consultant is especially necessary with regard to the technical adequacy of evaluation procedures and the legal and ethical propriety of evaluation activities.

Clearly, this evaluation of program evaluation services is worthwhile only to the extent that it is used in planning future evaluation activities. Hence, the final task of the Team during this phase is to prepare a summary report of this evaluation, delineating specific recommendations for changes in Team functioning or evaluation service provision for the following year. Such changes might include changes in the composition or operational procedures of the Team, elimination of certain evaluation procedures, adoption of new training approaches, or use of different methods for disseminating evaluation information. This summary report can be kept by the special services director and given to the new Team the following year.

Summary

This paper has provided a general overview of a systems approach to special education program evaluation that has been successfully applied by the authors for incorporating evaluation into special education systems. When used within the context of a planned change approach to special education, and with a recognition that primary concern is for development and improvement of special education services, the approach can be useful to special education practitioners in systems of various size and scope.

REFERENCES

Cox, M. Managerial style: Implications for utilization of evaluation information. *Evaluation Quarterly, 3*, 28-36, 1977.

Cronbach, L.J., & Associates. *Toward Reform of Program Evaluation*. San Francisco: Jossey-Bass, 1980.

Maher, C.A. Program evaluation of a day school for conduct program adolescents. *Psychology In The Schools, 19*, 45-57, 1981.

Maher, C.A., & R.E. Bennett. *Planning and Evaluating Special Education Services*. Englewood Cliffs, NJ: Prentice-Hall. (In press.)

Maher, C.A., & R.J. Illback. Planning for the delivery of special education services: A multidimensional needs assessment framework. *Evaluation and Program Planning*. (In press.)

Salvia, J., & J. Ysseldyke. *Assessment and Remediation in Special Education*. New York: McGraw-Hill, 1981.

CHAPTER 25

USING GOAL-REFERENCED DATA AGGREGATES TO REVIEW AND EVALUATE SPECIAL EDUCATION SERVICES

CHARLES A. MAHER AND ROBERT J. ILLBACK

P ROGRAM goals are important aspects of any system for planning and evaluating special education services (Maher & Bennett, in press). A goal-based approach lends direction to program planning and implementation by requiring explicit specification of desired program outcomes. Moreover, a focus on program goals also can provide several indices (a) of program planning and efficiency; (b) of staff compliance with service delivery procedures, and (c) of program effectiveness. Various kinds of goal-referenced data aggregates can be useful to a special education program manager in evaluating (a) quality of services provided, (b) staff performance, and (c) program goal attainment. This is the case whether the program is a special education school or department of special services, or a smaller unit such as a resource room or self-contained classroom.

The importance of program goals and objectives, and evaluating goal attainment, is apparent to most managers of special education programs (Maher, 1981; Rothman, 1980). What is not so clear, though, is how aggregate data from a goal-based approach to providing special education services can be used by managers to detect service delivery problem areas, and to improve service problems. This paper describes and illustrates various approaches to using goal-referenced data (aggregates) to review, to evaluate, and to improve special education services. These approaches will be discussed within the context of a special education day school for conduct problem adolescents, where concern existed among program managers and staff for evaluating various aspects of the quality of special education services.

Delineating the Data-base for Goal-referenced Evaluation

Within this school's special education service delivery system, each pupil had a number of goal-directed educational interventions, based on educational, social, or vocational goals usually stated as part of their IEPs. It was the school's philosophy that, if goals could not be articulated by staff, then the utility of an educational intervention may be questionable. Thus, if program managers or staff wanted information about which pupils were receiving goal-directed educational intervention plans, the following evaluation questions might be appropriate to answer:

(a) What is the average number of goal-directed interventions per pupil?

(b) Which pupils have fewer goal plans than the others?

(c) Are the small numbers of goal plans for these pupils justified, or should they be increased in number?

(d) If these small numbers of goal plans are justifiable, are these justifications documented in the pupil's records?

(e) Who are the pupils with large numbers of goal plans?

(f) What are the diagnostic, demographic, physical, medical, psychological and functional differences between and among those groups who have large numbers of goal plans and those having very few?

(g) If there are no obvious differences between and among those groups that justify a large number of goal-directed interventions for some and a relatively small number for others, what are the factors and determinants of this difference in amount of services/training being provided. Is this reasonable?

These kinds of questions can be answered by completion of a table similar to Table 25-I that focuses on pupils in a particular educational unit.

Obviously, all the questions related to the number and frequency of goal plans, and differences in numbers of goal plans among pupil groups, will not, and cannot, be answered by the statistics presented in Table 25-I. However, these statistics can serve as a jumping-off point for more incisive inquiries about the quality of services being provided to each pupil.

TABLE 25-I

NUMBER OF GOAL-DIRECTED INTERVENTIONS PER PUPIL

(1) *Pupil Name*	(2) *# of Instructional* *Goal Plans*	(3) *# of Related Service* *Goal Plans*	(4) *Total # of* *Goal Plans*
A.A.	6	3	9
C.J.	6	2	8
J.W.	7	3	10
D.B.	4	1	'5
M.J.	1	3	4
G.B.	2	5	7
R.J.	3	0	3
J.J.	5	1	6
R.B.	8	3	11
L.M.	5	4	9
Total	47	25	72
Average # of Goals Per Pupil	4.7	2.5	7.2
Proportion of Goal Plans in Instructional and Related Service Areas	65%	35%	100%

Using the Data-base for Program Monitoring

The goals related to the number of goal-directed interventions to be initiated or implemented by the staff of the various program areas may differ from one school or unit to the next. However, once a goal is set, a program manager may wish to observe that the goal is being attained and take corrective action if it is not.

By examining the statistics presented in Columns 2 and 3 of Table 25-I, a program manager can ascertain the proportion of goal plans that are in place within a particular program area. This procedure provides a simple and convenient indication of the utilization of goal-directed treatment plans in different units within the school district.

The reasons why more goal-directed intervention plans are instituted by some staff than others cannot be determined by these statistics. Nor do these statistics provide any guidelines on what corrective action to take. They do, however, indicate whether corrective action is, or is not, needed.

At times, simply communicating such statistics to the staff without any further comment or discussion leads to spontaneous corrective action. For example, if program staff realized that its goal-directed treatment plans are much lower in number than those being implemented in other areas, it may, without any necessity for further communication, rectify its deficiencies. This rather simple device of compiling and presenting comparative statistics on quality of care and quality of documentation can obviate the need for prolonged and occasionally unpleasant discussions and confrontations.

If a goal-directed framework for conceptualizing, implementing, and evaluating special education services is adopted by a school, one need not read the entire record of a pupil to determine if the individual is receiving intervention services. A quick determination of the number of goal plans in effect should be indicative of the education being provided. The absence of any goal plans can be accepted as evidence of the absence of any education in a particular area, e.g. reading, social skills.

The reasons for a particular child's admission to a special education school are varied, and not delineating a set of treatment goals could be considered justifiable in some situations. However, if a goal-directed intervention plan is indeed nonexistent for any particular pupil, a manager, team, or staff member may wish to document the reasons for such absences of intervention plans. A table, such as the one in Table 25-II, that can be compiled with relative ease, permits a program manager to determine the number of individuals without any intervention plans and to verify if such absences are documented.

Intervention vs. Programming

At this point, a differentiation should be made between *intervention* and *programming*. In a large number of schools, the daily or weekly schedule of a pupil is accepted as "proof" of intervention. In a goal-directed framework, it is expected that for each program prescribed for the pupil, such as might be stated on an IEP, an outcome goal be specified and a rationale for the entire goal be provided. If this is not done, the temptation to "program" individuals for services that they may not need, or from which they may not benefit (for cosmetic, budgetary, and logistic considerations, rather than for habilitative

TABLE 25-II

PUPILS WITHOUT ANY GOAL-DIRECTED
INTERVENTION PLANS

(1) *Pupil Name*	(2) *Reason for Absence Indicated in Writing*
L.S.	No
R.J.	No
S.M.	Yes
J.C.	No
M.M.	Yes
A.B.	Yes
F.H.	Yes
E.M.	No
B.S.	Yes
G.T.	Yes
C.C.	Yes
N.F.	No
P.D.	No
B.W.	Yes
E.U.	Yes
V.G.	No

reasons), becomes quite tempting, and practitioners may continue
to send pupils to program areas for months without thinking about,
specifying, or evaluating any ostensible benefits that the pupil might
derive from attending such activities. Therefore, the absence of goal-
directed interventions, i.e. expected outcomes prespecified in observable and measurable terms, can be viewed as an absence of educational interventions, not withstanding the number of hours of "programming" on pupils' IEPs, which can at times very efficiently serve
to mask (a) a lack of progress, (b) the need for various types of ser-

vices (c) a need for different environments, (d) unnecessary interventions, or (e) the complete lack of education.

Here again, as previously discussed, the individual and aggregate indicators based on goal-directed interventions do not provide the program manager with answers as to why certain deficiencies exist. Nor do such statistics specify what actions the program manager should or could take. They do, however, pinpoint exceptions or deficiencies that merit further investigation and may require corrective actions.

Assessing Intervention Efficiency

Tables 25-III and 25-IV present models that permit a program manager to examine some indices that *could* be indicative of the "efficiency" of various program areas. If, in a school, a general consensus has been established that all educational plans should specify an expected outcome as a result of the intervention, then each pupil receiving service in a program area should have at least one current goal-directed intervention specified by that program area. In Table 25-IV, Column 5 indicates the degree to which each program area seems to be complying with the goal-directed framework. Column 5 displays the average number of goal plans per pupil.

A program manager examining column 5 of Table 25-IV can very quickly determine the degree of compliance in different program areas. An investigation of the reasons for poor compliance can lead to corrective action. It should be mentioned that corrective action need not always be punitive or involve sanctions. In some instances, providing training and guidance to staff of a program area can very expeditiously remedy the deficiency. In other instances, individuals need to be instructed on how to budget their time. Sometimes, as indicated previously, merely presenting the statistics in Table 25-IV to all program staff "triggers" self-corrective activities by those programs that are not in compliance with standards to which they have previously agreed.

Interpreting the indicators of column 6 is somewhat more difficult. It could be assumed that a program manager may wish to see one goal per pupil. However, as the number of goal-based intervention plans per pupil increases, a point of diminishing return may be reached. For example, the program area of science, that seems to have six goal plans per pupil, may be undertaking too much.

TABLE 25-III

GOAL-DIRECTED INTERVENTION PLANS PER PUPIL BY PROGRAMS

Pupil Name	Couns	Math	LA	SCI	SStudies	WStudies	Read	LSkills	TOTAL
					Program				
L.B.	2	NA	1	1	0	NA	NA	1	5
R.M.	0	3	NA	NA	2	2	0	0	7
J.J.	1*	2	NA	2	NA	NA	0	4	9
B.L.	NA	3	1	NA	NA	NA	1	5	10
T.O.	NA	4	NA	2	3	3	1	2	15
P.H.	3	2	NA	2	NA	4	2	0	13
V.M.	0	NA	NA	3	1	1	2	3	10
E.P.	NA	NA	NA	3	2	1	1	1	8
G.B.	NA	3	4	NA	NA	1	0	2	10
S.W.	NA	1	NA	1	1	1	1	0	5
TOTAL	6	18	6	14	9	13	8	18	92

NA = not applicable, some pupils did not attend that program

TABLE 25-IV

INDICES ON GOAL-DIRECTED INTERVENTION
PLANS BY PROGRAM AREA

(1) Program Area	(2) # Of Pupils Enrolled	(3) # of Pupils with at Least One Goal Plan	(4) Total #of Goal Plans	(5) % of Pupils with Goal Plans	(6) x Number of Goal Plans Per Pupil
Counseling	15	7	7	50%	.5
Mathematics	25	25	52	100%	2/0
Language Arts	30	11	47	33%	1.5
Science	15	10	90	66%	6.0
Social Studies	16	1	1	6%	.06
Work Study	11	9	28	82%	2.5
Reading	22	22	37	100%	1.7
Life Skills	48	40	100	83%	2.0
TOTAL	182	125	362	69%	1.98 (x)

Perhaps by setting a large number of concurrent goals for a pupil, the attainment of goals is inhibited. Thus, in this instance, a lesser number of goal plans may be more "efficient" of staff time and more "effective" in the attainment of educational outcomes.

Utilizing a goal-directed educational framework for evaluating the efficiency of special educational services can also allow for more efficient personnel allocations. In a "traditional" nongoal-directed framework, it is not unusual to find the most assertive program manager acquiring the largest number of staff. In other instances, managers who "program" pupils, i.e. provide a number of hours of activities for a large number of pupils without specifying or attaining therapeutic outcomes, are allotted the largest contingent of staff. At times, such allotments are based on spurious statistics such as number of pupils seen or number of hours of "programming" provided per pupil. A more sensitive index for making personnel allocations would be the number of goal-directed interventions per pupil, which is based on pupil needs. When goal-directed interventions cannot be specified, the need for the services being provided should be questioned.

Indicators of Educational Outcomes

A goal-directed educational framework not only facilitates the review and evaluation of the efficiency of educational procedures, such as compliance with standards, number of goal-directed interventions, and the like, but it also enhances a manager or staff member's capability to evaluate the effectiveness of educational interventions.

If goal-directed interventions are to have educational viability, a certain percentage of these goals should be attained by pupils. If the large majority of goal-directed interventions results in failure, the utility of providing certain intervention services to those pupils can be questioned. In other instances, where a large number of goal plans are not attained, evaluation can focus on the attainability or degree of difficulty of those goals, as well as the effectiveness of the educational methods being used to attain those goals.

Table 25-V presents the number of goal plans that have been set and terminated for each pupil. Some of these goal plans were terminated because the goal was attained (column 3); others were terminated because of the lack of any discernable progress toward the goal (column 4).

The overall rate of goal attainment for all students is 40 percent. Obviously, there is no way to determine if this is an acceptable rate of educational success. However, once such data are compiled for the first time in a school, certain explicit objectives can be set or are implicitly accepted as standards. For example, if the rate of goal attainment was 40 percent in the first year of a goal-directed educational framework, one would expect that either this rate will remain stable or improve. A precipitous drop in rate of success to 20 percent or 30 percent in the second year would be a cue to a staff member or manager to start investigating the determinants of this decline.

Some staff and program managers can also use the 40 percent rate of success as a baseline to set up an objective for the coming year that stipulates a 65 percent or 70 percent rate of goal attainment. This process would be analogous to management by objectives, except that instead of being applied to intervening managerial pro-

TABLE 25-V

INTERVENTION GOALS SUCCESSFULLY
ATTAINED OR ABANDONED

(1) Pupil	(2) # of Terminated Goals	(3) # of Successfully Completed Goals	(4) # of Abandoned Goals	(5) Percent of Success	(6) Percent of Failure
M.A.	5	3	2	60%	40%
J.P.	2	0	2	0%	100%
V.L.	1	0	1	0%	100%
D.D.	10	7	3	70%	30%
B.E.	12	2	10	17%	83%
C.M.	8	3	5	38%	62%
K.O.	3	0	3	0%	100%
T.V.	4	3	1	75%	25%
N.T.	5	2	3	40%	60%
TOTAL	50	20	30	40%	60%

cedures, the objective is applied to educational outcomes.

Table 25-VI displays a model that can be used to examine goal attainment rates by program areas. Column 8 presents the rate of goal attainment in different program areas. In this example, it appears that 100 percent of the goals have been attained in social studies. This could be an indication that this program is doing an excellent job in planning for attainable goals and using treatment methods that are appropriate and conducive to goal attainment. A program manager may wish to evaluate the determinants of such a high degree of success. Further examinations might reveal that this high rate of success is spurious, as trivial goals are being set for pupils. Column 9 indicates that 92 percent of the goals set by the counseling program end in failure. This may be due to a variety of factors. It could be that the methods being implemented are not effective treatment methods. Perhaps the population being served consists of the most severely handicapped individuals. It could also be hypothesized that the goals being set by the program are too demanding and are, hence, unattainable. A further factor that might account for this low rate of goal attainment could be the premature abandonment of goal plans.

The number of goals attained per hour of programming (Column

TABLE 25-VI

GOAL ATTAINMENT RATES IN
PROGRAM AREAS

(1) Program	(2) # of Pupils	(3) Total # of Hours Programmed for All Pupils	(4) Goal Plans Implemented & Terminated	(5) $\bar{x}$ # of Goals Implemented Per Hour of Programming	(6) $\bar{x}$ Goals Attained Per Hour	(7) # of Goals Attained	(8) % of Goals Attained	(9) % of Goals not Attained
Life Skills	80	240	120	.5	.25	60	50%	50%
Work Study	15	30	15	.5	.3	10	75%	25%
Social Studies	20	60	5	.1	.08	5	100%	.0%
Counseling	20	40	30	.75	.05	2	8%	92%
Mathematics	31	40	75	1.9	1.1	44	59%	41%
Science	17	30	22	.7	.6	17	77%	23%
Language Arts	28	55	38	.7	.2	9	24%	76%
Reading	24	60	13	.2	.13	8	62%	38%
TOTAL	235	555	318	.6 ($\bar{x}$)	.3 ($\bar{x}$)	155	49%	51%

5) may not be the best index for reviewing the effectiveness and efficiency of educational programs, as different goals will require different amounts of time. This index can, however, provide data on the cost of attaining goals in different program areas. Some goals will be more costly to attain than others. If the needs of the pupil are such that specific types of interventions are not absolutely or definitely indicated, but rather one of several plausible intervention modalities are suggested, the program manager may opt for the more cost-efficient goals given particular resource limitations. Thus, a goal-planning framework can facilitate the determination of cost-effective intervention modalities, and lead to an augmentation of cost-effective habilitative services without necessarily diminishing the frequency, intensity, and duration of services.

Summary and Conclusion

The examples discussed above suggest that a goal-directed educational framework is not only an appropriate vehicle for specifying and monitoring individual intervention plans, but significantly facilitates pupil IEP reviews and program evaluations, based on aggregate data compiled from individual goal-directed educational plans. Such aggregate statistical reports do not, in all instances, provide the direct solutions for the exceptions and deficiencies that they uncover. Indeed, upon further investigation, it may be realized that statistics that seem indicative of deficiencies may be indicative of quality care. Thus, goal-referenced approaches must be used flexibly and creatively.

REFERENCES

Maher, C.A. Training of managers in program planning and evaluation: Comparison of two approaches. *Journal of Organizational Behavior Management, 3,* 45-56, 1981.

Maher, C.A., & R.E. Bennett. *The Planning and evaluation of special education and related services.* Englewood Cliffs, NJ: Prentice-Hall. (In preparation.)

Rothman, J. *Using research in organizations.* Beverly Hills, CA: Sage, 1980.

CHAPTER 26

ISSUES IN EVALUATING THE IMPACT OF SPECIAL EDUCATION

RANDY ELLIOT BENNETT AND CHARLES A. MAHER

APPROPRIATE education for handicapped children entails the provision of a variety of direct and indirect services for this population. These services can be broadly classified as assessment, instruction, related services, staff development, and administration (Maher & Bennett, in press). Evaluation of these various services is being increasingly seen as an important activity for local, state, and federal agencies as public demands for accountability in education increase and available resources decline (Maher & Illback, in press). Despite this growing concern, there has been little recent discussion in the professional literature about evaluating the impact of special education programs.

This paper discusses three issues critical to the evaluation of impacts or outcomes in special education. Though not unique to special education, these issues must nevertheless be addressed within that context if the effects of special services are to be accurately documented. These issues are the (a) importance of impact evaluation, (b) adequacy of currently available assessment tools, and (c) meaning or interpretation of outcome evaluation results.

The Importance of Impact Evaluation

In special as in general education, evaluation efforts have emphasized the determination of program impact with relative infrequency. Instead, evaluation efforts have typically tended to center upon program operations or processes, e.g. Blaschke, Note 1; Stearns, Green, & David, Note 2.

This paper is based in part on a presentation made at the annual meeting of the American Psychological Association, Los Angeles, August, 1981.

The focus of evaluation on the operations or processes of special education can be understood within the context of a number of factors. First, the legal and professional codes commonly used to plan, deliver, and evaluate services for the handicapped are markedly process-oriented. The most striking example of such a code is PL 94-142, which, with the exception of goal-oriented individualized education programs, mandates operations: due *process* guarantees for parents; *procedures* for conducting preplacement evaluation; the *provision* of a free appropriate education to handicapped children. The APA *Standards for Educational and Psychological Tests* (1974), which has been recommended for use in guiding special education assessment (Bennett, 1981a; Salvia & Ysseldyke, 1981), likewise describes acceptable *practice* for such operations as selecting, administering, and interpreting tests. The orientation of both the *Standards* and PL 94-142 would seem then, to direct the special education practitioner's attention to program activities as opposed to program outcomes.

A second factor related to the process-focus of special education program evaluation is the recency of national initiatives on behalf of educating the handicapped. PL 94-142, enacted in 1975, began to see implementation in 1977 (Office of Education, 1977). Though full implementation was targeted for 1980, the mandates of the law have yet to be fully carried out (Department of Education, 1980). Given the recency of program installation, the concern of special educators at local, state, and federal levels has understandably been with implementing, and evaluating the operation of, programs mandated by the law.

Third, a host of evaluation and interpretation problems exist that make the assessment of special education program impacts difficult. For example, because of the law's mandate for individualized education programs, handicapped children being served in the same group-instructional arrangement may not necessarily share common goals or receive comparable educational treatments. In addition, a lack of appropriate tools for assessing the handicapped and guidelines for interpreting program impacts, both discussed in subsequent sections of this paper, discourage the assessment of program outcomes.

The emphasis that has been placed on process in the evaluation of special education programs is in many ways appropriate. Process evaluation can provide valuable insight into whether a special education program (be it an assessment, instruction, related-service, staff development or administrative program) is being implemented as planned (Anderson & Ball, 1978). Additionally, such evaluation provides at least part of the information needed for understanding the relationship between program operations and effects and, hence, for developing and improving programs (Messick, 1975).

There can, however, be no doubt that outcomes and their documentation are central to the success of special education efforts. As a number of recent federal court suits have demonstrated, both parents and the courts believe program *effects* to be the "bottom line," not only in relation to instructional programs, e.g. *Armstrong v. Kline,* 1979, but also in relation to other educational services such as assessment, e.g. *Larry P. v. Riles,* 1979. Along with the concerns of parents of handicapped children and concerns of the courts, special educators must also recognize the importance of outcome documentation in satisfying the demands of the general public for educational accountability. Such documentation is of critical importance in times of decreasing resources that force greater and greater selectivity in the funding of human-service programs. Finally, and most importantly, it is only through attention to outcomes that effective programs can be identified and replicated, and ineffective or detrimental ones improved or discontinued.

The Adequacy of Currently Available Assessment Tools

A second issue of importance in the evaluation of special education outcomes, particularly instructional impacts, relates to the availability of appropriate assessment tools. Tools appropriate for assessment of the handicapped can be considered to be those judged technically adequate for use with these populations.

A major problem connected with judging the technical adequacy of available measures, however, is the lack of relevant, readily accessible technical data. Measures are not valid or reliable in and of themselves, but rather are valid and reliable when used for specific purposes with specific populations (Messick, 1975; *Standards,* 1974). Thus, the data needed for determining adequacy must come from studies of those measures with *handicapped* populations. Unfortunately, publishers' evidence for the adequacy of their measures is usually based on data from *general* populations, e.g. see the technical manuals for the *Peabody Individual Achievement Test* and the *Key Math Diagnostic Arithmetic Test.* Furthermore, although increasing numbers of population-specific studies are being independently conducted e.g. Dean, 1979, 1980, they have not yet been summarized in a way that allows the practitioner to easily judge the adequacy of particular measures for evaluating members of specific handicapped groups.*

Not only is there very little population-specific data on many commonly used special education measures, but there is also very little data on modifications, extended time, translation to braille or cassette, use of readers or recorders, routinely made to those measures (Ragosta, Note 3; Sherman, Note 4). For example, little data appears to be available to show whether such popular test modifications as braille measure the same constructs or predict to the same criteria as the original version of the test.

A second problem connected with the issue of the appropriateness of instruments for the handicapped is that no major effort has yet been undertaken to address the assessment needs of some special populations (Bennett, 1981b). This is particularly true for relatively small populations such as the deaf, blind, deaf-blind, and severely retarded. Major test publishers have little motivation to develop measures for use with these populations because the likelihood of their recovering development costs for such tools is very slight, and federal and foundation funds have not generally been made available for development efforts.

While the lack of readily accessible technical data and tools specifically constructed for use with the handicapped presents problems for the evaluation of instructional and related service outcomes, these deficiencies should not prevent attempts to assess special education program effects. Published and unpublished literature can be searched for technical data, measures can be constructed, and local adequacy studies undertaken. In addition, "multimethod" strategies of assessment can be employed (Ball, 1981; Bennett, Note 5; Cronbach & Associates, 1980; Maher & Illback, in press). In the absence of proven measures, the use of a number of

---

*Salvia and Ysseldyke (1981) have critiqued a wide range of measures commonly used in assessment of handicapped populations. Their critiques, however, are based upon information presented in instrument manuals and hence omit much relevant information about the utility of currently available devices.

unproven tools may provide the evaluator with significant information if results from the various measures all point, even if only weakly, to achievement of a particular outcome. Finally, measures possessing levels of reliability that would normally be considered low for individual assessment should not automatically be discarded (Joint Committee on Standards for Educational Evaluation, 1981). These measures can often be used for *group*-assessment purpose because measurement error dramatically decreases as the size of the group being evaluated is increased (Stanley, 1971). This means that measures of unknown or relatively low precision can be used given that moderate-size samples are available for program evaluation.

The Interpretation of Program Results

The final issue to be discussed in the evaluation of special education program outcomes centers upon the interpretation or meaning of program effects. What constitutes a meaningful effect in education is an issue that can be debated along a variety of dimensions including quantity, quality, and cost.

An initial problem in judging the quantity or size of program effects comes in selecting a frame of reference or standard against which to compare an observed impact. Standards for comparison can be broadly classified as absolute or normative. For example, effects can be compared to absolute criterion goals: an assessment program is judged effective if all referred cases are evaluated within a sixty-day time span; a resource program is considered successful if participants achieve an average of 90 percent of their skill goals.

A second type of standard against which effects can be judged is normative: the achievement of those in other programs. For example, the impact of a resource room program designed to foster reading skill development in learning disabled (LD) children might be compared with the effects achieved by other LD resource programs, other types of LD programs, e.g. special classes, or even the achievement of normal children in regular education programs, e.g. through the use of tests normed on representative samples from that population. This latter comparison is probably defensible only for mildly handicapped children, for whom a legitimate goal of special education is the achievement of skills possessed by their nonhandicapped peers (Goodman & Bennett, in press). It is clearly less appropriate for use in evaluating programs for the moderately or severely handicapped.

These two types of evaluation standard are not as clearly distinct as they might at first seem. For example, the extent to which a program achieves its *absolute* goals can be compared to an alternative program's achievement of the same outcomes (as when one approach designed to encourage perfect attendance for emotionally disturbed children is compared to another). Second, though seldom explicit, comparative notions almost always underlie the choice of absolute criteria. Criterion goals are typically set at given levels because those levels are thought reasonable in light of what is known about the success of other previous programs.

Once a frame of reference or standard of comparison is chosen, the evaluator is still faced with the problem of what value to place on the *size* of an observed impact. What interpretation should be offered if children in the district resource room program achieve an average of 93 percent of their goals, or move from the tenth percentile to the fifteenth relative to their normal peers, or out-perform by a half standard deviation children in the neighboring district's program?

Determining the educational significance of a program effect is in large part a matter of judgment (R. Wolf, 1979). Statistical procedures, however, can be used to aid the evaluator in reaching sound judgments. As a first step, standard inferential tests can be employed to determine the likelihood that observed impacts are due to chance. Effects large enough to be statistically significant, though, may not necessarily be of any real educational value. To help determine the size of effects beyond simple statistical significance, some authors, e.g. R. Wolf, 1979, recommend the use of estimators of the proportion of variance accounted for by group membership, e.g. omega squared. Sechrest and Yeaton (1981) have identified a number of limitations to such estimators including the fact that they suffer the general deficiency of depending upon the specific features of the evaluation design and its implementation, e.g. number of subjects, extent of variance present in the sample.

As an alternative to percentage-of-variance estimators, Sechrest and Yeaton (1981) recommend an approach that can be used in cases where data from a number of programs aimed at achieving comparable outcomes exist. In such cases, it is suggested that a mean and standard deviation be calculated or, for non-normal distributions, a frequency plot constructed, for the distribution of past program effects. The effect size of the program being evaluated can then be expressed in terms of its frequency of past occurrence and its significance judged in those terms. While the utility of this method for estimating special education program effects is currently limited, its value should increase as studies of special education program impacts become more numerous and diverse.

Besides the techniques described above, purely judgmental approaches, such as visual analysis, can be employed in assessing impact size. Reviewers expert in a given program area, e.g. instruction of the mentally retarded, can be asked to judge graphic presentations of evaluation results to determine the extent to which an effect "looks big" (Parsonson & Baer, 1978). While problems with this approach exist, e.g. interjudge agreement, a number of investigators have reported evidence supporting its value (Sechrest & Yeaton, 1981).

The second dimension of importance in interpreting program effects is quality. Quality of impact is associated with the nature of the variable or variables upon which an effect is observed (Ball, 1981). What constitutes an important or quality variable for handicapped children, in the judgment of some, will vary according to the unique characteristics of each handicapped child. However, some types of special education service *do* have common goals for all handicapped children (Maher & Bennett, in press). For example, student assessment is generally designed to provide information for decisions of identification/categorization or program planning/review. Even instruction, the most frequently individualized of special education services, is provided in group service delivery arrangements, e.g. resource rooms, special classes, which may emphasize one or another general content area depending upon the *collective* characteristics of the children served: communication skills for the deaf; mobility for the blind; reading for the reading-disabled. Additionally, certain instructional variables may be of importance for a variety of types of handicapped children. Reading goals, according to the Department of Education (1980), are contained in the individual education programs of approximately two-thirds of all special children. Other consequential variables undoubtedly exist.

Quality of impact can be assessed by surveying the opinions of subject-matter experts or analyzing the professional literature for evidence that the variables impacted upon by the program are indeed ones considered important to the development of handicapped children. In addition to the opinions of experts, feedback about quality can be sought from wider audiences, in particular parents, teachers, and other community members, as a means of "socially validating" the effects of a program (Kazdin, 1977; M. Wolf, 1978).

A third critical dimension in the interpretation of program results is the *cost* involved in achieving a particular outcome. A variety of approaches, derived in whole or in part from economics, have been suggested for analyzing cost-effect relationships in educational and human service programs. Levin (1975) has distinguished among three such approaches: cost-benefit, cost-effectiveness, and cost-utility analysis.

Cost-benefit analysis involves the direct comparison of program costs and benefits in terms of monetary value. The objective of this comparison is to arrive at some estimate of the "worth" of a program, where worth is related to the size and direction of the dollar-difference between program cost and benefit. A critical assumption of cost-benefit analysis is that prices can be obtained for both the inputs and outputs (effects) of a program. While this assumption is workable in business, where physical products are manufactured and prices set according to market conditions, it is less readily applied to the results of educational programs. What dollar value should be placed, for example, on increased reading skills for learning disabled students?

Cost-effectiveness analysis expresses the value of programs through comparison of their actual educational or psychological outcomes with monetary measures of input resources, e.g. teaching staff, materials and equipment, space. Cost-effectiveness analysis allows decision-makers to compare various alternative programs, e.g. mainstream program, resource room, special class, by displaying program effects relative to costs; for example, the more cost-effective of two reading programs consuming equal resources would be the one producing greater reading gains. Unlike cost-benefit analysis, cost-effectiveness analysis does not permit judgments of absolute program worth since costs and effects are not expressed in comparable units.

In contrast to both cost-benefit and cost-effectiveness analysis, *cost-utility* incorporates the decision-maker's subjective views as to the value of outcomes produced by alternative programs. Cost-utility analysis is particularly useful when a complex set of outcomes, not necessarily shared across all program alternatives, exists. As an example, this technique could be applied as an aid in deciding whether a resource program successful in fostering handicapped children's social skills is of greater value than a more expensive special class program that produces far better academic effects but less definitive social-skill improvements.

Though the application of the above methods to education has been widely discussed (Levine, 1981), their use in special education has been extremely limited. Hartman (1981) has pointed out that estimating costs for special programs is often difficult because cost determinants are typically embedded in the programmatic aspects of the educational process. Before a reasonable estimate of cost can be calculated, the components of the program, the nature, quantity and price of resources required, and the number of children served by each program unit must be identified. Recent controversies over what constitutes related services for the handicapped illustrate one of the basic problems encountered in estimating costs, though these problems are by no means intractable (see Hartman, 1981, for an example of one cost-estimation approach for special education).

A second, potentially more serious difficulty, relates to the measurement of outcomes, a topic discussed earlier in this paper. Clearly, the analysis of cost-effect relationships will be hampered to the degree that program impacts cannot be adequately determined. However, as noted earlier, impact measurement problems can be addressed in a number of ways. Their existence should not block attempts to evaluate either program results or the relationship between impact and cost.

Summary

Outcome assessment is an important, though underutilized, activity in special education program evaluation. The importance of this type of evaluation is underscored by recent litigative actions, public demands for the accountability of special services, and the need to identify effective programs for dissemination. Measurement problems encountered in assessing direct-service effects include the lack of readily accessible technical data and the absence of tools for evaluating low incidence populations. These problems can be addressed by searching published and unpublished literature for technical data, using multi-method combinations of unproven tools, and developing new measures where necessary. The interpretation of effects should focus on the quantity and quality of impacts and, to the extent possible, the costs incurred in their achievement.

REFERENCE NOTES

1. Blaschke, C. *Case Study of the Implementation of Public Law 94-142.* Washington, D.C.: Education Turnkey Systems, Inc., May 1979.
2. Stearns, M., D. Green, & J. David. *Local Implementation of Public Law 94-142: First Report of a Longitudinal Study.* Menlo Park, CA: SRI International, April 1980.
3. Ragosta, M. *Handicapped Students and the SAT* (Research Report No. 80-12). Princeton, NJ: Educational Testing Service, 1980.
4. Sherman, S. *Issues in the Testing of Handicapped People.* Paper presented at a meeting of the Association of Handicapped Student Services Personnel in Post-Secondary Education, Boston, July 1981.
5. Bennett, R. *A Multi-method Approach to Assessment in Special Education.* Paper presented at the annual convention of the National Association of School Psychologists, Houston, April 1981.

REFERENCES

Anderson, S., & S. Ball. *The Profession and Practice of Program Evaluation.* San Francisco: Jossey-Bass, Inc., 1978.
Armstrong v. Kline, 476 F. Supp. 583 (E.D. Pa, 1979).
Ball, S. Outcomes, the size of the impacts and program evaluation. *New Directions for Program Evaluation, 9,* 71-86, 1981.
Bennett, R. Assessment of exceptional children: Guidelines for practice. *Diagnostique, 7,* 5-13, 1981. (a)
Bennett, R. Issues in the educational assessment of children with learning and behavior disorders. *Journal of the International Association of Pupil Personnel Workers, 25,* 201-210, 1981. (b)
Cronbach, L., et al. *Toward Reform of Program Evaluation.* San Francisco: Jossey-Bass, Inc., 1980.
Dean, R. The use of the PIAT with emotionally disturbed children. *Journal of Learning Disabilities, 12,* 629-631, 1979.
Dean, R. The use of the Peabody Picture Vocabulary Test with emotionally disturbed adolescents. *Journal of School Psychology, 18,* 172-175, 1980.
Department of Education. *Second Annual Report to Congress on the Implementation of Public Law 94-142: The Education for All Handicapped Children Act.* Washington, D.C.: Author, 1980.

Goodman, L., & R. Bennett. Use of norm-referenced assessment for the mildly handicapped: Some basic issues reconsidered. In T. Miller & E. Davis (Eds.), *The Mildly Handicapped Student.* New York: Grune & Stratton. (In press.)

Hartman, W. Estimating the costs of educating handicapped children: A resource-cost model approach — Summary Report. *Educational Evaluation and Policy Analysis, 3,*33-47, 1981.

Joint Committee on Standards for Educational Evaluation. *Standards for Evaluations of Educational Programs, Projects, and Materials.* New York: McGraw-Hill, 1981.

Kazdin, A. Assessing the clinical or applied importance of behavior change through social validation. *Behavior Modification, 1,* 427-452, 1977.

Larry P. v. Wilson Riles. Opinion, U.S. District Court for Northern District of California (No C-712270 RFP), October 11, 1979.

Levin, H. Cost-effectiveness analysis in evaluation research. In M. Guttentag & E. Struening (Eds.), *Handbook of Evaluation Research* (Volume 2). Beverly Hills, CA: Sage Publications, 1975.

Levine, V. The role of outcomes in cost-benefit evaluation. *New Directions for Program Evaluation, 9,* 21-40, 1981.

Maher, C., & R. Bennett. *Planning and Evaluating Special Education Services.* Englewood Cliffs, NJ: Prentice-Hall, Inc. (In press.)

Maher, C., & R. Illback. Planning special education programs: A multidimensional needs assessment framework. *Evaluation and Program Planning.* (In press.)

Messick, S. The standard problem: Meaning and values in measurement and evaluation. *American Psychologist, 30,* 955-966, 1975.

Office of Education. Education of handicapped children: Implementation of part B of the Education of the Handicapped Act. *Federal Register, 42,* 42474-42518, 1977.

Parsonson, B., & D. Baer. Graphical analysis of data. In T.R. Kratochwill (Ed.), *Single Subject Research: Strategies for Evaluating Change.* New York: Academic Press, 1978.

Salvia, J., & J. Ysseldyke. *Assessment in Special and Remedial Education.* Dallas: Houghton-Mifflin, 1981.

Sechrest, L., & W. Yeaton. Assessing the effectiveness of social programs: Methodological and conceptual issues. *New Directions for Program Evaluation, 9,* 41-56, 1981.

Standards for Educational and Psychological Tests. Washington, D.C.: American Psychological Association, 1974.

Stanley, J. Reliability. In R. Thorndike (Ed), *Educational Measurement.* Washington, D.C.: American Council on Education, 1971.

Wolf, M. Social validity: The case for subjective measurement or how applied behavior analysis is finding its heart. *Journal of Applied Behavior Analysis, 11,* 203-214, 1978.

Wolf, R. *Evaluation in Education: Foundations of Competency Assessment and Program Review.* New York: Praeger, 1979.

BIBLIOGRAPHY

SELECTED BIBLIOGRAPHY OF SPECIAL
EDUCATION RESOURCES

Etta M. Bishop

Since the listings following each chapter identify the related print references, this selected bibliography emphasizes the listing of *non-print resources.*

BOOKS

Bayes, Kenneth, and Sandra Franklin. *Designing for the Handicapped.* Montreal: Society for Emotionally Disturbed Children, 1971.

Clark, Gary, and Warren White. *Career Education for the Handicapped: Current Perspectives for Teachers.* Boothwyn, PA: Educational Resource Center, 1980.

Drake University. *Adaptations for Teaching Secondary Handicapped Students.* Des Moines: Midwest Resources, Inc., 1981.

———.*Developing Secondary Level Individual Educational Plans.* Des Moines: Midwest Resources, Inc., 1981.

——— *Federal Legislation: What it Means for Educating Handicapped Students at the Secondary Level.* Des Moines: Midwest Resources, Inc., 1981.

———.*For Parents Only . . . Practical Advice to Parents on Special Education.* Des Moines: Midwest Resources, Inc., 1981.

———.*Glossary of Special, Career, and Vocational Education Terms.* Des Moines: Midwest Resources, Inc., 1981.

———.*Grading and Graduation Requirements for the Handicapped Secondary Student.* Des Moines: Midwest Resources Inc., 1981.

———.*Resources for Educating Secondary Handicapped Students.* Des Moines: Midwest Resources, Inc., 1981.

JWK International Corporation. *Administrator's Handbook on Integrating America's Mildly Handicapped Students.* Reston, VA: The Council for Exceptional Children, 1982.

Hale, Robert G., and Lotsee Smith. *Reading In Instructional Media and Special Education.* Boston: Special Learning Corporation, 1980.

Ontario Department of Education. *Designing Schools for the Physically Handicapped.* Toronto, 1974.

Ontario Department of Education. *Special Education Facilities: Schools and Playgrounds for Trainable Mentally Handicapped Children.* Toronto, 1971.

Petrie, Joyce Anderson. *Media and Mainstreaming: An Annotated Bibliography and Related Resources.* Syracuse: Syracuse University, 1979.

Research for Better Schools, Inc. *Clarification of P.L. 94-142 for the Administrator.* Philadelphia, 1980.

————.*Clarification of P.L 94-142 for the Classroom Teacher.* Philadelpia, 1979.

————.*Clarification of P.L. 94-142 for Paraprofessional and Support Staff.* Philadelphia, 1980.

————.*Clarification of P.L. 94-142 for the Special Educator.* Philadelphia, 1980.

Swann, Will. *The Practice of Special Education.* Great Britain: The Blackwell Press Limited, 1981

University of New Mexico. *Consumer's Guide to Personnel Preparation Programs: In-Service Programming and Public Law 94-142; Two Surveys.* Chicago: Instructional Dynamics International, 1979.

————.*Consumer Guide to Personnel Preparation Programs: The Training of Paraprofessionals for the Education of Low-Incidence Populations of Handicapped Children.* Chicago: Instructional Dynamics International, 1980.

————.*Consumer Guide to Personnel Preparation Programs: The Training of Paraprofessionals in Special Education and Related Fields.* Chicago: Instructional Dynamics International, 1980.

————.*Consumer Guide to Personnel Preparation Programs: The Training of Professionals in Physical Education and Recreation for the Handicapped.* Chicago: Instructional Dynamcs International, 1980.

————.*Consumer Guide to Personnel Preparation Programs: The Training of Professionals in Vocational Education for the Handicapped.* Chicago: Instructional Dynamics International, 1980.

————.*Consumer Guide to Personnel Preparation Programs: Thirty Projects/ A Conspectus.* Chicago: Instructional Dynamics International, 1980.

The following two sources include extensive bibliographies that will be useful to anyone involved with the planning and designing of learning environments and educational facilities.

Sleeman, Phillip J. and D.M. Rockwell. *Designing Learning Environments.* New York: Longman Inc., 1981.

————.*Instructional Media and Technology.* Stroudsburg, PA: Dowden, Hutchingson & Ross, Inc., 1976.

JOURNALS

Albright, Leonard; Susan E. Hasazi; Allen L. Phelps, and Marc E. Hull. Interagency Collaboration in Providing Vocational Education for Handicapped Individuals. *Exceptional Children, 47*:584, 1981.

Arends, R.I., et al. Educational Dean: An Examination of Behaviors Associated with Special Projects. *Journal of Teacher Education. 32*:14-20, 1981.

Braverman, Barbara. Say It With Captions. *Instructional Innovator, 25*:25, 1980.

Brown, Lou; Ian Pumpian; Diane Boumgart; Pat Vandeventer; Alison Ford;

Jan Nisbet; Jack Schroeder, and Lee Gruenewald. Longitudinal Transition Plans in Programs for Severely Handicapped Students. *Exceptional Children, 47*:624, 1981.

Chandler, H.N. Teaching LD Students in the Public Schools: A Return to the Closet?. *Journal of Learning Disabilities, 14*:482-485, 1981.

Chandler, H.N and V.R. Utz. Special Education and the Education Administrator: An Uneasy Alliance. *Journal of Learning Disabilities, 15*:54-56, 1982.

Clymer, E. William; Marsha Young, and Thomas J. Castle. Special Forms for Special Education. *Audiovisual Instruction, 23*:24, 1978.

Cooke, T.C. Experiential Approach to Developing Vocational Special Needs Competencies in Teachers. *Journal of Ind Teacher Education, 19*:36-44, 1981.

Fineman, S. We Need Principals Who Understand. *Principal, 61*:33-34, 1981.

Finkenbinder, R.L. Special Education Administration and Supervision: The State of the Art. *Journal of Special Education, 15*:485-495, 1981.

Frith, G.H. Paraprofessionals: A Focus on Interpersonal Skills. *Education & Training Mental Retarded, 16*:306-309, 1981.

Geoffrion, L.D. Computer-Based Exploratory Learning Systems for Handicapped Children. *Journal of Educ Tech Syst 10*:125-132, 1981-82.

Grimes, L. Computers are for Kids: Designing Software Programs to Avoid Problems of Learning. *Teaching Exceptional Children, 14*:48-53, 1981.

Hammond, Kathleen L., and Louis V. Messineo. The Design of Instructional Packages. *International Journal of Instructional Media 6*:271, 1978-79.

Hannaford, A. and E. Sloane. Microcomputers Powerful Learning Tools With Proper Programming. *Teaching Exceptional Children 14*:54-57, 1981.

Heller, Harold W. Secondary Education for Handicapped Students: In Search of a Solution. *Exceptional Children, 47*:582, 1981.

Irwin, Michael. Media, the Arts, and the Handicapped. *Audiovisual Instruction, 24*:33, 1979.

Johnson, R.E. Administration of Programs for the Handicapped. *Journal Special Educators, 18*:73-85, 1981.

Joiner, Lee M. and David A. Sabatino. A Policy Study of P.L. 94-142. *Exceptional Children, 48*:24, 1981.

Kahan, E.H. Aides in Special Education — A Boon for Students and Teachers. *Teaching Exceptional Children, 14*:101-105, 1981.

Lee, H.D. Use of In-Service Activities to Introduce Industrial Arts Teachers to Special Needs Students. *Man Society Technology, 41*:6-9, 1981.

Luchow, J.P. Preparing the Classroom Teacher for Mainstreamed Students. *Education Digest, 47*:9-11, 1981.

McConville, L.S. and R.J. Ritter. Recision and Consolidation; New Directions for This Federal Role in the Education of Handicapped Children. *Education & Training Mentally Retarded, 16*:284-387, 1981.

Masat, L.J., and F.K. Schack. Mainstream Teacher: Training is Not Enough. *Principal, 61*:28-30, 1981.

Messineo, Louis, and Ronald Loiacono. A Non-Textbook Instructional Model. *International Journal of Instructional Media, 6*:115, 1978-79.

————.An Ex Post Facto Design of a District's Instructional Program. *International*

Journal of Instructional Media, 6:77, 1978-79.

Messineo, Louis, and Phillip J. Sleeman. A Parents Guide to Special Education. *International Journal of Instructional Media,* 4:361, 1976-77.

Mitchell, B.M. Update on the State of Gifted/Talented Education in the U.S. *Phi Delta Kappan.* 63:357-358, 1982.

Nadler, Barbara; Myrna Merron, and William K. Friedel. Public Law 94-142: One Response to the Personnel Development Mandate. *Exceptional Children,* 47:463, 1981.

Neel, R. and F. Billingsley. Letter and the Spirit of P.L. 94-142. *Early Years,* 12:62-63, 1982.

Patton, Patricia L. A Model for Developing Vocational Objectives in IEP. *Exceptional Children,* 47:618, 1981.

Pekarsky, D. Normalcy, Exceptionality and Mainstreaming. *Journal of Education,* 163:320, 1981.

Schanzer, S.S. When Can We Justify Mainstreaming? *Principal,* 61:31-32, 1981.

Shapiro, H.S. Implementing P.L. 94-142 in the High School — A Successful In-Service Training Model. *Education,* 102:47-52, 1981.

Stilington, Patricia L. Vocational and Special Education in Career Programming for the Mildly Handicapped Adolescent. *Exceptional Children,* 47:592, 1981.

Sleeman, Linda B. Mental Retardation . . . An Annotated Bibliography. *International Journal of Instructional Media,* 4:117, 1976-77.

Smith, A. Special Education-By Any Other Name. *Clearing House,* 55:100, 1981.

Spencer, D. Unite in Fight for Special Education. *Times Education Supplement,* 3420:15, 1982.

Stodden, Robert A., and Robert N. Ianocone. Career/Vocational Assessment of the Special Needs Individual: A Conceptual Model. *Exceptional Children,* 47:600, 1981.

Swanson, L.F. Handicapped Students in My Classroom? *Momentum,* 12:25-26, 1981.

Taber, F.M. Microcomputer-Its Applicability to Special Education. *Focus Exceptional Children,* 14:1-14, 1981.

Thorkildsen, R. Educating Handicapped Students Via Micro-Computer/Videodisc Technology. *Educating & Training Mentally Retarded,* 16:264-269, 1981.

Tweedie, D. and H. Baud. Future Directions in the Education of Deaf-Blind Multihandicapped Children and Youth. *American Ann Deaf,* 126:829-834, 1981.

Vasa, S.F. and A.L. Steckelberg. Mildly Handicapped Students in Rural Schools. *Education Digest,* 47:32-35, 1981.

Whitmore, J.R. Lessons Learned from Dean's Grants for the Restructuring of Teacher Education. *Journal of Teacher Education,* 32:7-13, 1981.

Wimmer, Diane. Functional Learning Curricula in the Secondary Schools. *Exceptional Children,* 47:610, 1981.

Ysseldyke, J.E., et al. Participation of Regular Education Teachers in Special Education Team Decision Making: A Naturalistic Investigation. *Exceptional Children,* 48:365-366, 1982.

FILMSTRIPS WITH AUDIO CASSETTES

Dealing With Special Problems. Audio Visual Narrative Arts, Pleasantville, NY, 1977.

EASE Curriculum. Stanfield Film Associates, 1979.

Every Kid is Special-A Series. Westport Communications Group, Inc., Educational Enrichment Materials, Inc., Mt. Kisco, NY, 1977.

Educational Services. Parent's Magazine Films, Inc., New York, 1976.

Organizations & Associations. Parent's Magazine Films, Inc., New York, 1977.

Legal Rights. Parent's Magazine Films, Inc., New York, 1977.

Like You, Like Me. Avatar Learning. Encyclopaedia Britannica Educational Corp., 1979.

Overcoming Handicaps. Educational Direction, Learning Tree Filmstrips, 1979.

Parent to Child. Parent's Magazine Films, Inc., New York, 1977.

Parent to Parent. Parent's Magazine Films, Inc., New York, 1977.

Parents and School Policy. Parent's Magazine Films, Inc., New York, 1977.

Reinforcement in the Home. Parent's Magazine Films, Inc., New York, 1977.

Special Education Early. Parent's Magazine Films, Inc., New York, 1977.

Special Need, A Special Love-Children With Handicaps, Families Who Care-A Series. Parent's Magazine Films, Inc., New York, 1977.

Special World of Kids. Westport Communications Group, Educational Enrichment Materials, 1979.

VIDEO CASSETTES (3/4" color)

After Assessment. Lexington Public Schools, National Instructional TV Center, Bloomington, IN, 1975.

Annual Review. Indiana University Radio and Television Services, Indiana University Audiovisual Center, 1978.

Assessment. Indiana University Radio and Television Services, Indiana University Audiovisual Center, 1978.

Diagnosis And Educational Planning. Lexington Public Schools, National Instructional TV Center, Bloomington, IN, 1975.

Due Process Hearing, The. Indiana University Radio and Television Services, Indiana University Audiovisual Center, 1978.

Due Process Panel, The. Indiana University Radio and Television Services, Indiana University Audiovisual Center, 1978.

Early Assessment-Steps to Planning. Lexington Public Schools, National Instructional TV Center, Bloomington, IN, 1975.

Educating the Severely and Profoundly Handicapped. Indiana University Radio and Television Services, Indiana University Audiovisual Center, 1978.

Every Child Can Learn. Lexington Public Schools, National Instructional TV Center, Bloomington, IN, 1975.

Every Student is Different — The High School. Lexington Public Schools, National Instructional TV Center, Bloomington, IN, 1975.

Individualized Education Program Case Conference. Indiana University Radio and Television Services, Indiana University Audiovisual Center, 1978.

Integrating Handicapped Children in the Regular Classroom. Indiana University Radio and Television Services, Indiana University Audiovisual Center, 1978.

Larry P. Case, The. Indiana University Radio and Television Services, Indiana University Audiovisual Center, 1978.

Least Restrictive Environment Panel. Indiana University Radio and Television Services, Indiana University Audiovisual Center, 1978.

Least Restrictive Environment — Resource Rooms and Special Classes. Indiana University Radio and Television Services, Indiana University Audiovisual Center, 1978.

Least Restrictive Environment — Special Day and Residential Schools. Indiana University Radio and Television Services, Indiana University Audiovisual Center, 1978.

Like Other People. Didactic Films Limited, Perennial Education, Inc., Northfield, IL, 1973.

School for Me, A. AV-ED Films, Lem Bailey Productions, Hollywood, CA, 1975.

Teaching Children With Special Needs. Division of Instructional Television, Maryland State Department of Education, 1978.

Together They Learn. Lexington Public Schools, National Instructional TV Center, Bloomington, IN, 1975.

FILMS (16mm Sound)

Across the Silence Barrier. 57 min., color, WGBH-TV, Time-Life Films Multimedia Division, 1977.

Adaptation of Pscyhodiagnostic Findings to Teaching Materials. 25 min., b&w, Rocky Mt. Educ. Lab, Barbre Productions.

Adapting the Curriculum to the Child. 18 min., b&w, U.S. Office of Economic Opportunity, Modern Talking Picture Service.

Aids for Teaching the Mentally Retarded- A Positive Approach. 25 min., b&w, National Audio-Visual Center, 1970.

All My Buttons. 28 min., color, H & H Enterprises, 1973.

All The Way Up There. 27 min., color, Encyclopedia Britannica Educational Corp., 1980.

Am I Being Unrealistic? 25 min., color, British Broadcasting Co-TV, Media Guild, 1974.

And A Time to Dance. 10 min., b&w, Commonwealth Mental Health Research Foundation, 1972.

Angela's Island. 23 min., color, Films Incorporated, 1978.

As We Are. 29 min., color, Phoenix Film, 1973.

Assessing A Young Child. 25 min., color, British Broadcasting Co-TV, Media Guild, 1974.

Assist Program I: A Training Film for Paraprofessionals of the Moderately Handicapped. 75 min., color, Indiana University Developmental Training Center.

Assist Program II: A Training Package for Instructional Associate Mainstreaming. 46 min., color, Indiana University Developmental Training Center.

Auditorially-Handicapped Child, The-Deaf. 29 min., b&w, National Educational Television, Indiana University Audiovisual Center.

Autistic Syndrome I. 42 min., b&w, Stichting Film Co.

Autistic Syndrome II. 40 min., b&w, Stichting Film Co.

Autistic Syndrome III. 35 min., b&w, Stichting Film Co.

Autistic Syndrome IV. 42 min., b&w, Stichting Film Co.

Balthazar Scales of Adaptive Behavior Part I and II. 35 min., color, University of Wisconsin Bureau of Audiovisual Instruction, 1974.

Battered Child. 58 min., b&w, National Educational Television, Indiana University Audiovisual Center, 1969.

Bertha. 36 min., color, Joseph P. Kennedy, Jr. Foundation, 1974.

Best Things In Life. 25 min., color, University of Connecticut, 1960.

Blind Teacher In A Public School. 24 min., color, 1976.

Board and-Care. 27 min., color, Sarah Pillsbury and Ron Ellis Prod., Pyramid Films, 1980.

Born To Succeed, Part I — The Concept of Number. 32 min., color, Hampshire Communication Corp., 1971.

Born to Succeed, Part II — Arithmetic. 32 min., color Hampshire Communication Corp., 1971.

Boy Named Terry Egan. 53 min., color, Columbia Broadcasting System, Carousal Films Inc., 1973.

Broken Bridge, The. 43 min., color, British Broadcasting Co-TV, Time-Life Films Multimedia Division, 1970.

Can I Come Back Tomorrow? 29 min., color, California State College at Los Angeles, University of Southern Calif Dept. of Cinema.

Child is a Child, A. 7 min., color, Aims Instructional Media Services Inc., 1973.

Child With Cerebral Palsy. 44 min., b&w, Prentice-Hall, Inc.

Children Are Not Problems — They Are People. 27 min., color University of Kansas, 1975.

Children Lost and Found. 60 min., color, University of Minnesota, 1975.

Children of Promise. 24 min., color, Iowa State Educational Association, 1977.

Child's Quarrel With The World. 22 min., color, Films Incorporated, 1977.

Chris. 19 min., color, Films Incorporated, 1974.

Club Five to Eight. 14 min., color, University of Kansas, Bureau of Child Research.

Color Her Sunshine. 21 min., b&w, Public Television Library, Indiana University Audiovisual Center, 1970.

Conversations with Deaf Teenagers. 14 min., color, U.S. Bureau of Education for Handicapped, National Audiovisual Center, 1973.

Craig. 19 min., color, Films Incorporated, 1974.

Crime of Innocence. 27 min., color, Paulist Communications, 1974.

Cry Help! 83 min., color, National Broadcasting Co., 1970.

Curb Between Us. 15 min., color, Barr Films, 1975.

David. 28 min., color, Canadian Broadcasting Corp., Filmakers Library, 1980.

David. 19 min., color, Films Incorporated, 1974.

Day For Justin. 28 min., color, Brigham Young University, 1970.

Day In The Life of Bonnie Consolo, A. 17 min., color, Barr Films, 1975.

Deaf Child Speaks. 16 min., color, University of California Extension Media Center, 1973.

Dee (Larsen's Syndrome). 10 min., color, Encyclopedia Britannica Educational Corp.

1978.

Development of Perceptual Motor Skills in a Profoundly Retarded Child. 16 min., color, Kansas University of Child Research, 1971.

Disruptive Behavior. 16 min., color University of Wisconsin Bureau of Audiovisual Instruction, 1972.

Dyslexia: Prevention and Remediation, A Classroom Approach. 20 min., color, Indiana University Audiovisual Center.

Ears to Hear. 28 min., color, Canadian Broadcasting Corporation, Film Marketing Library, 1975.

Eddie. 27 min., color, Paulist Communications, Media Guild, 1974.

Education for the Deaf (Parts 1 & 2). 51 min., b&w, British Information Service, Film and Publication Division.

Education of the Visually Handicapped. 29 min., color, University of Wisconsin Bureau of Audiovisual Instruction, 1973.

Educational Needs of Young Deprived Children. 26 min., b&w, U.S. Office of Educational Opportunity.

Elizabeth (Visual Impairment). 10 min., color, Encyclopedia Britannica Educational Corp., 1976.

Entering the Era of Human Ecology. 20 min., color, University of California Educational Media Center, Media Guild, 1976.

Everything But Hear. 16 min., color, Clarke School for the Deaf, 1970.

Film on Early Intervention, A. 26 min., color, Instructional Media Services, 1979.

Finding My Way. 8 min., color, Films Incorporated, 1975.

First Steps. 24 min., color, National Film Board of Canada, 1977.

Fitting In. 25 min., color, University of Wisconsin Bureau of Audiovisual Instruction, 1976.

Fred's Case: A Stimulus. 10 min., color, Indiana University Developmental Training Center.

Fulfillment of Human Potential. 18 min., color, McGraw-Hill Book Co., 1979.

Gifted Child. 40 min., color, Time-Life Films Multimedia Division, 1970.

Graduation, A Follow-Up: What Happens to the Retarded Child When He Grows Up? 17 min., color, James Stanford, 1972.

Graduation Day. 15 min., color, Parsons State Hospital and Training Center, 1973.

Greene Valley Grandparents. 10 min., b&w, Center for Southern Folklore, 1971.

Grouping, 15 min., color, University of Wisconsin Bureau of Audiovisual Services, 1972.

He Comes From Another Room. 28 min., color, Mental Health Training Films Program, 1973.

Head to Toe. 9 min, color, Motivational Resources, 1973.

He's Mentally Retarded. 8 min., color, Educational Media Associates, 1975.

Help For Mark. 18 min., color, Prentice-Hall, Inc., 1970.

Hey Look At Me. 12 min., color, West Virginia University, Screenscope, 1970.

Hidden Handicap. 23 min., color, American Broadcasting Co-TV, McGraw-Hill Book Co., 1976.

Horizon of Hope. 15 min., color, University of California Extension Media Center, 1971.

If A Boy Can't Learn. 28 min., color, Lawren Productions, 1972.

I'll Find A Way. 26 min., color, National Film Board of Canada, Media Guild, 1977.

In A Class . . . All By Himself. 50 min., color, National Broadcasting Co., Films Incorporated, 1972.

In This Dark World. 29 min., b&w, National Film Board of Canada, International Film Bureau.

Including Me. 59 min., color, Capitol City TV Producers, Media Five Film Distributors, 1976.

Individualized Education Program. 30 min., color, Indiana University Radio and Television Services, Indiana University Audiovisual Center, 1978.

Individualized Instruction. 17 min., color, University of Wisconsin Bureau of Audiovisual Instruction, 1972.

Introduction to Speech and Language Disorders. 23 min., color, State University of Iowa, 1975.

Invisible Handicap: Dyslexia. 15 min., color, Columbia Broadcasting System, Carousal Films, Inc., 1975.

It's Cool to be Smart. 23 min., color, McGraw-Hill Book Co., 1978.

It's Okay to be Deaf, Denise. 28 min., color, Viewfinders, 1975.

Janet is a Little Girl. 28 min., b&w, University of California Extension Media Center, 1972.

Jennifer. 19 min., color, Films Incorporated, 1974.

Jennifer is a Lady. 26 min., color, New York University.

John (Cystic Fibrosis). 10 min., color, Encyclopedia Britannica Educational Corporation, 1978.

Just For The Fun Of It. 18 min., color, Aims Instructional Media Services, Inc.

Kai (Speech Impairment). 10 min., color, Encyclopedia Britannica Educational Corporation, 1978.

Keeping Safe. 28 min., color, Journal Films, 1979.

Language of the Deaf. 16 min, color, Columbia Broadcasting System, Carousal Films, Inc., 1977.

Learning Disabilities. 30 min., b&w, National Broadcasting Co., Films Incorporated, 1971.

Lend A Hand. 60 min., color, University of Wisconsin Bureau of Audiovisual Instruction, 1977.

Let's Be Friends. 6 min., color, Avatar Learning, Inc., Encyclopedia Britannica Educational Corp., 1977.

Let's Talk It Over. 6 min., color, Avatar Learning, Inc., Encyclopedia Britannica Educational Corp., 1977.

Like Everybody Else. 32 mn., color, Stanfield House, 1975.

Like Ordinary Children. 25 min., color, Heritage Visual Sales, Ltd., 1975.

Lily — A Story About a Girl Like Me. 14 min., color, Davidson Films, Inc., 1977.

Lisa! Pay Attention. 22 min., color, A-V Explorations, Inc., 1970.

Look Beyond the Disability . . . 29 min., color, University of Kansas, Bureau of Child Research, 1974.

Madison School Plan. 18 min., color, Aims Instructional Media Services, Inc., 1971.

Mainstreaming in Action. 27 min., color, Togg Films and The Center of Human

Policy, Encyclopedia Britannica Educational Corp., 1979.

Mainstreaming Techniques: Life Science and Art. 12 min., color, McGraw-Hill Book Co., 1979.

Making Their Senses Make Sense. 24 min., color, University of Alabama.

Man That Gravity Forgot, The. 9 min., color, Coronet, 1979.

Mark (Learning Disability). 10 min., color, Encyclopedia Britannica Eductional Corp., 1978.

Mary (Hearing and Speech). 10 min., color, Encyclopedia Britannica Educational Corp., 1978.

Matter of Incovenience. 10 min., color, Stansfield, 1973.

Mimi. 11 min., b&w, Billy Bud Films, 1972.

Minority of One. 28 min., color, Films Incorporated, 1976.

Moderate Retardation in Young Children. 43 min., b&w, Western Reserve University.

Movigenic Curriculum: An Experimental Approach To The Solution of Learning. 40 min., b&w, University of Wisconsin Bureau of Audiovisual Services.

Multi-level Teaching For Normal and Handicapped Children. 20 min., color, Kansas University Bureau of Child Research, 1977.

Music Child, The. 46 min., b&w, Benchmark Films, Inc., 1976.

My Brother David. 25 min., color, Heritage Visual Sales, Ltd., 1975.

Nature of Retardation. 27 min., color, Psychological Films, 1973.

New Sight for the Blind. 17 min., b&w, National Educational Television, Indiana University Audiovisual Center.

Nicky: One of My Best Friends. 15 min., color, McGraw-Hill Book Co., 1975.

1972 Special Olympics. 16 min., color, University of California, Media Guild, 1976.

Non-Slip. 25 min., color, University of Kansas, 1975.

Observation, The. 30 min., color Van Praag Productions, Inc., 1970.

Operation Behavior Modification. 40 min., b&w, University of Kansas.

Operation Dry Pants. 30 min., color, Southwest Film Lab, Inc.

Out of Left Field. 7 min., color, American Foundation for the Blind.

Overview. 30 min., color, Maryland State Department of Education, 1975.

PACA: Paraprofessionals As Change Agents. 30 min., color, University of Kansas, Bureau of Child Research, 1976.

Paige (Down's Syndrome). 10 min., color, Encyclopedia Britannica Educational Corp., 1978.

Peer-Conducted Behavior Modification. 25 min., color, University of California at Los Angeles, Media Guild, 1976.

People You'd Like to Know: An Introduction. 20 min., color, Encyclopedia Britannica Educational Corp., 1979.

People You'd Like to Know Series-C.J. (Social Emotional Disturbance). Encyclopedia Britannica Educational Corp., 1976.

People You'd Like to Know: Diane (Amputee). 10 min., color, Encyclopedia Britannica Educational Corporation, 1976.

Perceptual Movements and Activities, Part I. 17 min., color, Morten Moyer Productions, 1972.

Perspectives on Language Training. 30 min., color, University of Kansas, 1975.

Place Among Us. 27 min., color, National Broadcasting Co., 1970.

Principles of Parent-Child Programs for the Pre-School Hearing Impaired. 26 min., color, Pennsylvania State University.

Public Law 94-142: Equality of Opportunity. 21 min., color, Instructional Media Services, 1977.

Puzzle Children, The. 59 min., color WQED, Pittsburgh, Indiana University Audiovisual Center, 1976.

Question of Values — Down's Syndrome. 24 min., color, Edward Feil, 1973.

RAFE: Developing Giftedness in the Educationally Disadvantaged. 20 min., color, BFA Educational Media.

Randy's Up — Randy's Down. 21 min., color, Kansas University Bureau of Child Research, 1978.

Reading is for Us Too. 29 min., color, University of GUELP, Macmillan Library Services.

Results, The. 28 min., color, Van Praag Productions, Inc., 1970.

Santa Monica Project. 28 min., color, New York State Department of Education, 1970.

Sara Has Down's Syndrome. 17 min., color, John Friedman, 1974.

School Is for Children (Adult Edition). 17 min., color Aims Instructional Media Services, Inc., 1973.

Sensoritonic Readiness Program. 22 min., color, Pathway School Resource Center.

Socialization. 19 min., color, University of Wisconsin, 1972.

Special Children, Special Needs. 22 min., color, Thomas Craven Film Corp., Campus, 1973.

Special Education: Blind, Deaf, and Physically Handicapped. 11 min., color, Educational Communications Inc., 1976.

Special Education Techniques: Lab Science and Art. 24 min., color, McGraw-Hill Book Co., 1979.

Special Me. 25 min., color, Center for Mass Communications of Columbia University Press, 1972.

Specific Learning Disabilities: Evaluation. 28 min., color, Davidson Films, Inc., 1975.

Specific Learning Disabilities in the Classroom. 23 min., color, Davidson Films, Inc., 1975.

Specific Learning Disabilities: Remedial Programming. 32 min., color, Davidson Films, Inc., 1975.

Splash. 20 min., color, Documentary Films, 1972.

Suffer the Little Children. 50 min., color, National Broadcasting Company, 1972.

Symbol Boy. 5 min., color, Benchmark Films, Inc., 1976.

Talented, the Gifted and the Genius. 30 min., b&w, National Education Association.

Talking Typewriter. 20 min., color, Responsive Environment Corporation.

Teaching Children Who Are Retarded. 20 min., color, University of South Dakota.

Teaching the Young Mongoloid Child to Communicate. 26 min., color, Harris County Center for the Retarded Inc.

Teaching Triad, The. 19 min., color, Dubnoff Center, Aims Instructional Media Services, Inc., 1974.

Teaching Verbalization by Contingency Management. 14 min., color, Westinghouse Learning Corp.

They Are Not Expendable. 24 min., color, American Educational Films, 1970.

They Call Me Names. 22 min., color, BFA Educational Media, 1972.

They Can Be Helped. 22 min., color, International Film Bureau.

Those Other Kids. 26 min., color, University of Minnesota.

Time for Georgia. 14 min., b&w, New York University, 1971.

Time's Lost Children. 29 min., color, KPBS-TV, San Diego, Indiana University Audiovisual Center, 1973.

To Laugh, To Play, To Learn — Part I — An Introduction to Learning Disabilities. 27 min., color, Aims Instructional Media Services Inc., 1977.

Training Resources and Techniques. 25 min., color, Kansas University Bureau of Child Research.

Two, Three, Fasten Your Ski. 17 min., color, Phoenix Films, 1975.

Visual Perception Training in the Regular Classroom. 23 min., b&w, Aims Instructional Media Services Inc., 1970.

Visualization: A Key To Reading. 25 min., color, Soundings Films, 1972.

Walter. 16 min., color, University of Southern California Department of Cinema, Churchill Films, 1973.

Watch Us Move. 21 min., color, University of California Extension Media Center, 1974.

We Can Grow. 13 min., color, Comminico, Inc., ACI Media, 1970.

Where Your Money Goes. 28 min., color, Journal Films, 1979.

Who Are These People? 22 min., color, Gifted-Talented Institute, Heron House, 1977.

Why Billy Couldn't Learn. 42 min., color, California Association for Neurologically Handicapped Children.

Why Wait? 20 min., color, Oregon State Board of Health.

Window Full of Cakes, A. 20 min., b&w, Commonwealth Mental Health Research Foundation, 1974.

You Have Something to Offer. 16 min., color, McGraw-Hill Book Co., 1976.

Young Fingers on a Typewriter: A New Concept in Learning. 36 min., color, University of California Extension Media Center, 1975.

INDEX

A

Administrator (*see also* Principal)
role of, 67, 214, 218, 234-235, 241
Allen, C., 172
Alternative schools (*see also* Counterculture schools)
popularity of
reasons for, 57
American Foundation for the Blind, 102, 107
American School for the Deaf, 81
Anderberg, J.R., 142, 151
Anderson, J.R., 137, 151
Anderson, R.H., 34, 38
Anderson, S., 267, 274
APA *Standards for Educational and Psychological Tests*
purpose of, 266
Apprenticeship
description of, 232
Armstrong, J., 153, 160, 161, 63, 164, 171
Armstrong v. Kline, 10, 267
Aschner, M., 153, 154, 171, 172
Assessment (*see* Assessment tools, Needs assessment; Testing)
Assessment tools
adequacy of
impact evaluation and, 267-269
special populations and, 268
Austin, Mary C., 68

B

Baer, D., 271, 275
Bailey, R.B., 142, 152
Ball, S., 267, 274
Barbe, Walter B., 68
Barr, Robert D., 54, 60
Barth, R.S., 113, 121
Bates, Herman III, 212
Belch, P., 153, 156, 172
Bell, R.W., 60, 61

Bennett, R.E., 238, 248, 252, 253, 264, 266
268, 274, 275
Bennion, Junius L., 95
Bereano, Philip L., 15, 24
Berkell, Arthur, 110
Berko, J.J., 136, 137, 161
Berliner, D., 154, 172
Bernazza, A.M., 186, 191
Blaschke, C., 265, 274
Blessington, John, 60
Bloom, Benjamin S., 19, 21, 24, 34, 38
Bloomer, R.H., 186, 188, 191
Bourne, Lyle E., 19, 20, 24
Bowe, Frank, 105, 107
Bower, Gordon, 21, 24, 137, 151
Bracht, G.G., 71, 75
Bradley, Robert H., 49, 59, 60
Brown, C.T., 151
Bruner, Jerome, 214, 226
Buterbaugh, James G., 94

C

Cahen, L., 154, 172
Caldwell, Bettye M., 49, 59, 60
Career Activity Team (CAT)
description of, 224-226
Career education (*see also* Vocational Education)
agencies and organizations relevant to
involvement of, 216
approaches to
description of, 223-226
community involvement in
importance of, 218
Curriculum Development and Dissemination Center for
establishment of, 217
financing of
methods of, 216, 219
goals and objectives of
development of, 216, 219-220

289